Psychology for Nurses and the Caring Professions

"This beautifully written book . . . clearly explains the application of psychological concepts and theories to health and succinctly summarises key issues. Each chapter also provides a series of vignettes capturing the kind of real-life situations health and social care professionals will encounter in their own practice and a set of thought-provoking exercises . . . These will be invaluable in developing critical thinking skills and growing the capacity to provide the kind of empathic care which is the heart of person-centred practice."

Dr Wendy Cousins, Course Director, University of Ulster School of Nursing, UK

"I have recommended earlier editions of this book and now am delighted to say that this latest edition is even better. The authors continue to clearly explain the relevance of psycho-logical theories, models and approaches to nursing care but now, through the use of frequent reflective activities, vignettes and a 'psychosoap' family, students are also highly encouraged to identify how the theory will help them to become the high quality holistic practitioners they desire to be."

Anthony Duffy, Nurse Tutor, College of Human and Health Sciences, Swansea University, UK

"This new edition embraces innovation in student learning. The use of the 'psychosoap' provides a structure which is meaningful and insightful. The chapter exercises have 'realworld' application and can be used to understand your own and others motivations, beliefs and values. Unlike many psychology texts . . . this book offers real 'food for thought' and provides the building blocks which link theory to practice. It will also be a valuable resource for those who like to 'dip in' to a book."

Philip Larkin, Professor of Clinical Nursing, and Joint Chair, University College Dublin and Our Lady's Hospice & Care Services, Ireland

"This new edition continues to improve the reader's experience, providing comprehensive insight into the complex subject of psychology. It is user friendly, underpinned by research findings and will enable the reader to apply its concepts personally and professionally. It is a text which is well designed for student use and application and it has employed a number of innovative features . . . An excellent resource, which I would highly recommend."

Siobhan McCullough, Lecturer, School of Nursing and Midwifery, Queen's University Belfast, UK

Psychology for Nurses and the Caring Professions

FOURTH EDITION

Jan Walker, Sheila Payne, Nikki Jarrett and Tim Ley

Open University Press

Open University Press
McGraw-Hill Education
McGraw-Hill House
Shoppenhangers Road
Maidenhead
Berkshire
England
SL6 2QL

email: enquiries@openup.co.uk
world wide web: www.openup.co.uk

and Two Penn Plaza, New York, NY 10121-2289, USA

First published 1996
Reprinted 1997, 1998, 1999, 2000, 2001 (twice), 2002
Second edition published 2004
Third edition published 2007
Reprinted 2008, 2011
First published in this fourth edition 2012

A catalogue record of this book is available from the British Library

ISBN-13: 978 0 335 24391 4
ISBN-10: 0 335 24391 6
eISBN: 978 0 335 24392 1

Library of Congress Cataloging-in-Publication Data
CIP data applied for

Typeset by Graphicraft Limited, Hong Kong
Printed and bound in Spain by Grafo, S.A.

The McGraw-Hill Companies

Contents

Tables

Figures

Preface

In this new edition we have made explicit our use of the parallels between the everyday experiences of people receiving health and social care and those that care for them, particularly student practitioners. Although it sounds crazy, it is easy for professional carers to think and act as if those receiving care are in some way a different species from those of us that provide care. By making clear some of the commonalities that exist in the experiences we all have, we hope to help our readers develop the empathy that is a cornerstone of person-centred practice.

Those who choose to enter caring professions are naturally concerned for the well-being of others, but there are many ways that this concern can be expressed. A commonly encountered idea of caring is that the carer is active and does what is necessary, while the receiver remains a passive recipient of that care. However, we know that we ourselves value our own independence and that the majority of us value our capacity to do things for ourselves. Therefore it is a reasonable starting assumption that this will be true for many of those that we care for. We may know people who have learned to become dependent on another person (such as a parent or spouse) for everyday tasks. Dependence can be an easy habit to acquire but it is rarely in the interest of the person who is dependent. This is true for us, it is true for our friends, and it is true for those we care for.

If one observes good quality health and social care, or thinks critically about how things could be in an ideal situation, it is possible to see how optimal caregiving is actually a reciprocal interaction between the person giving care and the person receiving care, working together to achieve the best outcomes. In such situations the person being cared for has kept their independence, been given and exercised choices and been involved in planning and care delivery. Observations such as this may sometimes challenge common practices in health care. This book provides an invitation to become a thinking, critical carer.

In common with earlier editions of this book, we have illustrated the application of ideas by frequently relating them to events in the lives of a fictitious family, a 'psychosoap'. Each of the events we describe is a fictionalized account of things that have really happened in health and social care environments.

New in this edition are:

- Summaries of ideas at regular intervals, typically after each half chapter.
- Exercises interspersed within each chapter. These exercises are often invitations to observe, and/or reflect on, events in care environments and relate them to ideas in this book.
- New material, including ideas regarding: resilience, well-being, positive psychology, social perception and the distinction between deliberative and intuitive information processing.

We want 'psychology' to be more than a set of theories to learn (and then probably forget) before getting on with the 'real' business of health and social care. We hope this encounter with psychology will be enlightening and engaging, and contribute to your development as a reflective person. It is with this aim in mind that we have written the new edition of this book.

Dedication and acknowledgements

Tim Ley would like to dedicate his contribution to this book to Annie and Pa, and to thank Terry Lawrence for the difference she made to his teaching.

The authors would like to extend their thanks to the reviewers of this new edition whose sound advice helped to improve and enhance the final version. They especially wish to thank: Julie Apps, Lecturer at the School of Nursing, Midwifery and Social Work, University of Manchester; Siobhan McCullough, Lecturer at the School of Nursing and Midwifery, Queen's University Belfast and Dr Wendy Cousins, Course Director at the University of Ulster.

Chapter 1

Psychology in health and social care

Key topics

- Relevance of studying psychology
- Schools of thought in psychology
- Psychology in practice: people and practice
- How to make effective use of this book
- Introducing the 'psychosoap' family

Introduction

Our purpose throughout this book is to offer ideas from psychology that can be applied to your work in health or social care. Our objectives are to enable you to:

- apply evidence-based psychology to enhance your therapeutic work;
- become a reflective thinker who does not draw on simplistic explanations for the behaviour of others;
- work more effectively as a member of a multiprofessional team;
- promote and protect the health and well-being of patients or clients and their caregivers;
- preserve your own health and well-being.

In this chapter, we introduce you to some of the different perspectives used to study psychology, which we draw on in later chapters. We use a framework that is designed to help you reflect on your experiences in practice, starting with a vignette that captures the sort of situation we all face at some time.

Vignette

Anna is a student nurse on community placement who is being driven by her supervisor, a community nurse, to check on Mr Smythe, an elderly patient who is partially sighted and has recently been diagnosed with Type 2 diabetes. As they drive, Anna is asked to recall what had been said in lectures about the management of Type 2 diabetes. At the same time, Mr Smythe is trying hard to remember the instructions the nurse had given him at her previous visit.

Anna and Mr Smythe both want to present a positive image to the community nurse; they are both trying hard to recall important information and they are both in new situations that give rise to some anxiety. The community nurse is well aware of these parallels and reflects on how she can help the two of them to gain confidence and move forward.

The vignette above introduces some of the many topics we address in later chapters, for example:

- Why are Anna and Mr Smythe concerned about the image they present and how can they be put at ease?
- Why is it difficult to recall information and what can be done to make remembering information easier?
- Why are both Anna and Mr Smythe anxious and what can be done to help them both respond to their situations effectively?

The vignette embodies the important point that the basic ideas from psychology apply to us all, whether we work in health or social care, or are students or patients. If you are an undergraduate student, or have been working in health or social care for a long time, you will remember the transition to becoming a student, including meeting new people and responding to a new set of demands and expectations. The similarities and differences between the situation faced by somebody starting their studies and somebody experiencing illness for the first time are worth reflecting on. If you stop to consider what you have found difficult and what has helped you to deal with life changes, this will help you to understand better the world of your patients. Psychology has an important contribution to make to this process.

What is psychology?

Psychology is the study of human behaviour, thought processes and emotions. It can contribute to our understanding of ourselves and our relationships with other people, if it is applied in an informed way. To do this, psychology must take account of the context of people's lives. Certain sets of beliefs and behaviours are risk factors for illness; therefore some knowledge of public health and the public health agenda is essential. Those we care for come from a variety of different social and cultural backgrounds and have different world views and frameworks of meaning. These shape beliefs and behaviours that may place some people at greater or lesser risk of illness than others. Therefore, in order to apply psychology effectively to health and social care, some knowledge of sociology is essential. In order to understand the link between psychological and physiological processes, some knowledge of the biomedical sciences is also essential. Therefore psychology sits alongside these other disciplines to make an important contribution to the health and well-being of the population. But it is important to note that the psychology we draw on has evolved mostly from western philosophy, science and research, and needs to applied with some caution when applied to people from other cultures.

Why is psychology important in health and social care?

Those of us who work in the caring professions spend most, if not all, of our working lives interacting with other people. A key part of our job is to promote health and well-being. Many people are familiar with the following broad definition of health: 'a state of complete physical, mental and social well-being and not merely the absence of disease or infirmity' (WHO 1946). If this is seen as an important goal, those working in health and social care need the knowledge and skills to help people work towards achieving it. There are many ways in which psychological theory and research can contribute to improvements in health and social care. They can help us to:

- appreciate how people's understandings and needs vary, so that we can try to ensure that the individualized care we provide is both appropriate and optimal;
- understand how our own thought processes can sometimes lead us to incorrect assumptions about others;
- gain a better understanding of communication processes so that we can identify ways of improving the therapeutic relationship and work more effectively in inter-professional and inter-agency contexts;
- identify factors that affect how people cope with such situations as acute and chronic illness, pain, loss, and the demands of everyday life, so that we can help them, and ourselves, to cope better and reduce the risks of stress-related illness;
- inform us about factors that influence people's lifestyles and what makes it so hard for people to change health-related behaviours, such as smoking, diet and exercise;
- apply evidence-based interventions to enhance health, well-being and quality of life.

Schools of thought in psychology

There are a number of schools of thought in psychology which are quite different from each other. They influence the ways in which academic psychologists work and the ways in which psychology is applied in practice. These schools of thought reflect the separate traditions from which psychology has evolved:

- *Developmental psychology* is the study of the changes to the way individuals interpret and respond to the world around them as they mature throughout their lifespan (see Chapter 3). Developmental research has helped to establish age-appropriate interventions.
- *Cognitive psychology* is the study of cognition (mental processes) including memory, perception and information processing (see Chapter 4). Cognitive therapies aim to change the way the individual thinks about a problem.

- *Behavioural psychology* (based on behaviourism) is the study of learning by observing the direct effects of external contexts and events on behaviour and behaviour change (see Chapter 5). Behavioural therapies aim to change behaviour by altering the context and the consequences of the behaviour, for example by introducing treats for 'good' behaviour.

- *Social psychology* is the study of how social settings and social interactions influence the behaviour of individuals, either alone or in groups (see Chapters 2 and 6). Most cognitive and behavioural therapies take account of social influence when planning therapeutic changes, hence the use of the term 'social cognition' (see Chapter 9).

- *Psychoneuroimmunology and cognitive science* use modern technologies to study mind–body links between human thoughts and emotions, and physiological and immune responses (see Chapter 7). Research in this field has shown psychological interventions to be effective in disease reduction.

- *Psychodynamic psychology* (developed from psychoanalysis) aims to explain how past experiences exert unconscious influences over an individual's current thoughts and emotions. Therapies aim to uncover these influences so they can be dealt with at a conscious level. Psychodynamic therapies have been used mainly in the treatment of anxiety and depression. We refer to therapies used in the management of anxiety and depression in Chapters 5 and 8.

- *Humanistic psychology and narrative psychology* involve the subjective study of individual human experience (see Chapters 2 and 8). Humanistic and narrative approaches involve listening in a non-judgemental way to individual accounts. They are based on the assumption that humans have an innate capacity to solve their own problems. They provide the rationale for encouraging personal reflection as a problem-solving tool in practice. Person-centred counselling is commonly used in the treatment of distressing, but not major, psychological problems. Narrative approaches which encourage life review are used predominantly in later life (see Chapter 3).

Figure 1.1 illustrates how these different schools of thought relate to each other in terms of their contribution to the psychology of human experience.

Each approach gives us a unique insight into human psychological processes. It is not a matter of deciding which approach is 'true', but which ones are likely to be most useful in a given situation, or how insights from different perspectives can be used together to explain what appears to be happening. In therapeutic settings, many psychologists use an eclectic approach, which means selecting the combination of explanations and therapeutic approaches that best seem to suit the needs of the individual client.

In Table 1.1, we illustrate the application of these approaches to substance use, based on the potentially harmful use by a teenager, Joe, of an imaginary leisure drug nicknamed RAT. RAT could be a form of tobacco, alcohol, cannabis, heroin, crack cocaine or whatever the latest fashion drug happens to be.

Table 1.1 is intended to illustrate, in a very simple way, how each psychological approach can address an important aspect of substance use. When we consider the behaviour of other people, we frequently attribute it to a single cause and this is particularly true if we feel negative towards

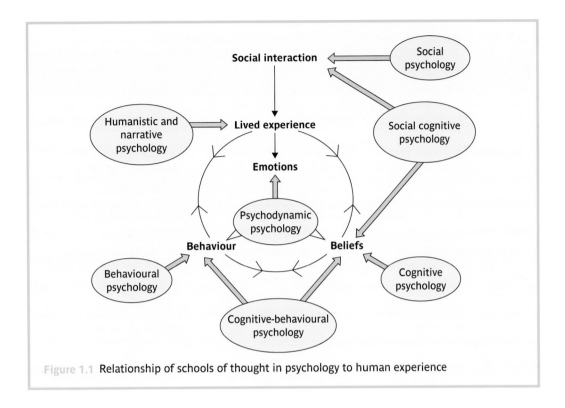

Figure 1.1 Relationship of schools of thought in psychology to human experience

the behaviour in question. Our attitude is very likely to be influenced by our knowledge of Joe's sex, age, education, employment, family or health status, by our own sex, age, education and health status, by whether RAT is a legal or an illegal substance and whether or not it leads to antisocial behaviours.

If we answer the question 'why does Joe use RAT?' by suggesting that 'Joe cares little about its consequences', we might assume that little can be done to stop Joe from using it. But the real answer is likely to be far more complex and far more demanding of our knowledge and skills. The ability to reflect on a range of influences and explanations in practice enables us to think of therapeutic interventions that could help someone like Joe in very many ways. Try out the following exercise and see how you get on.

Think of a habit that you would like to change. It might be 'not taking enough exercise', or 'eating the wrong food', or 'spending too much time on your phone'. Substitute this behaviour for the use of RAT in Table 1.1 and see how many different explanations you can find for why you do this. Then see if you can come up with any ways that might help you to make a change.

Exercise

Table 1.1 Psychological explanations and interventions for Joe's use of RAT

Psychological approach	Possible explanations for Joe's use of RAT	Possible ways of reducing or eliminating Joe's use of RAT
Behavioural explanations focus on the immediate consequences of behaviour	Joe finds RAT pleasurable and relaxing	Substitute alternative and equally pleasurable ways of relaxing
Cognitive explanations focus on incorrect or distorted beliefs	Joe does not believe that taking RAT causes any harm	Help Joe to reconsider his beliefs about the effects of RAT
Social psychology focuses on the way people interact with each other	Joe likes to spend time with friends who take RAT	Help Joe to manage social situations in which RAT is used
Developmental psychology focuses on the ways individuals change as they mature throughout their lives	Joe enjoys engaging in what are seen by older people as 'risk' behaviours, such as RAT	Help Joe to see that he is likely to view RAT differently in future years
Psychophysiology focuses on the interaction between physiological and psychological processes	Joe is physiologically addicted to RAT (his body needs it to function)	Introduce a less toxic replacement for RAT
Psychodynamic explanations focus on unconscious impulses and conflicts, often arising from childhood experiences	Taking RAT may be a comfort measure to compensate for needs that were not met in infancy	Focusing on Joe's emotional needs may help him to find alternative ways of meeting these
Humanistic psychologists help people develop their own inner resources to achieve their potential	There may be some underlying reason driving Joe's need to use RAT	Offer counselling support to help Joe explore his feelings about RAT and his reasons for using it

You will find relevant and detailed information throughout this book that will help you address these issues in more depth.

Psychology as a science

Modern psychology is a 'science'. Indeed, many courses in psychology are offered under the heading of 'cognitive science'. When people think of science they usually think in terms of physical sciences like physics. A good definition of 'a science' is that it is a discipline that tests its ideas first by making predictions, and then testing whether these predictions are true. Most of psychology, with its emphasis on research-based evidence, is clearly a science according to this definition.

Having read our example of substance use, those of you who have studied natural sciences such as physics or chemistry will probably have found psychology rather confusing. You will be used to making absolute predictions. For example, if you burn hydrogen you can predict with certainty that you will produce water. But humans are individuals. We are all different and behave in unpredictable ways. This means that psychology cannot possibly predict how any one individual will respond to a specific event or situation.

For ethical reasons, it is nowadays impossible to place humans or animals in experimental situations that could adversely affect their long-term well-being (although we give several examples of old experiments that did just that!). So psychologists have had to find alternative and imaginative ways of testing their predictions. We have selected a few of these experiments to illustrate key points in the forthcoming chapters. What is clear is that psychology can shed important light on behaviours that are difficult to understand, as in the case of substance use. Psychological research may even help us to predict and test therapeutic approaches that are effective for the majority of people.

Psychology in practice

In this section, we distinguish between the professionals who are trained in the administration of psychological interventions. We also provide a psychological justification for the use of reflective practice for everyone working in the fields of health and social care.

Professionals trained to provide psychological interventions

Those working in health and social care are likely to encounter a number of different types of psychologist. All have a first degree in psychology that is approved by their professional body and are trained in the use of research methods. They are distinguished from each other by the focus of their postgraduate training which nowadays is mainly at doctoral level. The following definitions are based on those given by the British Psychological Society (www.bps.org.uk):

Clinical psychologists aim to reduce psychological distress and to enhance and promote psychological well-being by helping those with mental and physical health problems including anxiety, depression and relationship problems.

Health psychologists promote positive ways of changing people's attitudes, behaviour and thinking in relation to both health and illness.

Counselling psychologists work with clients to examine mental health issues and explore the underlying problems that may have caused them, including bereavement, relationships and mental health problems.

Occupational psychologists help organizations to get the best from their workforce and improve the job satisfaction of individual employees.

Educational psychologists aim to help children and young people who experience problems that hinder their learning.

Sports and exercise psychologists work with participants in both team and individual sports. Exercise psychology is primarily concerned with the application of psychology to increase exercise participation and motivational levels in the general public.

Other types of psychologist include forensic (criminal) psychologists, neuropsychologists and teachers and researchers in psychology. The roles of some psychologists overlap with those of other health care professionals who have similar aims, including:

- *Counsellor* is similar to a counselling psychologist, except that there is no minimum standard of training, which can vary from a few days to several years and focus on one or several different psychological approaches.
- *Psychoanalyst* is someone who has trained in psychoanalysis under the supervision of an approved psychoanalyst. All approved psychoanalysts can trace the provenance of their trainers back to Freud. All analysts undergo psychoanalysis themselves as part of a lengthy period of training.
- *Psychodynamic psychotherapist* has undergone a period of intensive training, including personal analysis and supervised practice, and bases his or her approach on a psycho-dynamic model.
- *Psychiatrist* is a medical doctor who, since qualifying, has specialized in the diagnosis and treatment of people with mental health disorders. Psychiatrists have the right to prescribe drugs, the authority to admit people to hospital and sometimes use physical interventions such as electroconvulsive therapy (ECT).
- *Cognitive behaviour therapist* is a qualified health or social care professional, such as a mental health nurse, who has completed undergraduate or postgraduate specialist training in CBT. All clinical and counselling psychologists are trained to offer CBT.

Why is reflective practice so important?

Reflective practice is encouraged as part of education for all of the health and social care professions and psychology provides an important reason for this. For many years, some psychologists have accepted the idea that humans have two ways of processing information: one is unconscious and automatic; the other is conscious and deliberate or intentional. These different processes have a profound effect on our beliefs and behaviour. We compare these processes in Table 1.2, which we refer back to on many occasions in later chapters.

Table 1.2 Comparison between automatic and deliberate thought processing (Evans 2008)	
Automatic processing	**Deliberate processing**
Implicit	Explicit
Unconscious or preconscious	Conscious
Rapid	Slow
Automatic	Controlled
Low effort	High effort
Intuitive	Deliberative or thoughtful
Dependent on past experience of similar situations	Dependent on ideas

Our beliefs about others and our reactions towards others result from a mixture of automatic and deliberate processing. Deliberate processing is generally essential for the delivery of high-quality, individualized care. But automatic processing tends to take over as we are professionally socialized into stereotypical ways of thinking (see Chapter 2). Automatic processing also tends to take over as we gain in experience; for example, Benner (1984) described an expert as someone who has an intuitive grasp of each situation and no longer needs to waste time on considering alternatives. Intuition can be extremely useful, but there are obvious dangers when we rely on it too much. Reflection forces us to consider alternatives and offers protection against the negative effects of automatic processing. One of the main purposes of this book is to encourage you to reflect on your practice to enhance your learning and, in particular, to consider the impact of your practice on those you care for.

Making effective use of this book

This book has a number of features that, when combined, distinguish it from standard textbooks on psychology and health psychology. These are intended to enhance your learning experience and help you to relate psychological theory and evidence to practice. They include the following:

- A glossary at the back includes most terms that might be unfamiliar to a non-psychologist.
- At the start of each chapter, we have included an introductory vignette to focus your attention on important issues to be addressed.
- Examples illustrate key points and raise questions for you to consider. All of the situations we portray are taken from real life observations.
- Details of published research are used to support or supplement the information we give in the text and help to explain how psychological knowledge is arrived at.
- Summary tables appear at intervals throughout each chapter. These include theory-based practice guidance where appropriate.
- Exercises are intended to consolidate your understanding of the ideas we have introduced. You can do these alone, or with friends, or as part of a formal learning group on your course.

We have included two types of practical exercise:

- Those that enable you to relate the content of the book to your personal life.
- Those that enable you to relate the content of the book to what you observe or hear in practice.

In both types of exercise, the aim is the same – we want you to be able to apply the material in the book to your practice. But we recognize that it is not sufficient to understand the ideas in this book if you cannot relate them to real life situations. The abilities to reflect and to empathize are essential requisites for the provision of excellent care – the sort of care you would want your loved ones to receive. To achieve this, you need to be able to draw parallels between your own experiences and those that you work with and care for.

Introduction to the 'psychosoap'

In order to understand psychology, it is important to appreciate how it can be applied in different contexts. To do this, we give case scenarios drawn from our own experiences of practice and research, as well as those of our students and other informal contacts. It is essential for ethical reasons that we use pseudonyms and disguise individual identities at all times. To present a different pseudonym in each of our scenarios would be very confusing. So we have woven our examples into a family scenario that we use throughout the book, as in a soap opera.

Figure 1.2 contains the family tree for our 'psychosoap' family. We have also included a thumbnail sketch of each family member to help you make sense of the overall scenario.

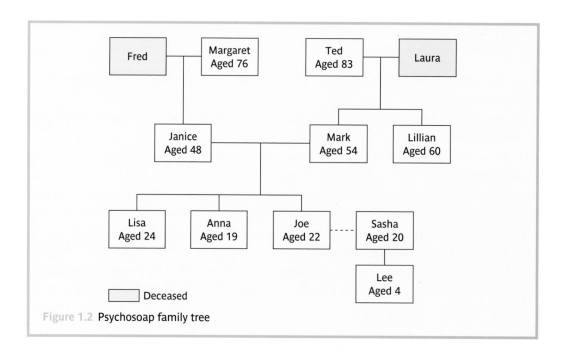

Figure 1.2 **Psychosoap family tree**

Psychosoap family background

Anna is currently studying for a degree programme in nursing, while living at home.

Lisa, Anna's older sister, is a qualified social worker working in an inner city area.

Anna and Lisa have a brother, **Joe**, who drifted after leaving school at the age of 16. He is currently unemployed and lives with his girlfriend **Sasha** and her son, **Lee**. Sasha is pregnant with Joe's baby.

Janice and **Mark** are parents to Lisa, Anna and Joe. Mark recently retired early because of the onset of Type 2 diabetes, hypertension and angina. Janice works as a health care assistant in a local nursing home for older people.

Janice's mother is **Margaret** who lives on her own in a town not far from Janice and Mark. She was born in the West Indies and came to this country when she was in her twenties. Here she married Fred who was then a postman. Fred died in an accident when Janice was 4 years old.

Mark's father **Ted** is a former factory worker. He is a widower whose wife died three years ago. He has chronic heart disease and has recently given up his home to live with Janice and Mark.

Mark's sister **Lillian** is unmarried and lives alone close by. She has recently been undergoing medical tests.

Further reading

The following textbooks are updated about every five years, so look out for the latest editions. There are a lot of alternatives, so you may prefer to be guided by your lecturers.

Background

Hughes, B.M. (2011) *Conceptual and Historical Issues in Psychology*. London: Prentice Hall.

Introductory psychology

Gleitman, H., Reisberg, D. and Gross, J. (2011) *Psychology*, 8th edition. New York: W.W. Norton.

Gross, R. (2010) *Psychology: The Science of Mind and Behaviour*, 6th revised edition. London: Hodder Education.

Health psychology

Marks, D.F., Murray, M., Evans, B., Willig, C., Woodall, C. and Sykes, C.M. (2005) *Health Psychology: Theory, Research and Practice*, 5th edition. London: Sage Publications.

Morrison, V. and Bennett, P. (2009) *An Introduction to Health Psychology*, 2nd edition. Harlow: Pearson Education.

Perceptions of self and others

Key topics

- Attitudes, stereotyping and the self-fulfilling prophecy
- Attribution and sources of bias
- Prejudice, discrimination and stigma
- The construction of self and identity
- Self-esteem, body image and personality

Introduction

In this chapter, we address the following questions:

- How do we form impressions of other people?
- What are the social influences that help to determine how we feel about ourselves and how we present ourselves to others?
- Why do we justify our own behaviour differently from the way we explain other people's behaviour?

The first part of the chapter considers our perception of other people, since this can have a profound effect on those we care for. The second part is about the sense of self, which has a major influence on how we feel and on what we do in almost every situation.

First, we invite you to take a few minutes to reflect on the following vignette.

Anna walked into the foyer of the hospital where there were many people moving around. There were nurses, visitors and porters. There were some people who were clearly patients: old people, young people, those who had recently had surgery and some who simply looked worried or unwell. As she looked at all these people, she automatically categorized them: old or young, patient or staff.

John was sitting in a wheelchair, leaning to one side, wearing a hospital bed gown. He was feeling very self-conscious about his appearance and aware of the rapid transition he had recently made from senior manager to just another patient.

Anna felt proud of her new role as she stopped to pull up John's blanket. At the same time her uniform also made her self-conscious. She realized that other staff might recognize her to be a novice because of subtle differences in the way she presented herself.

This vignette serves to illustrate that our perception of ourselves is greatly affected by the way we believe we are perceived by others. This process is rapid and efficient, but not always accurate. It is called stereotyping.

Stereotyping and attitude formation

As the vignette shows, we often perceive others according to the groups that we assign them to. Much of the information that we hold about other people is represented in stereotypes. A stereotype is a common set of beliefs or assumptions about a particular group of people. It is an example of a mental framework or 'schema' (see Chapter 3 for more on mental schemas). We learn these stereotypes without conscious effort and we are often unaware that we are using them. The stereotypes we use may draw on group characteristics that have some foundation in fact or experience, or they may be acquired from the media or through conversations within our network of family and friends.

Most stereotypes are based on selective attention to a limited number of characteristics which emphasize differences rather than similarities between groups. Group stereotypes are often based upon features such as age, gender, or ethnic, national or regional background. These characteristics are usually exaggerated and generalized at the expense of individual attributes. For example, it is not unusual for people in the UK, USA (and other countries) to have negative traits attributed to them according to their regional accent (Wales 2000; Hartley 2005).

Stereotypes lead to assumptions that fail to reflect the great variations within any group of people and are often very misleading when applied to an individual group member. This reflects a tendency to perceive the group that we belong to (our in-group) as more varied than groups we do not belong to (out-groups). In other words, we tend to think about members of our own group according to their individual characteristics, but members of other groups by a limited number of stereotypical group characteristics (this phenomenon is known as 'out-group homogeneity'). Many stereotypes are in fact positive. For example, many people share the idea that doctors are 'intelligent' and mothers are 'caring'. The following example illustrates the pervasiveness and impact of stereotypical assumptions.

The effects of stereotypical beliefs

Stern and Hildebrandt (1986) studied the reactions of women who were introduced to some full-term babies that were assigned the label of either 'full term' or 'premature'. Even though they looked the same, the full-term babies labelled as 'premature' were perceived as less cute and were less well liked than those labelled as 'full term'.

The label of prematurity not only changed the woman's perception, it changed the way she interacted with the baby, and this in turn changed the baby's behaviour.

Most of us who are interested in caring for others would agree with the idea that each person should be treated as an individual. Yet we often find that our emotional response (our gut response) does not always match up to that belief. The mothers in Stern and Hildebrandt's study would probably have been truly surprised to learn that they treated 'premature' babies differently from 'full-term' babies. The reasons for these discrepancies may be found in the two systems of processing, automatic and deliberate, we described in Chapter 1 (see Table 1.2). It would appear that we lack control over certain thought processes because they occur automatically, without our being consciously aware of what we are doing. Because of this, some might argue that they reveal certain hidden or implicit beliefs or assumptions that we would not consciously admit to but are evident in our attitude.

Attitudes

We all make frequent reference to attitudes and assume that we know what this means. Attitudes are subjective evaluations that predispose people to behave towards an object or person in a positive or negative way. The object in question may be a topic, such as a favourite television programme or teenage pregnancy, but it is commonly a person or group of people. For example, babies are usually portrayed in a very positive way, while older people have often been portrayed in a negative way. Attitudes are generally conceptualized as consisting of three classes of response:

- *cognitive*:   beliefs about the object;
- *affective*:   emotional feelings towards the object, based on a positive or negative evaluation;
- *behavioural*:   actions directed at the object.

Attitudes are formed through feedback from a range of different experiences. They are culturally shaped through formal socialization processes, including child rearing, schooling and professional training. They may also be the product of identification with social groupings such as religious, kinship or friendship groups. These groups exert strong influence or 'peer pressure' on the behaviour of group members. Conformity to 'social norms' laid down by the group is very strong and attitudes towards 'others' may be hostile (see Chapter 6).

Strong attitudes can be quite hard to suppress, even if we want to, because they tend to 'leak' via non-verbal behaviours. These include subtle changes in facial expression, gesture or posture, which make them difficult to hide from others. And as with stereotypical beliefs, we can hold and express some attitudes without being consciously aware of them.

Revealing implicit assumptions

Jost *et al.* (2004) used a method known as the Implicit Association Test (IAT) to test for positive and negative ideas associated with the concepts of ability and disability. They found that the behaviour of people taking the test sometimes showed that they had implicit ideas that were quite different from their explicit views. For example, one participant who had been an advocate of disability rights was quite distressed to find that he associated disability with certain negative qualities.

The idea of implicit thoughts can be quite uncomfortable, but did this participant need to worry about the results of that experiment? The IAT assesses associations between abstract ideas, in this case 'disability' or 'ability' and 'positive' or 'negative'. Making abstract associations is quite a different activity from responding to an actual person. Person-centred care is based on the understanding that an individual cannot be summed up by a single term such as 'disabled'. The respondent in Jost's experiment (Jost *et al.* 2004) may have had more positive associations with ability than disability, but would still have understood that 'disability' is only one small aspect of a person who is, in many regards, 'able'. This is the response that we advocate here. If we consciously take note of the whole person, rather than one particular characteristic, then the implicit associations found by Jost and others will be less important.

Nevertheless, it is important to recognize that implicit responses to others do exist and may on occasions lead us to experience emotional reactions that are unexpected and unwelcome. Education and close contact with groups who are marginal within our society enable us to understand the origins of negative attitudes and stereotypes, so that we can counter them in ourselves and others.

Overcoming negative attitudes and stereotypes

When Anna was still at school she went to help at a club for people with learning disabilities and was shocked at her own negative emotional reactions to the people she met there. It was only after continuing to work at the club that her view changed. Gradually the unusual appearance and behaviour shown by some of the people she met became less important to her. The things that had initially produced a negative reaction became interesting and even endearing characteristics, in a similar way to the likeable oddities of some of her friends.

As we have already shown, first impressions are very important in generating positive or negative attitudes. The ability to acknowledge negative reactions when they arise makes it easier to put these to one side and try to focus on the positive characteristics of those we work with and care for. As we noted in Chapter 1, reflection is an important tool for recognizing and dealing with these sorts of issue. And when recording or reporting personal information, it is a good idea to imagine that the patient or client is reading over your shoulder, or listening to what you say. The inability to recognize and deal with negative attitudes towards members of particular groups in society is important causes of prejudice, discrimination and stigmatization.

Prejudice and discrimination

Negative stereotypical attitudes are the main cause of prejudice and discrimination. Prejudice refers to the combination of negative beliefs and attitudes towards an individual or group, and discrimination to the negative behaviour associated with prejudice. Both prejudice and discrimination were implicit in the reactions of the mothers in Stern and Hildebrandt's study.

It is well recognized that certain groups in society are more likely to attract negative stereotypes, hence the need for laws that ban 'isms', such as racism, sexism and ageism. Cultural and religious affiliations have long been a source of prejudice because those stereotypes, like any other, overlook the variety of people within any particular group.

'We treat them all the same'

Vydelingum (2006) observed lack of attention to cultural differences and needs in the care given to Asian patients in a western general hospital. Examples included the failure to appreciate that lowering of gaze was a sign of respect, or that pain expression or tolerance might be different. The congregation of large numbers of visitors round the bed was seen as 'flouting the rules' and certain dietary requirements were viewed as irrational.

While some of these attitudes appeared to have racist undertones, staff claimed to be entirely fair because all patients were treated the same. But when encouraged to reflect on these issues, staff became more thoughtful and more aware of the consequences with respect to meeting individual needs. Vydelingum observed that reflexivity opens the way for improving cultural competence.

This example illustrates a real dilemma. By treating all patients the same for the sake of fairness, individual cultural and religious needs were overlooked. But there are clearly times when individual rights, such as having large numbers of visitors, might be seen as violating the rights of others to privacy and dignity. The ability to recognize when and how to deal with these issues requires insight and tactful negotiation.

Stigma

Goffman (1963) introduced the concept of stigma to refer to the distinguishing feature(s) of an individual or group that mark them out as different from the rest. A stigma can be a neutral feature, such as a facial blemish or abnormal body shape, which is interpreted by others in a negative way. Or it can represent an intentional sign of group membership, such as a hairstyle or dress code. Stigmas encourage stereotypical perceptions and reactions by others, a process referred to as stigmatization. It is possible that having any sort of distinguishing feature, such as wearing a head scarf or hijab, having visible tattoos, or using mobility aids may lead to labelling and stigmatization.

Research

Living with a facial disfigurement

As long ago as 1982, Rumsey *et al.* conducted an experiment on public transport to study the willingness of passengers to sit next to someone who had a large simulated birthmark on their face. The results were startling. When the birthmark was facing them, passengers tended to leave the adjacent seat empty until other seats were filled.

Strauss *et al.* (2007) studied the impact of facial disfigurement on the lives of adolescents. Congenital causes included birthmarks and cleft lip; acquired causes included burns. The findings were confirmed by a parent.

20 per cent were teased about how their face looked.

12 per cent felt left out of doing things with peers because of their looks.

11 per cent had been in a fight during the last month because of how they looked.

Girls felt the stigma more keenly than boys.

It appears that people who have a physical difference, whether congenital or acquired, are probably quite right to fear being stared at, ignored or avoided. Therefore, professionals need to understand these processes and have some knowledge of how best to help people deal with such situations.

Exercise

If you have the opportunity, why not replicate Rumsey's experiment? Alternatively, ask a friend to take you out in a wheelchair while you both observe the reactions of the public, shopkeepers and bar staff. Swap places and compare notes. Or devise your own experiment to test reactions to visible difference.

It is always helpful to be able to put yourself in the shoes of people who are stigmatized in order to understand what it is really like. Useful reviews of these issues, together with advice for professionals on how to help adolescents and adults with disfigurements, were provided by Newell (2002 a, b) and Rumsey and Harcourt (2004). Social skills training to help people deal with the social anxiety of facial disfigurement appears to offer benefits. Face transplant might appear to offer hope for those with the most severe facial disfigurements. But Rumsey (2004) suggested that the recipients most likely to benefit cosmetically are also likely to be among those most psychologically vulnerable and therefore ill-equipped to deal with the uncertainties of surgery.

The stigma of mental illness

A classic study by Rosenhan (1973), 'On being sane in insane places', illustrated how a diagnosis of mental illness, once established, can be difficult to shake off. In Rosenhan's study, several 'normal' people, including a psychologist and a paediatrician, presented themselves at a psychiatric clinic complaining of hearing voices. During their assessment, all of their behaviour was normal apart from their claims to have heard voices. All were diagnosed as having major mental illness, in most cases schizophrenia, and were admitted to hospital. Following admission, they stopped complaining about the voices, but in most cases it took several weeks to convince staff that they were in remission and well enough to be discharged. Only fellow patients were suspicious about their true identities.

People with mental health problems are probably the most stigmatized group in society. Even those who have suffered an episode of depression or other less serious mental illness are perceived by others to be less trustworthy and intelligent, more incompetent and dangerous, with the result that they suffer serious socio-economic disadvantage, social exclusion and higher levels of stress (see the review by Link and Phedan 2006). Some physical illnesses, such as epilepsy, HIV and cancer, have been similarly stigmatized in the past. Recent literature has focused on stigmatizing attitudes towards obese children and adults and demonstrated how these can impact on both mental and physical health. For example, Puhl and Latner (2007) demonstrated how negative health consequences of obesity, including blood pressure, in children are mediated by the stress of being stigmatized (see Chapter 7 on stress).

The 'bariatric' patient

Anna was assigned to look after Dennis, a 40-year-old patient who had multiple health problems and was labelled 'bariatric' (grossly obese). His care was difficult because of his size, so some permanent ward staff tried to avoid him. Behind the curtains, he burst into tears. He was aware of the negative attitudes towards him and was ashamed of his weight. He had always been large but had gained weight after his mother died a few years ago and he was left on his own. Anna began to see that the more isolated he became, the more he had turned to food for comfort. His stigmatization and isolation on the ward was unlikely to help him address his problems.

Within health and social care, diagnostic labels and indicators of social deprivation are assessed using 'valid and reliable' methods of assessment that purport to be objective. The resulting categories are intended to assist with social, psychological or medical treatment or management, but can have unintended harmful consequences because they often focus exclusively on what a person cannot do, and ignore what they can do. Some categories, such as geriatric and bariatric, can easily become terms of abuse.

In the following sections, we focus a little more closely on explanations for the tendency to develop negative stereotypes.

Sources of negative bias in social perception

The negativity effect

It has been known for a long time that we pay more attention to negative information about people than we do to positive information. This is known as the negativity effect. One possible reason for this is that negative information serves a warning function; it tells us when we need to respond with caution. For example, when we have a negative impression about a person we tend to avoid them. This can involve physical avoidance, as in the examples we gave earlier. But there are also more subtle forms of 'social avoidance'. For example, although staff may have to give care to a patient, they may choose not to engage with them for any longer than is necessary to accomplish the task.

Example

Who gets most visits? When caring for older people in the community, it seems logical that time should be allocated on the basis of need. Yet when Anna was out on community placement, she observed that the community nurse seemed to spend more time with people who were welcoming and cheerful than with those who expressed real emotional needs in a negative way.

Both physical and social avoidance mean that care workers will never have the opportunity to discover if their negative impressions are correct. A person may be really likeable but unless we get to know them we will never get to know this (Smith and Collins 2009). The failure to discover that our negative impressions are mistaken relates to the more widespread phenomenon of 'confirmation bias'.

Confirmation bias

When we form an idea, we have a tendency to look for evidence that supports the idea (confirming evidence) rather than seek evidence to test the possibility that the idea is incorrect (disconfirming evidence). For example, if something leads you to believe that a patient or client is 'nice' or 'awkward', you will tend to look for and find evidence that confirms this. Once again, this can happen without deliberate intent.

Exercise

When you have the opportunity, listen to the way members of staff describe patients at hand-over. How often do you hear a judgemental term such as 'that nice old lady', or 'that difficult patient' or 'that lovely looking young man' or 'this delightful child'?

- Reflect on the implications of any positive and negative descriptors used.
- Focus also on non-verbal expressions of attitude, including tone of voice and facial expression.

Then think about your own feelings towards the patients referred to in the light of the descriptions you have heard. Can you think of evidence to disconfirm or confirm those descriptions?

Confirmation bias goes well beyond social psychology. Researchers often pay more attention to evidence that confirms their hypothesis than to evidence that seems to contradict it – or they come up with cogent reasons for the failure of their hypothesis. Positive findings (those that support the researcher's hypothesis) are much more likely to be written up for publication than negative findings. This is why those undertaking a 'systematic review' of the literature are obliged to seek out and consider unpublished as well as published research findings.

Exercise

Next time you write an assignment, think carefully about the references you use and how you use them. Do you look for references that support the point you want to make? Or do you look for evidence to counter your argument? Which do you think is likely to test or extend your understanding of a subject?

The self-fulfilling prophecy

This is perhaps the best known form of bias. The self-fulfilling prophecy refers to a predictive form of labelling that becomes true, either by direct or indirect means. Take the example of the babies in the study by Stern and Hildebrandt, which we outlined earlier in this chapter. It was clear that the women had different attitudes and expectations of babies labelled as premature and were therefore likely to respond differently to them. Had those women been responsible for bringing up the babies, those labelled as full term were likely to have shown a different developmental pattern to those labelled as premature, even though they were no different to start with. This offers one explanation for the effect of nurture versus nature (upbringing versus inherited characteristics) that we consider in Chapter 3. People treated in a positive way tend to respond in a positive way, while those treated in a negative way are more likely to respond in a negative way. The effects of this 'self-fulfilling prophecy' were well illustrated in a series of classic social psychology experiments conducted by Rosenthal and colleagues in the 1960s.

Teacher expectations in the classroom

Rosenthal and Jacobson (1968) examined the effect of teachers' expectations on children in a classic classroom experiment. The result became known as the 'Pygmalion effect'.

At the beginning of the school year, students took an IQ test and were then randomly (regardless of the actual results) labelled as either clever or ordinary. The teacher was told to expect that the clever ones would make rapid progress. Students took a repeat IQ test at the end of the year.

Students labelled 'clever' were found to have made greater gains in IQ, compared to the others. Observations suggested that students labelled as clever received more attention, more encouragement and more positive feedback from the teacher than the other pupils.

It is worth remembering that, in the fields of health and social care, the self-fulfilling prophecy may be an important determinant of patients' and clients' behaviour. If we expect someone to be nice we pay them more attention and they respond in a more positive way to us. Try to remember that next time you approach someone who has been labelled as difficult.

Unpopular patients

In the early 1970s, Stockwell (1984) reported the findings of a classic nursing study which sought to identify the characteristics of 'unpopular' patients. Factors that accounted for their lack of popularity with nursing staff included physical features, physical defects, nationality, length of stay, complaints, and the need for time-consuming care. Other factors include perceptions of low social worth or value (Johnson and Webb 1995).

Taylor (1979) observed that 'good patient' behaviour involves being quiet, passive and undemanding. But these characteristics can also be indicative of dependence and depression.

Being passive is not conducive to recovery (see Chapter 8 on resilience). Yet those who are vocal about expressing their needs frequently become unpopular with care staff.

Next time you are on a placement, listen to the way members of staff talk about individual patients or clients. Who are the least popular ones? Why are they unpopular? How are they treated?

See if you are able to spend a little time with one of these patients, encourage them to 'tell me a little about yourself and your life'. How does their story make you feel?

Attribution theory

We have already referred to some psychological processes that seek to explain how stereotyping and prejudice occur. Attribution theory offers additional insight. According to attribution theory, we all have a basic need to understand why things happen. We want to have an idea about why people, including ourselves, behave the way they do; and we want to know the cause of events such as our becoming ill (see Chapter 9). Attribution theory proposes that decisions about causality involve three separate dimensions:

- *locus*:   internal–external (myself, or someone else);
- *stability*:   stable–unstable (always, or just on this occasion);
- *globality*: global–specific (in all situations, or just in this situation).

[The dimension 'internal–external locus' is similar to 'locus of control' (see Chapter 5), although it refers to beliefs about responsibility for cause, whereas locus of control refers to beliefs about responsibility for achieving future outcomes. The two are closely related.]

Attribution theory is illustrated in the following example:

Anna failed her first assessment. How might she explain this? Here are some of the possibilities:

1 Internal, stable and global attribution for failure: Anna decides she is just no good at anything.
2 External, unstable and specific attribution for failure: on this occasion, Anna believes the task was an unfair test of her ability.
3 Internal, unstable and specific attribution for failure: on this occasion, Anna reckons she did not work hard enough.

Which of these is most likely to lead to successful resubmission?

Example

The attributions people make are likely to determine their future course of action.

- If Anna holds internal, stable and global attributions for failure (I am no good at anything), this belief may cause her to leave the course.
- If Anna made external, unstable and specific attributions (it is their fault for setting such a poor test on this occasion), she may blame the module leader. This will help her to feel better about her failure, but will not motivate her to work harder for resubmission.
- On the other hand, if Anna makes internal, unstable and specific attributions (it was my own fault on this occasion because I didn't work hard enough), she is well placed to address the reasons for her failure and ensure that she works harder to achieve a pass next time.

There is evidence from research in health care that internal locus of control tends to be associated with better health outcomes in a variety of situations, probably because these attributions are associated with a greater sense of personal responsibility for self-management (see Chapters 8, 9 and 10).

Attribution bias

Attribution theory helps us understand how we make judgements about the actions of others. If someone is anxious, we may attribute their anxiety to their personality (internal, stable and global attributions). Or we may, if we have taken a little time to find out the reasons for their anxiety, attribute this to specific worries or concerns about their illness or what is happening at home (external, unstable, specific attributions). The attributions we make have important implications for the way we respond to others. All too often, we draw on stereotypes (negative, stable and global attributions) when making these judgements.

There is a tendency to systematic bias in the way we draw inferences about the causes of other people's behaviour when compared to our own. Ross called this the fundamental attribution error. When making a judgement about someone else's behaviour, he defined the fundamental attribution error as:

> the tendency for attributers [those making a judgement] to underestimate the impact of situational factors and to overestimate the role of dispositional [personality] factors.
>
> (Ross 1977: 183)

Closely related to this is the actor–observer effect, which is defined as the 'pervasive tendency' for people to attribute their own actions to the demands of the situation, while those observing are likely to attribute the actions to stable personal dispositions (personality traits). Malle (2006) has suggested that these forms of bias are more likely when trying to explain negative outcomes.

Examples of attribution bias

- If I make a mistake, it is because I was given the wrong information or instructions. But if somebody else makes the same mistake, it is because they are stupid, didn't listen or were careless.
- If I am anxious about an illness symptom, there must be a physical cause, even if the doctor cannot find one. But if a patient is worried about an illness symptom for which there is no apparent cause, he or she must be a hypochondriac.

On the other hand, the 'self-serving' or 'self-enhancing' bias refers to attributions for success-ful outcomes. For example, leaders tend to attribute the success of their group or organization to their own leadership expertise (a stable internal attribution for success), thus enhancing their personal reputation. But if the group or organization suffers a failure, they are more likely to lay the blame at an unexpected system fault (unstable, external attributions for failure).

Quite out of character, Anna forgot to report an incident to her mentor, who was held responsible for her omission. When he drew Anna's attention to her mistake, she knew that it was because it had been a very busy morning and she had been asked to attend to a patient who was very distressed.

Her mentor could have used this situation as an opportunity to discuss ways of prioritizing demands and ensuring that important tasks were not overlooked. Instead, he gave the impression to the ward manager that Anna was unreliable.

Attribution bias is an important cause of victim-blaming judgements. An example is the tendency to blame individuals for their plight, rather than focusing on the effect of health and social inequalities. Thus the poor are blamed for their poverty and the sick are blamed for their failure to follow a healthy lifestyle. Similarly, when mistakes occur in health or social care settings, there is a tendency to place blame on an individual, rather than examine the policies, procedures, environment or culture that impacted on their behaviour. As a consequence of this, people are reluctant to report errors when they occur and the structural or environmental causes remain unaddressed. In the interests of patient safety, attempts are being made to introduce a no-blame culture into the NHS. This would encourage the reporting of mistakes or errors, without the assignment of personal blame, so that organizational causes can be identified and addressed.

Perception of others

The following are suggestions about how you might reflect on your own experience of reacting to stereotypes. If you are to do this exercise properly, it will take real honesty on your part, and it may be uncomfortable. We suggest that you keep a record of your thoughts and (anonymized) observations as they happen. You may want to keep this private, if that allows for a more honest reflection.

- Are there certain 'types' of people that bring up negative feelings for you?
- If so, make a special effort to notice what actually happens when you meet people in this category. Do this for several individuals, either at college or on placement or both. Write down how you feel when you meet them.
- See what happens as you get to know them better. Do they match your first expectations? Write down your thoughts. Did you change your mind or do you now have a better idea what it is that prejudiced you against this sort of person?

Table 2.1 Summary: factors that affect the perception of others

Concept	Implications
Automatic processing of information is unconscious, rapid and effortless	Leads to implicit assumptions that may be incorrect, and stereotyping
Deliberate processing requires conscious effort and explicit assumptions	Necessary when providing individualized care. Reflection encourages deliberate processing
Attitudes: subjective evaluations that determine what we believe, how we respond emotionally and how we behave towards topics, people or objects	Negative attitudes are often overcome once we learn more about the subject or individual
Stereotyping: categorization of people according to group membership rather than individual characteristics	Leads to positive or negative attitudes towards all members of a group, depending on the stereotype used
Prejudice: negative attitudes towards all members of a group	Leads to discrimination against all members of the group
Discrimination	Negative behaviours towards individuals or groups, based on group membership
Out-group homogeneity	Tendency to think people in other groups are all the same
Negativity bias: tendency to attach undue importance to negative information about people	Once we have negative information about a person, we tend to avoid them
Confirmation bias: tendency to seek information to confirm rather than test our perceptions	We need to get to know individuals and make up our own minds, rather than being biased by prior information
Self-fulfilling prophecy	The predictions others make for us alter the way they treat us and tend to make their predictions come true
Primacy effect	First impressions count
Causal attributions include locus (self or other), stability (just now or always) and globality (in all situations or just this one)	An individual's causal attributions influence whether or not they will take personal responsibility for their actions
Attribution error or bias	Tendency to blame individuals for mistakes, rather than look for situational causes Tendency to excuse our own mistakes but blame others for theirs

So far, we have examined our judgements about other people and the effects that these have upon them. In the following section, we turn round and focus on our sense of self and the factors that contribute to its development.

The self-concept

We start with three vignettes that highlight links between the public presentation of self and the private self.

Examples

Lisa visited Sara, a single mother who was struggling to cope in difficult circumstances and had been diagnosed with postnatal depression. Sara had been given antidepressants which she had so far refused to take, saying *'I don't want to take them because of what they say about me.'*

Ted had arthritis pain and had been given painkillers and anti-inflammatory medication to take. At the start of a long holiday weekend, Ted complained of persistent stomach pains. Janice thought this was probably a side-effect of the tablets and advised him to stop taking them. But Ted was worried about what his doctor would think of him if he stopped them without medical advice.

Anna was struggling to finish an assignment. She was not sure exactly what was required but was reluctant to ask her tutor for fear of being seen as stupid.

In these examples, Sara, Ted and Anna each respond in different ways to what they perceive to be the expectations of others. We have already presented good reasons to be concerned about what other people think of us. Social psychologists go further by asserting that, from the time we are born, our sense of self is actually formed by the feedback we receive from others and the way we are treated by others. In the following sections, we present various ways of thinking about the sense of self and its development, together with some of their implications. Each of these perspectives offers a slightly different explanation for the development of the self-concept, but they should not be seen as mutually exclusive.

The 'looking glass self'

According to this idea, put forward by Cooley in 1902, we learn to see ourselves as we perceive others see us. From an early age our parents and others confer labels on us, such as good-looking or hard-working. We internalize these labels and use them to define ourselves. Positive labels make us feel good about ourselves and can motivate us to do well. Negative labels make us feel bad about ourselves and can reduce our belief in ourselves. This provides an important link between the perceptions others have of us and our perceptions of ourselves.

Exercise

Think of the labels you grew up with and those you have acquired more recently. Do you think any of these have turned into self-fulfilling prophecies?

Compare your own labels with those attached to your siblings, if you have any, or your friends. What impact, if any, do you think these have had on your lives?

Most of us remember labels placed on us by our parents and others during childhood. These are often used to distinguish between siblings. In our psychosoap family, Lisa was labelled as 'bubbly', Anna as the one who worked hard and her younger brother, Joe, was labelled from an early age as lazy. Such labels may or may not reflect the 'truth', but once internalized can become self-fulfilling prophecies. This may help to explain why Lisa is outgoing and popular, Anna is anxious to achieve success in her training as a nurse, while Joe failed to achieve at school and remained unemployed. Some of these acquired 'traits' may remain relatively stable, while others change as we encounter new social or professional groups or enter into new relationships.

Social identity theory

According to social identity theory (Tajfel 1982), our identity must balance the need to be similar to our reference group with the need to be a unique individual. In other words, we need to balance our social identity against our personal identity. A reference group is a group that we belong to by virtue of circumstance, such as the school we attend, or a group we choose to belong to, such as our chosen profession, or even a group we aspire to belong to. Our choice of reference group may be determined by the way we want to see ourselves, but equally our group membership (or aspiration) can determine how we see ourselves, how we evaluate our self-worth and how we behave. For example, young people may get caught up in antisocial behaviour in order to maintain their self-worth as equal members of their group or gang.

From an early age, children become very aware of the need for a group identity and are often afraid of dressing or acting differently from their peers for fear of victimization. As they approach their teens, they often seem torn between the need to assert their own individual identity and the need to conform to their reference group. Distinctive or rebellious group identities often emerge at this time, with particular styles of dress and behaviour. Later, new identities are forged in relation to work, parenthood, economic status and ageing and during their lives most people develop several different identities.

Anna has recently acquired a new identity as a nurse. With this comes a uniform, bedside manner, code of conduct, and set of expectations. But when she goes off duty and out with her friends, she assumes quite a different identity.

Her identity as a nurse is quite different from her sister Lisa's as a social worker. While they both assume caring roles, their respective professional groups have quite different ways of thinking and behaving.

Anna and Lisa are able to share a lot in terms of their family and social identities, but find each other's professional identities quite difficult to understand.

The identities we confer on others, based on stereotypical assumptions, are often rejected. For example, one 80-year-old might refer to another 80-year-old as 'that poor old soul' because they mentally distance themselves from being old. As a result, many older people decline to join seniors clubs. It becomes clear that, in many circumstances, people just don't see themselves the same way that others see them. It is a mistake to assume that individuals share common attributes or have anything in common with each other just because they happen to belong to a particular age or social group, or any other group.

Self-stereotyping

The reverse can also be true and we may learn to see ourselves in terms of the stereotypes conferred on us by others. These 'self-stereotypes' can be important in determining the way we feel about ourselves and the way we behave.

Living up to a stereotypical identity

In a study by Finlayson *et al.* (2005), low income African-American women who took part in a health survey were randomized to state their ethnic origin either before or after completing the health questionnaire. Those who were asked to state their ethnic origin *before* completing the questionnaire were more fatalistic about health outcomes and performed less well on assessments of their health knowledge than those who stated their ethnic origin after completing the questionnaire.

This study seems to support the view that people who are reminded of their group membership tend to behave in a manner that is consistent with the group stereotype. This may help to account for some of the differences in health-related and social behaviours shown by different social groups in the UK.

Social comparison

Social comparison theory (Festinger 1954) proposes that we construct our sense of self by making comparisons between our personal attributes and those of other people. That someone is 5 feet 8 inches tall is a statement of fact, but whether they consider themselves tall or short depends on who they compare themselves with. For example, they might consider themselves tall if a woman and short if a man.

When we are young, we tend to accept the labels conferred on us. But as we get older, we make our own comparisons with those who are important to us and who make up our reference group. Making downward social comparisons (seeing oneself as better, or better off, than others) tends to boost our self-esteem (feelings of self-worth) and maintains our sense of well-being. For example, people who are older or disabled are often heard to comment that there are lots of others worse off. This seems to help them feel better about their own situation.

Our self-concept and self-esteem depends to some extent on our choice of reference group. For example, those who gain a place at the University of Poppleton might consider themselves very successful if they are from a family with no history of going to university, but a failure if they are from a family where there is a strong tradition of winning Oxbridge scholarships. Media role models play an important part in influencing individual self-concept and self-esteem at both ends of the age spectrum by setting standards of expectation for such things as body shape, complexion, material acquisitions and status.

Social role theory

According to Goffman (1959), an important part of the self-concept is determined by the different social roles people play. We all play a large number of social roles during our lifetime, as illustrated in the following example.

Example

Anna has various roles as friend, daughter, aunt, nurse, part-time barmaid and girlfriend. Some of these are a familiar, taken-for-granted part of her life, though recently she returned to live at home and found that her role as daughter has changed because of her increased independence and confidence. However, she is still learning her role as nurse and frequently faces feelings of uncertainty and self-consciousness.

Goffman (1959) likened the experience of living to a drama that takes place in the theatre of everyday life (this is often referred to as the 'dramaturgical model'). Thus our social roles may be seen as the roles in a play and the social environment as the stage set. For example, in Chapter 6 we describe the Stanford prison experiment in which participants acted in accordance with their assigned role as either prisoner or prison guard. Goffman suggested that any one person will have available to them a number of different social roles according to the setting they are in at the time.

Goffman outlined how we use various props to help sustain our roles and present the image we wish to portray. He termed this 'impression management'. Clothes, hairstyle, make-up, perfume and mobile phone are all examples of the props we use to portray the public image we wish to present. The doctor's stethoscope and white coat are part of the props used to create the image of the doctor. In fact, the performance of some 'bogus' doctors has been so convincing that it has taken a long time before their lack of medical knowledge or expertise has exposed them. Each profession has its own set of props and behaviour into which newcomers are initiated and socialized. These are often learned by modelling (copying) rather than formal instruction (see social learning, Chapter 5). However, we eventually learn to regulate and modify our own behaviour as necessary.

Exercise

In our introductory vignette, we referred to the belief that an experienced member of staff might be able to recognize a novice by subtle differences in self-presentation.

- Apart from formal signs of status, see in how many ways you might be able to identify a newcomer into your own profession.

We often meet patients or clients in situations where they are deprived of their normal props or set. In our initial vignette, there was nothing to indicate what roles John, in the wheelchair, might have held in 'real life'. Knowledge of these other roles and identities can significantly influence the attitudes of those caring for them. For example, in order to ensure that she commanded greater respect, a colleague reminded staff that her elderly mother had until recently held the role of magistrate.

Adapting to changing roles

While certain aspects of our identity remain relatively stable over time, our roles can vary quite significantly during the course of our lives (see Chapter 3). Some people find it more difficult than others to make a transition between these different roles. Most of these role changes are a result of choice though others, like illness, divorce or job loss, are not. Some find it easier to adapt to changes in role than others (see also Chapter 8 on resilience).

During Janice's lifetime, she has had to adjust from being single to being married and becoming a parent; from being the mother of young children to having adolescent offspring and then to being alone with her husband. She was a caregiver to her mother-in-law, Laura, and now cares for Ted. Her role changed from being financially 'dependent' to chief wage-earner after Mark retired. Her role as wife and lover has changed over the years, as their relationship has matured, since she has aged and since Mark's health has deteriorated.

Example

Illness and disability interfere, often unexpectedly, with the ability of an individual to continue with previous social roles. For example, people who have lived independent lives suddenly become dependent on others. With new social roles comes adaptation to a new set of social rules and a new sense of self. An early study, Linville (1987) found that people vary in their ability to perceive themselves differently in different situations. Linville showed that having a complex self-schema that varies in response to different situations appears to make people more adaptive and resilient to stress-related illness and depression. Flexibility and resilience refer to the ways that people have become accustomed to think about things. It is influenced by their genetic make-up, their socialization, and their exposure to different life experiences. Openness (or not) to new ideas is characterized as a personality trait. But we have shown that many, if not most, of the difficulties people experience when adjusting to new roles are caused not by personal weaknesses, but by the attitudes of others.

Constructing the self

Another theory designed to accommodate change is that of Kelly (1955) who proposed that as we grow up we learn about ourselves and the world around us in much the same way that a scientist produces and tests theories. According to Kelly, we organize this knowledge into a series of dimensions called personal constructs that define our sense of self. Examples might include 'intelligent', 'attractive', 'outgoing', if these are important to us. We identify ourselves somewhere between positive and negative in relation to each one. For example, the labels others attach to us are not just internalized without question, but are put to the test in an attempt to confirm them. This offers one explanation for how stereotypical prophecies can become self-fulfilling.

Kelly went further to propose that anxiety and depression might be caused by a discrepancy between the 'ideal self' (the attributes the individual aspires to have) and the 'real self' (the attributes they perceive themselves to have). Kelly worked therapeutically, using what he termed 'repertory grid' analysis (see example in Figure 2.1) to help people realign these aspects of the self and improve their sense of self-worth.

Changing self-constructions

When Anna was a teenager, she was desperate to be interesting, attractive and outgoing, but rated herself negatively when compared to her selected significant others, as in Figure 2.1. This made her feel quite depressed. Based on Kelly's approach, a therapist would work with her to focus on her positive characteristics and encourage her to try out new roles that facilitate positive comparisons with others.

	Myself as I am (actual self)	Myself as I would like to be (ideal self)	Brother	Best friend
Interesting (✓) Dull (✗)	✗	✓	✓	✓
Attractive (✓) Plain (✗)	✗	✓	✓	✓
Outgoing (✓) Shy (✗)	✗	✓	✓	✓

Figure 2.1 Anna's **repertory grid**

The narrative self

Finally, a recent focus in psychology has been on what is termed 'the narrative self'. According to this approach, our identities are made up of the stories we construct about ourselves. We each have our own unique life story that encompasses the past, present and future. Our life story represents our map, our destination and our purpose. This narrative provides a sense of continuity over time. We use it to justify our actions and our existence. Within our life story, there are lots of smaller stories, based on various sub-plots that are constructed for different audiences, such as family, friends or colleagues. These define us as someone who is unique and they distinguish us from others. These stories may not be entirely factual because, as Murray (2003) explains, we construct narratives that help us to make sense of our life experiences and our aspirations.

Exercise

Try constructing a short story (no more than 500 words) that represents an important aspect of yourself, with the intention of presenting it to someone you have not met before.

How might this story differ from a story you might have told for someone close to you, whom you have known for a long time?

Major life-changing events, including chronic illness, disability or loss, cause what is termed biographical disruption because these events challenge both our story line and our sense of self (see also Chapter 3). Frank (1995) argued that illness calls for its own story and each story demands a listener. Listening to someone's account of their illness tells us a lot about the way they see themselves in the context of their illness and their life. It helps us to see them as individuals and tells us about the challenges they face.

Exercise

Set aside at least half an hour to spend with an individual patient or client who has experienced an illness or social problem and invite them to 'tell their story'.

- What does their account tell you about how the individual wants to be seen by others (for example, as a hero or a victim)?
- What does it tell you about their sense of self-worth? You may find it helpful to reflect on this as you read the next section on self-esteem.

Self-image

Self-esteem

Self-esteem reflects a critical personal evaluation of self-worth and is a central component of psychological well-being. Research evidence supports the view that there are stable elements of self-esteem which are formed early in life, though subsequent life experiences may serve to raise or lower self-esteem. There is no single theory of self-esteem. Accounts depend very much on the field of psychology they are drawn from and the different explanations are not mutually exclusive:

- According to personal construct theory, self-esteem reflects the degree of discrepancy between the ideal self (what an individual would like to be) and the actual self. The greater the discrepancy, the lower self-esteem.
- A psychodynamic psychologist might view self-esteem as resulting from the type and strength of attachment relationships formed in early life (see Chapter 3 on development).

- Drawing on social comparison theory (Festinger 1954), self-esteem is influenced by the extent to which we feel our beliefs and behaviour are valued by others who matter to us. This is often referred to as the 'social norm' (see the theory of planned behaviour in Chapter 9).

- According to Bandura's social learning theory (Bandura 1997: Chapter 5), self-esteem comes from the confidence in one's ability to be able to achieve important goals. Personal efficacy is an important determinant of self-esteem in western societies that value individual effort and personal achievement. In contrast, in eastern cultures esteem is gained through personal contribution to collective endeavour (Abrams and Hogg 2004).

Feedback on self-worth commences at birth and is particularly important during the formative years. Therefore childhood experiences in the family and in peer groups are very important (see Chapter 3). Changes in adult life, particularly changes in work or family roles, are important influences on self-esteem. Injuries or alterations to the body can also have important positive or negative effects on self-esteem, as evidenced by demand for cosmetic surgery.

Body image

Our bodies are important determinants of our identity and self-esteem. Bodies have certain unique features that remain relatively stable over time and by which other people recognize us. Other body features change with age and life experiences. Work as health or social care professionals brings us into contact with many people who have to deal not only with life changes but with changes to their actual bodies. Some of these are abrupt results of trauma, disease processes or surgery. Other changes are insidious, as in disease processes such as rheumatoid arthritis or chronic heart disease, those caused by exposure to toxic environments, or ageing processes such as the menopause. All types of bodily change can result in the need to change the self-concept and may seriously challenge an individual's sense of identity.

Body image is described as having three components: body reality, body ideal and body presentation.

Body reality

Body reality refers to the physical structure of the individual's body. Basic aspects of our body reality, such as our height, eye and hair colour and body shape, are determined by genetic factors. Other aspects of body structure, such as weight and skin texture, change over time from infancy to old age. Nevertheless, most people retain a sense of continuity in relation to their own bodies. Sudden disruptions require adjustment, whether these are the result of trauma or disease, or were deliberately engineered, for example by cosmetic surgery.

Body ideal

Body ideal is part of an individual's ideal sense of self. It is likely to be gender-specific and age-specific, but is strongly influenced by social norms that define appropriate size, shape and contours. Magazines and other media provide a lot of information about 'appropriate' body shape, size and colour, for example urging women to be slim, suntanned or have large breasts. A brief look at a history of fashion book shows how women's, and to a lesser extent men's, ideal body shapes have varied over time. There are also cultural differences in what is considered desirable. Discrepancies between body reality and body ideal lead to dissatisfaction and have been blamed for serious health problems, such as eating disorders.

Anna's friend, Suzy, judges herself to be fat in relation to her ideal self when she is in fact of normal weight in relation to population norms. Considering herself to be fat makes Suzy feel bad about herself, even though all her friends think she looks great. Suzy has tried unsuccessfully to stick to a healthy diet and exercise plan in order to lose weight so she has recently started skipping meals completely. Anna is very concerned that she has an eating disorder and has encouraged her to seek help from the college counsellor.

The effect of body image on self-esteem is influenced by the roles that are important to the individual. For example, a mastectomy scar may damage self-esteem in the role of lover, but be of little importance in the role of, say, accountant.

Changed body image and self-esteem

Al-Ghazal *et al.* (2000) compared the impact on body image and self-esteem of different types of breast cancer surgery (local excision, mastectomy and mastectomy plus breast reconstruction) for women aged between 20 and 70. In all age groups, mastectomy was associated with poorer body image and lower self-esteem. The research team concluded that breast reconstruction should automatically be offered to all women undergoing mastectomy.

This study was conducted retrospectively and it is possible the findings were influenced by the women's treatment preference. For example, those who opt for mastectomy alone may do so out of fear of recurrence. An earlier prospective study by Morris and Ingham (1988) indicated that providing choice, rather than the type of operation performed, improved both physical and psychological functioning.

Body presentation

Body presentation includes the characteristic ways in which the body moves or functions in social situations, including gestures and physical actions. Some innate responses, such as smiling or laughing when we are happy, are shared by all people. Other responses, such as hand waving, nodding or winking, are acquired (learned) from childhood onwards and have different meanings in different cultures. We use both innate and acquired responses in a largely unconscious way and feel very awkward if we try to suppress or change them.

Each culture has its own norms of body presentation in terms of what is acceptable and what is not. For example, the avoidance of eye contact and lowering of gaze are signs of respect in some cultures and disrespect in others. In multi-ethnic societies, this can cause particular misunderstandings as we highlighted in the example from Vydelingum's study (2006). Another common problem is the use of body space. In some cultures people stand close while talking to each other in a way that is likely to make most Europeans feel uncomfortable.

If you can, talk to relatives, friends or acquaintances who grew up in other cultures or even different parts of the country. See how many examples you can identify where the norms of body presentation and social interaction differ from your own.

Certain conditions give rise to social misunderstandings as a result of lack of control over body movements. For example, someone who has Parkinson's disease may show very little facial movement, which can make them seem quite disinterested in what is going on around them. People who have cerebral palsy or Tourette's syndrome are often ridiculed because they are unable to control their body movements. Having a body that does not conform to the norms of a society or reference group can lead to adverse consequences that cause psychological harm. People are often quite ingenious when it comes to finding solutions to practical problems caused by their disability but may be crushed by feelings of humiliation or social rejection.

Personality

We give little space in this book to the topic of personality because the inappropriate use of personality labels can (and does) lead to stereotyping and stigmatization within health and social care systems. A trait is a relatively stable set of individual characteristics that include patterns of thought, adjustment and behaviour that are partly inherited, strongly influenced by experiences during childhood, and to some extent modified through adult experiences. Longitudinal studies appear to confirm that about 40 per cent of personality is genetically determined and 60 per cent is environmentally determined (Borkenau *et al.* 2001).

The names most commonly associated in psychology with the measurement of personality are Cattell and Eysenck. However, the personality measure most commonly used in health psychology is the 'Big Five', which measures the following five traits (Costa and McCrae 1992):

- *neuroticism:*   anxious, tense, worrying, unstable;
- *extroversion:*   active, assertive, enthusiastic, outgoing, talkative;
- *agreeableness:*   appreciative, forgiving, generous, kind, trusting;
- *conscientiousness:*   efficient, organized, reliable, responsible, thorough;
- *openness (or creativity):*   artistic, curious, imaginative, insightful.

Costa and McCrae used the term 'undercontrolled' style to describe those who have high neuroticism and low conscientiousness scores. They claimed that these individuals are at the mercy of their own impulses, drives and urges, leaving them at a heightened risk of unhealthy or antisocial lifestyles.

The 'Big Five' in social context

Jonassaint *et al.* (2011) found significant associations between Big Five personality traits and socio-economic status (SES) in an American sample of healthy adults aged 18–50 years. The authors reported that higher levels of parental education were associated with lower individual scores on neuroticism, higher conscientiousness, higher extroversion and higher openness to new ideas. They found no effects of parental education on agreeableness. In view of the known relationship between education, SES and health, these findings may be relevant to both health and social care.

Friedman (2000) offered three possible explanations for links between personality and health:

- Certain personality types may be associated with emotional and physiological mechanisms that lead to certain diseases, for example coronary artery disease and cancer (see Chapter 7 on stress).
- Personality traits may set a trajectory towards health or disease. For example, those who are more sociable may develop better support networks (see Chapter 8 on resilience).
- Personality may be associated with motivational forces that draw people towards certain behavioural norms such as risk-taking, substance use or unemployment.

In Chapter 3, we review parenting practices that may also have an important bearing on the development of different response styles.

Stability and change in personality

Srivastava *et al.* (2003) conducted a cross-sectional internet survey of adults aged 21–60 using the Big Five personality measure. They found that conscientiousness and agreeableness increased throughout early and middle adulthood at varying rates. Neuroticism declined among women but did not change among men.

We regard the utility of these findings in terms of individual care as highly dubious. In fact, we suggest it is dangerous for those working in the caring professions to believe that an individual's personality tells them anything meaningful or reliable about the way that individual is likely to respond in different or difficult circumstances. If we believe that the way an individual behaves is a consequence of their personality, we will probably believe that they are unlikely to change. The attribution of difficulties or failures to an individual's personality, rather than their circumstances, may simply be a convenient way of absolving us from our responsibility, as care professionals, to engage in person-centred care.

Table 2.2 Summary: factors that affect self-perception	
Concept	**Explaining the self**
The looking glass self (Cooley 1902)	Much of what we think of as our 'self' is actually defined by the ways that other people view us and respond to us
Labelling	The labels we and others attach to ourselves can become self-fulfilling prophecies
Social identity theory (Tajfel 1982)	Our identity reflects, in part, the need to be similar to our reference group(s)
Self-stereotyping	The way we learn to see ourselves is influenced by the social stereotypes we identify ourselves with
Social comparison theory (Festinger 1954)	Our construction of our sense of self is influenced by the comparisons we make between our own attributes and those of other people
Social role theory (Goffman 1959)	An important part of our self-concept is determined by the different social roles we play
Adaptation	Certain aspects of our identity remain relatively stable over time, even though our roles vary significantly during the course of our lives
Personal construct theory (Kelly 1955)	We learn about ourselves and the world around us in much the same way that a scientist produces and tests theories
The narrative self	Our identities are made up of the stories we construct about ourselves
Self-esteem	Self-esteem reflects a critical personal evaluation of self-worth
Body image	Our bodies have certain unique features that remain relatively stable over time and form important determinants of our identity and self-esteem
Personality	All of the above factors influence what we know as our personality. Personality types can give rise to stereotyping and are not helpful in the context of care

Further reading

Goffman, E. (1959) *The Presentation of Self in Everyday Life.* London: Penguin.

Goffman, E. (1963) *Stigma: Notes on the Management of Spoiled Identity.* Harmondsworth: Penguin.

Rumsey, N. and Harcourt, D. (2004) *The Psychology of Appearance.* Maidenhead: Open University Press.

Stockwell, F. (1984) *The Unpopular Patient.* London: Croom Helm.

Development and change across the lifespan

Key topics

- The child's development of thinking, understanding and reasoning
- Social development, attachment and parenting
- Development and change in adult life
- Age, ageing and end of life

Introduction

In order to be able to communicate effectively with people of all ages, it is important to know how their interpretation and ability to relate to others is influenced by their level of cognitive, moral and social development. Cognitive development refers to development of thinking and understanding about the world. Moral development refers to the ways in which children evaluate issues and justify their behaviour. Social development focuses on the development of relationships with others. This chapter focuses on these questions:

- How do children of different ages learn about complex issues such as those related to health, illness and the body?
- Why are attachment relationships so important to human health?
- What is meant by healthy, successful or positive ageing?

The following vignette is based on a scene witnessed by a health visitor. It illustrates a number of important points related to these questions. See if you can identify what these are.

Lee, aged 4, was telling Margaret, his 76-year-old great-grandmother, that he would soon have a new brother or sister. He hoped it would be a brother to play football with. He explained that the baby was in Mummy's tummy and he was waiting for it to hatch through her belly button. He hoped the doctor would zip her up properly so Mummy could take him swimming again. Margaret described afterwards how this evoked memories of the birth of her own daughter, Janice. She commented that she would have loved another child, but it was not to be.

This vignette focuses on a moment of intimacy between an older and a younger person who have a close relationship. It highlights the child's understanding of the body and its functions. It tells us about the self-centred nature of a young child's thought processes. And it illustrates the process of reminiscence that is common in later life. In this chapter, we address continuity and change in the way people understand and respond to events from the beginning to the end of life.

Theoretical background

It is important to remember that a theory is simply a system of ideas or principles that are used to explain what is happening and, if possible, predict what is likely to happen. Many former theories of child and lifespan development were 'stage' theories, based on an assumption prevalent during the mid-twentieth century that psychological development follows a fixed sequence of separate steps. For example, early in the twentieth century, Freud introduced the idea that children pass through a series of psychosexual stages until they reach puberty. According to this theory, failure to move successfully from one stage to the next would cause 'fixation' and affect later psychological adjustment (for example, see Gross 2010). While few psychologists now support this particular view, Freud's important contribution to psychology was to highlight the influence of childhood experiences on adult psychological adjustment.

Freud's theory of development stopped at puberty, but Erikson proposed an 'epigenetic' stage theory of human development (one in which the stages are determined by an interaction of genetic and environmental influences) that extended across the lifespan. Drawing on psychoanalytic theory, Erikson proposed that an individual is unable to progress from one stage to the next until certain 'crises' have been overcome and psychological adaptations accomplished (Erikson 1980). Many of the challenges faced by adults are, we feel, better addressed under the headings of stress and coping (Chapter 7). Nevertheless, Erikson's ideas continue to inform research into adult developmental processes, most notably the psychology of later life.

In contrast to Freud and Erikson, Piaget (1952) was interested primarily in cognitive development – the development of thinking and reasoning. He rejected biological theories that assumed developmental changes to be entirely 'pre-programmed'. He also dismissed behaviourist theories (Chapter 5) which proposed that children learn entirely through reward and punishment. He based his theory of cognitive development on direct observation of his own children, from which he proposed a developmental framework that until quite recently informed educational, health and social care practices. Piaget assumed that each child progresses through certain stages of development in a fixed sequence, each building on learning acquired at the previous stage. Like Freud, Piaget stopped short at adolescence, at which point he assumed the capability for adult reasoning was attained.

Although psychologists no longer subscribe to stage theories, we have included Piaget's theory because it continues to offer useful practical applications for general purposes. But we also offer the work of Vygotsky as a flexible and useful addition to our understanding about the ways in which children and adults can be helped to learn and develop throughout the lifespan.

The development of thinking and understanding

Piaget's theory of cognitive development

According to Piaget, the child is born with certain hard-wired reflexes, such as sucking and crying, with which they interact with the world around them. As children interact with the physical and social environment, they develop mental representations called schemas (see also Chapter 4), which form the building blocks of understanding and reasoning. Just as in a building, it is not possible to build the second floor before the building blocks for the first floor are in place. Schemas may be behavioural (e.g. learning to tie shoelaces), symbolic (use of representations, such as language and numbers) or operational (e.g. learning to add up or subtract). The sequential development of schemas imposes a constraint on the child's ability to understand and to reason at each developmental stage.

According to Piaget, schemas are developed through a process of 'assimilation' and 'accommodation'. New information about the world is assimilated (incorporated) into existing schemas until these schemas no longer provide an adequate interpretation for what is happening. At this point, existing schemas are altered or modified to 'accommodate' new information.

Face recognition in babies

It has long been known that, within days of birth, babies are able to distinguish the human face from other images and can distinguish their mother's face from those of strangers. This led developmental psychologists to propose that babies are born with an innate 'face-recognition schema' which assimilates information from different faces to accommodate facial discrimination.

However, more recent experiments (Coulon *et al.* 2011) indicate that, shortly after birth, infants are able to discriminate unfamiliar talking faces. Their experiments led them to propose that the mother's face may be recognized soon after birth because they have already assimilated information about her voice while still in the womb.

Piaget proposed that the process of assimilation and accommodation underpins cognitive development. His own observations led him to define a series of invariant developmental stages. We have highlighted the main stages in Table 3.1.

Table 3.1 Piaget's stages of development

Stage of development	Competence
0 to 2 years: sensorimotor stage	Gain sensory information through the mouth and hands to learn about the properties of objects around them
	Learn to recognize and later label familiar objects
	Learn that objects continue to exist when they are out of sight
2 to 7 years: pre-operational stage	Influenced by how things look, rather than by logical reasoning
	Learn to use imagination and language (symbolic thought)
	Become self-aware, but remain egocentric (unable to see how things look from the point of view or perspective of someone else)
7 to 11 years: concrete operational stage	Capable of using logical reasoning
	Can view things from the perspectives of others
	Understand the concept of relativism (taller, hotter), reciprocal relationships and number conservation*
	Have difficulty in dealing with abstract concepts**
11 years: formal operational stage	Capable of engaging in abstract thought
	Able to manipulate ideas and follow a hypothetical argument, using logic and without reference to a concrete object

*An example of number conservation is: If I start out with two oranges and you have none, when I give you one of my oranges there are still two oranges in total.

** A child who has difficulty with abstract concepts would probably view health in terms of not feeling poorly.

Clearly, much change takes place within these age bands and Piaget subdivided them into a series of sub-stages. For those who are interested, these are detailed in any specialist text on child development.

A key skill that needs to be learned during childhood is the ability to understand that other people do not necessarily see or appreciate things from the same point of view. Applied literally, this refers to what other people can see. But it also refers to the ability to understand and empathize with the feelings, beliefs and attitudes of others.

Seeing things from a different perspective

One of the best-known examples of Piaget's experiments is the 'three mountains' experiment (Piaget and Inhelder 1956). The child was seated in front of a table, on which stood a model of three mountains and a doll. The child was shown a selection of photographs and asked to choose the photograph of the view the doll is likely to see. Very young children did not understand the task. Until around the age of 7, the child selected his or her own view, rather than that of the doll. This appeared to demonstrate that children at this stage are unable to see things (literally) from the perspectives of others. Piaget termed this 'egocentrism'.

The 'three mountains' experiment subsequently came in for criticism because the task is complex and uses a scene that is not part of most children's normal experience. Donaldson (1978) demonstrated by using familiar objects, such as teddies and building bricks, that children of the same age or younger are able to accomplish the task. Children in her study were able to hide a 'naughty teddy' behind building bricks so that the doll could not see it, demonstrating that the child is able to take the doll's perspective (literally).

A problem with these experiments is that they focus only on visual perception, whereas the term 'egocentrism' is normally applied to the inability to understand someone else's feelings. Further experiments using dolls led Donaldson to conclude that young children are often quite good at understanding how other people are feeling and what they might be thinking or planning to do (Donaldson 1990). In other words, many young children have the ability to empathize with others and cannot be truly held to be 'egocentric'. In the field of health and social care, these findings imply that young children's understanding can be disrupted by unfamiliar objects or surroundings and quite young children are likely to be affected by the feelings and emotions of those around them.

Finding the right way to explain

When Sasha first became pregnant, she experienced a lot of morning sickness and became very tired, which made her tearful. At this time, Lee became upset when left at the nursery, telling the staff that Mummy was poorly. With encouragement and help from the nursery staff and the health visitor, Sasha tried to reassure Lee and explained things to him using simple examples so that he could understand. She worked out a routine with Joe that enabled them to help Lee feel more secure until this phase of her pregnancy passed and things were back to normal.

When questioned, it is quite difficult to tell if young children are saying what they really believe, or what they think adults want to hear, particularly if they feel that their knowledge is being put to the test. Professionals who wish to explain things to children in this age range using play must make sure that they use familiar objects. They also need regularly to check out the child's understanding by asking them to describe what is happening, rather than asking direct questions, as happened in Piaget's experiments.

Piaget's theory remains influential in the contexts of education and child care, because the notion of developmental stages provides a simple rule of thumb for children's levels of understanding that is easy to apply.

Vygotsky's sociocultural theory of cognitive development

Vygotsky was a Russian contemporary of Piaget, although his work was little known in the west until more recently. Like Piaget, Vygotsky acknowledged children as active explorers of the world around them and that they learn in incremental steps. But while Piaget seemed to view this as a mainly solitary activity, Vygotsky was interested in the role of social interaction and language in the child's development. Vygotsky (1978) argued that children are particularly likely to learn from others when there is only a small gap between what they are able to do on their own and what they could do with a little help from someone more skilled. Vygotsky called this gap the 'zone of proximal development'. Essentially, this means that the child learns 'one small step at a time, with help and guidance'.

The term 'scaffolding' is used to describe the interactive process whereby the amount of help and guidance given is tailored to the individual's responses, so that they can gradually achieve more and more. These concepts have been influential in education with the introduction of active, guided participatory learning. They have also led to the introduction of peer teaching, where older children who are more skilled are encouraged to teach those at a slightly lower level of skill development.

Facilitating learning using 'scaffolding'

Lee was having difficulty opening a box and became very frustrated. Joe observed that the cause of Lee's frustration was his failure to distinguish the top of the box from the bottom. If Joe had assumed that Lee was not old enough to open the box for himself, he might have taken it and opened it for him. Instead, Joe showed Lee where he was going wrong, and then gently guided him while he did it himself. In this way, Lee learned a new skill that would enable him to open the box for himself in future.

An important and useful feature of Vygotsky's theory is that, unlike Piaget's theory, it has no upper age or stage limit, so this principle applies equally to adult learning. In the field of health it has influenced the introduction of patient-led programmes (see Chapter 9).

Vygotsky's theory predicts greater flexibility in the ways individuals learn. Children will achieve greater understanding about certain issues if they have had more opportunities for learning about these within their social environment. This explains why some children with health problems appear to be very advanced for their age in terms of their knowledge about their body, illness, drugs or procedures, while others have little knowledge or understanding. Thus, when giving information and explanations, professionals need to take account of each individual child's experience and understanding. They should not be guided solely by the child's age and developmental stage.

Understanding medical information

Veldtman *et al.* (2000) sought to evaluate knowledge and understanding of illnesses in children and adolescents, aged between 7 and 18 years, who had congenital and acquired heart disease. They found that less than a third had a good understanding of their illness; 77 per cent did not know the medical name of their condition and 33 per cent had a wrong or poor understanding of their illness. Even some older adolescents had an entirely wrong concept of their disease. Of particular importance is their finding that understanding was not directly related to age.

Rushforth (1999) reviewed the available evidence in order to enhance information-giving and consent-taking for children in hospital. She proposed that children's understanding is often related to the explanations they have been given. For example, in relation to pain, they were more likely to be able to explain why an injection hurts than why they have a headache. She suggested that this is because adults are more likely to spend time explaining an injection. She also pointed out that ambiguity in the English language can lead children to make misinterpretations. For example, a child might hear IV as ivy. Rushforth argued that many childhood fears related to illness originate from such simple misconceptions. Therefore, it is essential to check the child's existing level of understanding before giving any further information. (Drawing on Vygotsky, the same applies to adults; see also Chapter 4 on memory and information-giving.)

Finding the right level of explanation

Sasha has been trying to explain to Lee that she is expecting another baby. She has told him that there is a baby growing in Mummy's tummy. But when Lee asked how the baby got in there, Sasha was not sure what to say. It is unlikely, at the age of 4, that he will be able to understand an abstract concept such as conception. There are some very good books that help to explain pregnancy and childbirth to young children and Sasha has decided to get one from the library next time she is in town. This will enable her to find out what Lee already knows and help her to provide the 'scaffolding' around which he can develop his learning on this subject.

In Table 3.2, we summarize practical reasons for assessing the individual's level of cognitive ability.

Table 3.2 Developmental implications for communication	
Approximate age range/cognitive capability	**Practice implications**
0 to 2 years Pre-verbal	All communication is through the principal caregiver(s) Attention may be diverted by distraction during or after an intervention
2 to 7 years Language, objects and events are taken at face value Interpretations and reasoning are limited	Assess current level of understanding Help parents to understand the child's limitations when giving explanations Pointing, pictures, stories and play are helpful ways to promote understanding
7 to 12 years Able to understand direct cause and effect relationships Reading and comprehension skills variable	Assess understanding of verbal and written information Build explanations on existing knowledge and understanding Avoid abstract concepts – keep verbal and written explanations simple and to the point Involve parents and encourage reasonable expectations of the child
12 to 15 years Able to engage in logical reasoning	Check out the child's understanding of what is happening and the likely outcomes or consequences Child may consent to their own treatment if they can demonstrate full appreciation of what is involved
Age 16+ Achieves adult reasoning	Entitled to consent to treatment within the terms of the 1975 Mental Capacity Act

Children and even many adults will tend to reply 'yes' when asked if they understand something, so this is an inappropriate way of assessing knowledge and understanding. Verbal and literacy levels vary widely within the child and adult population, so it is important to invite each individual to 'tell me . . .' or 'show me. . . .'. A less threatening way is to invite a young child to 'tell [Mummy, Daddy or sibling] . . .' or 'tell [favourite toy] . . .'.

Exercises

Look back at the vignette at the start of this chapter.

● How might you explain Lee's understanding of the birth of the new baby?

● Can you foresee any problems that might arise from his expectations of the birth?

● If so, can you think of any ways of helping to overcome these?

The development of moral reasoning

As children grow older, the development of moral reasoning is important because it is associated with independence of thought and action, the ability to tell right from wrong and to resist peer pressure where necessary.

Research

Developing moral reasoning

Kohlberg was interested in how children learn to tell right from wrong. He studied how boys from the age of 10 dealt with moral dilemmas such as theft and criminal damage (Kohlberg 1969).

Younger boys conformed to adult rules, but evaluated the goodness or badness of an act by its consequences. They tended to reason that if it is possible to 'get away with it', then it couldn't be that bad.

Older children tended to obey the rules of their social group in order to gain praise and avoid censure.

By the age of 16, adolescents tended to demonstrate commitment to a set of principles shared with a reference group.

By contrast, the highest level of adult moral reasoning involves the development of a self-chosen moral code and set of ethical principles.

Based on these observations, Kohlberg developed a stage theory of moral reasoning, as summarized below.

Like Piaget, Kohlberg proposed that these stages are fixed in terms of sequence. But unlike Piaget, he claimed that they are not linked directly to chronological age. In fact, he believed that few actually attain the highest level of post-conventional morality.

Table 3.3 Kohlberg's stages of moral reasoning

Approximate age range/ level of moral development	Features
2 to 7 years Pre-conventional morality	Right and wrong are distinguished by the consequences of their actions The main aim is to achieve rewards and avoid punishment Obedience to authority becomes an important value
7 to teenage years Conventional morality	The child wants to be thought of as a 'good' person, so will aim to please Behaviour is judged to be 'good' or 'bad' on the basis of social rules set down by the society or subculture in which the child lives (including their peer group or gang)
Adulthood Post-conventional morality	Democratically agreed laws and social rules are obeyed because they are seen to be for the public good At the highest level of development, people adopt a set of ethical principles based on personal conscience

An important criticism of Kohlberg has been that his work is culture-specific, limited to a set of western values that prevailed at a particular point in time. It is possible to argue that since Kohlberg made his observations in the 1960s, punishment for bad behaviour has largely disappeared and younger children are now much more ready to challenge the moral codes of their parents. Older children may be less likely to be influenced by the moral rules of society and more likely to be influenced by the social code of their peer group. This is particularly noticeable where taking risks or behaving badly is considered 'cool'.

The influence of peer pressure

Sasha had a very strict upbringing but went to a school where she mixed with children from a variety of different social and cultural backgrounds. By the time she was 15 years old, her closest friend boasted of having sex and encouraged her to do the same. She knew her parents would be angry and upset, but one evening at a party a boy she was infatuated with persuaded her to have sex with him. She did not know how to ask him to use protection and she became pregnant.

Example

Peer pressure is a strong influence on teenage behaviours and is likely to take priority over adult 'rational' arguments. Based on his observations of boys, Kohlberg argued that with respect to behaviours such as smoking, drug-taking and alcohol consumption, younger boys need careful parental monitoring to make sure that they don't 'get away with it'.

Children's understandings of death and dying

According to Piaget's theory, children at the pre-operational stage of development may find it impossible to accept the permanence of death.

Example

What does death mean?

Lee has a friend, James, also aged 4, whose father was recently killed in a road accident. James's mother told him that his daddy had died and he was later taken to visit the grave. But a few weeks after that, he said to his mother, 'Now please can we go and dig daddy up?'

Rushforth (1999) suggested that children may be unable to accept death in terms of the impact on the family until adolescence. Viewed from the perspective of Kohlberg's pre-conventional and conventional stages of moral reasoning, it is possible that a child may see the death or permanent departure of someone they love as a punishment for their own misdeeds. Rushforth has therefore argued that the greatest disservice we do is to try to protect children from the realities of events such as death. In seeking to fill gaps in their knowledge, their imagination may be far worse than reality. It is worth reflecting that even adults have difficulty in accepting death as permanent unless or until they have seen the body or obtained concrete evidence of the death. An abstract concept such as death can be addressed through stories, but may be more easily understood and ultimately less frightening if learned about through the death of a pet. This assumes that family members are themselves willing to confront the reality of death. Discussions of children's understandings of death and dying from a number of different perspectives can be found in Talwar *et al.* (2011).

The importance of play

Both Piaget and Vygotsky noted the importance of play in cognitive, motor and social develop-ment. During the pre-conventional and conventional stages of moral reasoning, play also offers opportunities to enact and resolve moral conflicts. Play in the form of experimentation starts at an early age when babies repeat acts that have a direct effect on their environment and those in it, such as hitting a hanging mobile to make it turn, or making a noise to attract the caregiver's attention. Piaget argued that play enables babies to practise motor, cognitive and social compe-tences and thereby achieve mastery. Both Piaget and Vygotsky noted that children use symbolic or pretend play to act out different roles and situations. This enables them to learn to cope with a variety of possible situations, including emotional crises, interpersonal conflicts and social roles. For example, playing at doctors and nurses, or mothers and fathers, is a good way to learn about different aspects of the social world in which they live.

Preparation through play

Example

Sasha has been encouraging Lee to play at mothers and fathers with his friend, in preparation for the birth of his new brother or sister. Boys are often discouraged from playing with dolls, but Sasha has provided him with an old doll of her own that cries and wets its nappy. She hopes that he will be better prepared and less jealous once the baby is born. Meanwhile, Joe has been encouraging Lee to play football and other 'boys' ' games to build up a special type of relation-ship between stepfather and son and distract from the extra attention required by the new baby.

Play has been promoted as a useful way of preparing children for medical procedures. There is some evidence that this can be effective if it is tailored to suit an individual child's needs (Watson and Visram 2000). Play therapy is an accepted intervention for use with emotionally or behaviourally disturbed children, although a meta-analysis of research findings by LeBlanc and Ritchie (2001) showed play therapy may take as many as 30 sessions to achieve optimum improvements in such outcomes as self-concept, anxiety and behavioural problems.

Social development

Social development refers to the development of human relationships. The human infant is dependent on adults for all its needs in the early years. Therefore, there are good reasons why babies need to establish a close relationship with their mother and/or other principal caregiver(s). The early behaviourist view was that a bond of attachment to the mother occurred because she provided food and comfort. This explanation was discounted at an early stage when Harlow (1959) demonstrated through experiments with rhesus monkeys that a baby monkey preferred soft physical contact with an inanimate object, even when it did not deliver milk. Harlow's studies also confirmed that female monkeys who had no experience of mothering subsequently neglected or abused their own children. These experiments identified that a close bond between the child and principal caregiver is an important requirement for normal social development.

Having observed permanent negative effects of separation at birth on other species, psychologists once believed that there might be a critical sensitive period soon after birth when it was essential for mother and baby to 'bond'. Klaus and Kennell (1976) studied the effect of increased infant–mother contact soon after birth and found that close physical contact just after birth stimulated caring responses in the mother. As a result, maternity units encouraged women to hold and suckle their babies as soon as they had been born.

However, Rutter (1979) noted the propensity of adoptive parents to develop strong attachments with older babies. This cast doubt on the notion of a sensitive period for attachment. Babies undoubtedly benefit from a close relationship with their principal caregiver, but this may take place at any time during the early weeks or months and may involve one or more care providers.

Attachment

Attachment refers to the strong emotional bond which is formed with the principal caregiver(s) in infancy and usually remains lifelong. The name most closely associated with early studies of attachment in human infants is John Bowlby. Bowlby (1969) noted that human babies exhibit a number of behaviours that have survival value because they engage the adults who will meet their needs. These include:

- crying, cooing, babbling and smiling – called signalling behaviour;
- clinging, non-nutritional sucking and maintaining eye contact with caregiver – called approach behaviour.

Bowlby's theory of attachment is based on an interactional model. This means that attachment is not dependent solely on the infant's responses or those of the mother. Rather, each influences the other. Therefore, a depressed mother who is unable adequately to respond to the infant's demands for attention may change the baby's normal response. Similarly, a very small pre-term infant may be unable to produce responses like crying or smiling that elicit adult attention.

Bowlby suggested that the quality of the attachment relationship formed in infancy provides a template for subsequent intimate and social relationships. Therefore the failure to develop strong emotional bonds in infancy or childhood may damage the ability to develop close relationships in adult life.

Separation

By the age of between 7 and 12 months, Bowlby noted that babies become very distressed at the absence of their mother or primary caregiver. He termed this 'separation anxiety'. At this age, infants also become very wary of strangers and may protest vigorously if they approach too close. Bowlby emphasized that separation from the primary caregiver before the age of 5 years might damage the mental health of the child. His research was used to argue that women should not go out to work and leave their babies with other caregivers. More recent studies have identified that attachment to multiple caregivers is possible. There is no evidence of adverse effects of other types of child care arrangements on the child, provided stable and good quality sources of care are provided.

Until the 1960s, when a child was admitted to hospital it was common for the mother to be asked to leave the child and only be allowed to visit for limited periods. This was because children were observed to become extremely distressed each time their mothers had to leave. James Robertson worked closely with Bowlby in the late 1940s and, with his wife, made a series of harrowing films that revealed the true nature and extent of distress shown by separated young children (Robertson and Robertson 1967–73). The stages of separation were marked by:

- protest – anger and loud crying;
- despair – withdrawal and less vigorous crying;
- detachment – later, the child outwardly displayed cheerful behaviour but remained emotionally distant.

As a result, children's units reversed their policies and now encourage mothers, or other close caregivers, to stay if possible for the duration of the child's admission. Of course, this can cause separation problems for other children in the family, depending on the availability of alternative trusted caregivers. Special attachment and play objects can afford comfort and security when children have to spend time on their own in hospital.

Feeling safe and secure in hospital

Ångström-Brännström *et al.* (2008: 310–16) undertook a qualitative study to find out what gave comfort to children who had a chronic condition while they were in hospital. They reported that the children took their own toys, blankets and clothes with them to the hospital. One said: 'I have my doll with me. She's sick – can you see? And she also has to do blood tests . . . I can talk to my doll if my mother is not here.' One of the girls packed her own backpack with some special things whenever she went to the hospital: 'I always take some of my own things with me – this book, my [toy] dog, and some other things.'

Research

Types of attachment

It was observed that not all children respond in the same way when separated from their mothers. This led to a series of experiments into different types of attachment relationships and their effects on separation.

Experiments with strangers

During the 1970s, Ainsworth (Ainsworth *et al.* 1978) initiated a series of classic experiments on the nature of attachment and stranger fear, called the 'strange situation experiment', as in the following scenario. The child and mother are placed in a room full of toys. A strange person comes into the room and talks to the mother. Then the mother exits from the room, leaving the child with the stranger. Finally, the mother returns. The child's reactions to each of these situations are observed through a one-way mirror. Based on the child's responses to these events, three main classifications of attachment were identified (based on Ainsworth *et al.* 1978; Cassidy and Shaver 1999). They are referred to as secure, avoidant and ambivalent attachment styles.

Research

- *Secure attachment.* The child uses the parent as a secure base for exploration, plays happily with the toys, reacts positively to strangers and returns to play. Play is reduced during the parent's absence and the child is distressed. On the parent's return, the child seeks contact and then returns to play.
- *Avoidant attachment.* The child avoids physical intimacy with the parent and maintains emotional neutrality. Plays with toys, unaffected by the parent's whereabouts in the room. The child is not distressed on separation and, on the parent's return, ignores her or may move away. If the child is distressed, they are as easily comforted by the stranger as the parent.
- *Ambivalent attachment.* The child protests strongly on separation. The child is fussy and wary in the parent's presence and has difficulty leaving her. On reunion, the child seeks contact in a babyish way, but at the same time struggles against the parent and appears angry. The child remains uninvolved in play.

Subsequent research sought to identify features of parenting associated with these styles of response.

- The parents of children who were securely attached appeared more responsive, showed more affection including touching, smiling and praise and more social stimulation.
- Those whose children showed avoidant attachment or insecure attachment showed much lower levels of these types of interaction.

These observations indicate that maternal or parental warmth is an important prerequisite for secure attachment. Follow-up studies have indicated that securely attached children are more likely to be initiators of play as well as active participants in play, more curious and eager to learn, and show more empathy towards other children. Those who have insecure attachment relationships tend to be socially withdrawn and less curious (Maccoby 1980). However, Maccoby noted that (at least until the age of 3) insecure relationships can change if the quality of the parental response improves.

It is important to reflect that the quality of the attachment relationship reflects a two-way interaction. The temperamental disposition of the child may affect the mother's behaviour, just as the mother's behaviour may affect the responses of the child. For example, some babies cry a lot and resist being held and cuddled, which can make it difficult for the mother to form a close relationship.

Support for lone parents

Sasha was only 16 when Lee was born and had no further contact with the father. Her parents came from a culture that did not tolerate premarital sexual encounters and Sasha was forced out of their home into temporary accommodation. Lee cried a lot, which made Sasha feel inadequate. She became depressed and unresponsive. The health visitor observed these problems and also noticed signs of insecure attachment in Lee's behaviour. After discussion with the social worker, Sasha was put in touch with a mature registered childminder so that she could receive support from an experienced mother. This also allowed her to continue with her education and attend parenting classes. This enabled Sasha to build her self-confidence as a mother and also build up a more secure relationship with Lee.

Recent attention has focused on the child's 'theory of mind' and the impact that attachment and parenting has on its development. Theory of mind refers to the ability to appreciate the relationship between someone's mental state (beliefs and emotions) and their behaviour (Sodian 2011). The ability to be able to understand how other people think and feel is essential for successful social development. In view of variations in theory of mind among children of different ages, psychologists were interested to understand if this was influenced by attachment relationships and parenting.

Research

The relationship between theory of mind and attachment style

Meins *et al.* (2002) used the Strange Situation experiment to identify attachment style in a group of 57 children aged six months. When these children were 2 years old, they were introduced to a play situation in which a series of games were used to assess their 'theory of mind'.

The children whose mothers were more sensitive to their needs and commented appropriately on their mental state were more likely to demonstrate secure attachment at six months. This early maternal behaviour, which the researchers termed 'mind-mindedness', predicted more mature development of theory of mind in the child later on. The researchers suggest that mothers of children who demonstrate secure attachment treat their children as individuals who have minds.

An intrinsic absence of, or deficiency in, theory of mind has been implicated in the development of autistic spectrum disorders – there is no suggestion that parental behaviours are to blame for this.

The influence of parenting styles on development

It is evident from the previous sections that home is the centre for children's learning, and relationships within the home offer a template for the development of future behaviour and interpersonal relationships. Distinct styles of parenting have been identified, based on a series of studies originally conducted by Baumrind (1967, 1971). These include authoritative, authoritarian, permissive and uninvolved parenting.

- *Authoritative parents* are characterized as setting reasonable standards and enforcing them firmly, consistently and fairly without the need for physical punishment. They monitor the child's behaviour and help the child to conform to standards of behaviour by providing explanations, guidance and feedback, and encourage self-direction.
- *Authoritarian parents* expect obedience, show less warmth and use less communication. They set absolute standards, often using physical punishment. They attempt to control the attitudes as well as the behaviour of the child and discourage argument.
- *Permissive (indulgent) parents* are indulgent towards the child's impulses, desires and actions and make little attempt to regulate the child's behaviour. They attempt reasoning, but avoid any exercise of control and make few demands on the child.
- *Uninvolved (neglectful) parents* show little regard for the child's well-being or behaviour.

Exercise

Drawing on the descriptions of parenting above, reflect on your own upbringing and compare it with those of people you know well. In what ways are they similar or different? Do you think that the parenting styles you experienced have influenced any of your own characteristics or those of your friends?

The effects of these parenting styles have been the subject of a large amount of research over the past two decades. Cumulative evidence indicates that children brought up in families that provide emotional warmth and authoritative parenting are less likely to engage in antisocial or delinquent behaviour and legal or illegal substance use. Close parental monitoring of the teenager's activities by supportive parents appears to be an important factor. Youngsters who perceive their parents to be permissive or neglectful are likely to use larger quantities of all street drugs and to start using them at a younger age (Montgomery *et al.* 2008).

Parenting and adolescent behaviour

A meta-analysis by Hoeve *et al.* (2009) of the effects of parenting style on adolescent behaviour identified neglectful or rejecting parenting as an important predictor of delinquent behaviour. Those who received supportive parenting (warmth, affection and acceptance) and whose activities were closely monitored were less likely to engage in delinquent behaviour. One reason may be that adolescents who have a good relationship with their parent(s) are more likely to disclose their activities, friends and whereabouts. Poor relationships with the same-sex parent (fathers and sons, mothers and daughters) were particularly important predictors of delinquency.

Development in adolescence

Adolescence refers to the period between childhood and adulthood. It is a key time of development that was overlooked by major stage theorists including Freud and Piaget – perhaps because it is difficult to define and understand. The onset of adolescence, if defined as the onset of puberty, is subject to variation between cultures and within the same culture over time, due to environmental influences such as diet. Entry to adulthood, in contrast, is culturally determined. Some cultures have initiation rights that determine the end of childhood and give access to the rights and privileges of adulthood. In western cultures, there are many markers by which adulthood may be defined: biological markers such as the attainment of ultimate height and completion of pubertal changes; legal markers such as attaining the right to have legal sexual intercourse, get married, smoke, drink alcohol, hold a credit card and vote; status markers such as marriage, having a family and home ownership. Between these markers lie many contradictions. For example, it may be possible to get married or join the British Army, but not buy alcohol or vote. And in an age when young people are encouraged to attend university, many remain financially dependent on their parents until well into their twenties and some into their thirties.

Different individuals mature in different ways at different rates and the situation is further complicated when they have a learning difficulty that delays cognitive and moral, but not physical, development. These issues create confusion for the adolescent, and pose dilemmas for those providing services that were designed for either children or adults, or which transfer from one to the other at a fixed age. For example, within health care, neither children's wards nor adult units are best suited to the needs of adolescent patients, while automatic discharge from social care at age 18 can have damaging consequences for a group who are not sufficiently mature to cope without support. Dealing with the transition from adolescence to adulthood poses particular problems for those who have a severe learning difficulty, for whom there appears to be a prolonged period of childhood and delayed adolescence.

Growing up with a severe learning difficulty

Todd and Shearn (1997) interviewed the parents of adults with moderate to severe learning difficulties who were aged between 17 and 44 years, in order to address the issue 'when is an adult not an adult?' The conflict is summed up by one parent as: 'He looks and sounds like a man. But when you look and listen more carefully you realize he's just a child. You've got to treat him like an adult in one way, and like a child in another.' One mother observed of her 32-year-old son: 'I think he's going through his adolescence now. He's beginning to find his feet.' The study highlights some of the conflicts between the adult body and child's mind. Those with learning difficulties appear torn between being dependent and wanting to be independent; wanting to do normal things, such as get married, but being rejected as 'different' by others.

In Vygotskian terms, adolescence may be regarded as a time of intense social, intellectual and behavioural learning; a period of apprenticeship for the autonomy of adult life and the responsibilities that go with it. It is also a period during which youngsters attempt to discover their identities and roles in life, socially and at work. It is a time when adolescents rebel against parental constraints and values and seek to establish their own identities within peer groups (Chapter 2) – we have already focused on some aspects of parenting that facilitate successful transition.

Well-being in adolescence

The security afforded by having emotionally warm and involved parents has been shown to be important in protecting against adolescent depression (Taris and Bok 1996).

Contributory causes of teenage depression

A longitudinal study by Waatkaar *et al.* (2004) confirmed that teenage depression is associated with broken friendships, death or serious illness of a close friend, parental divorce, problems with a teacher, family member in trouble with the police and drug/alcohol problems within the family, most of which appeared to impact more on girls who reported more depressive symptoms than boys.

Further analysis appeared to show that negative life events tended to occur after the onset of depression, *not the other way round*. They pointed out that life events do not occur 'out of the blue' but are often the consequence of family lifestyle.

Studies such as these confirm the importance of warm, secure relationships, early in life. Authoritative parenting helps to establish good role models, prepare adolescents to avoid unnecessary risks, resist negative peer pressure and deal with difficulties as they arise. Good relationships with parents enable the adolescent to view close monitoring as caring, rather than controlling, behaviour. Adolescents who live in deviant, chaotic or disrupted families, or who lack family support, are more likely to develop low self-esteem and mental health problems. They are also more likely to link up with peer groups that encourage antisocial and risk behaviours.

A review by Asarnow *et al.* (2001) suggests that interventions for adolescent depression should begin with assessment and management of such issues as substance misuse, family dysfunction and maternal depression. Substance use may, in some instances, be a form of self-medication used to deal with rejection. Prevention is better than cure, and Greenberg *et al.* (2003) in the USA found strong evidence that long-term school-based and youth development programmes, which are student-focused and relationship-orientated, are capable of improving social behaviour, school attendance and performance, and mental health in adolescents. However, the message is that it is best to start such programmes before youngsters start to experiment with risky behaviours. As health and social care professionals, an important role is to find ways to listen to, support and encourage youngsters and youth groups to find adaptive ways of dealing with important issues. We summarize the effects of different parenting styles in Table 3.4.

Table 3.4 Influence of parenting styles on emotional and behavioural development

Parenting style	Parenting characteristics	Likely or possible effects
Authoritative	Set standards of expectation Give explanations and feedback Do not use physical punishment Are consistent and fair Encourage self-direction Monitor activities	Higher levels of self-esteem, self-confidence and achievement Internal locus of control More independent and altruistic Likely to adhere to parental values Less likely to engage in delinquent or criminal behaviours Less likely to use legal and illegal substances Less likely to suffer from depression
Authoritarian	Expect obedience to absolute standards Show less warmth Use less communication Use physical punishment Attempt to control attitudes and behaviour Discourage argument	Have a more negative self-concept Are less well able to regulate their own behaviour Tend to obtain poorer school grades May follow parental example in the use of physical force
Permissive (indulgent)	Make few demands on the child Attempt reasoning but make no attempt to curb the child's impulses or desires Make little attempt to regulate the child's behaviour	Children tend to be immature Less able to take responsibility or self-regulate their behaviour Do worse in school May show aggression if the parents are permissive towards aggressive behaviour
Uninvolved (neglectful)	Show little regard for the child's well-being or behaviour	Infants show insecure, avoidant attachment Adolescents show disturbed, impulsive, antisocial patterns of social relationships Most likely to develop depression

Seen in these contexts, naughty, deviant or delinquent patterns of behaviour in children and adolescents need careful and empathetic investigation, rather than a rush to judgement.

Development in adult life

People continue to develop throughout their lives and not just during childhood as the developmental theories of Freud and Piaget might have us believe. Erikson and Levinson both proposed stage theories of lifespan development. Levinson *et al.* (1978) described a series of life transitions that reflect common patterns of changing family and work roles across the lifespan. For example, young adults move away from home, make and break new friendships, establish and negotiate sexual relationships, get a job, start a family. In early middle life, people may have to reappraise life goals in the light of achievements, or the failure to achieve previously determined goals. This might include having or not having children, career progression or change, adjustments in lifestyle or expectations, maintaining relationships or separations, dealing with success or failure. Later middle life often includes physical changes associated with the menopause for women, the demands of caring for older parents, loss of parents, children leaving home (or staying at home), separation or divorce and increasing concerns about health. Difficulties in adapting to these sorts of changes are commonly referred to as a 'mid-life crisis'.

Many of the major life changes faced by adults are included in the Holmes and Rahe (1967) list of major life events (see Chapter 7 for more details). This was designed as a measure of exposure to stress, though some of the events described are now rather out of date. However, neither stage theories nor the measurement of stressful life events explain *how* adults are able to negotiate successful transitions between different roles and circumstances. A theory that attempts to address this was put forward by Baltes and Baltes in 1990 (Coleman and O'Hanlon 2004). They called it 'selective optimization with compensation' (generally referred to as SOC, but not to be confused with sense of coherence; see Chapter 7).

Based on goal theory, Baltes and Baltes proposed three fundamental processes by which individuals actively manage their lives:

- *selection* refers to the development of a set of personal goals that focus commitment to the acquisition of skills and resources;
- *optimization* refers to the degree of effort the individual invests in trying to achieve these goals;
- *compensation* refers to flexibility in trying out alternative means of achieving goals when previous means are no longer available (Bajor and Baltes 2003). It also refers to the willingness to re-evaluate goals that are no longer attainable and identify new ones (see Chapter 9 for examples in relation to chronic illness).

Some indicators of these processes are given in Table 3.5. You will find similarities between these responses and locus of control (Chapter 5).

Wiese *et al.* (2002) found evidence that these processes are predictive of well-being in the context of both family and work. In many ways, these positive strategies resemble the active coping strategies designed to gain and maintain control, referred to in Chapter 7. This model is potentially of considerable use in practice, both for our own benefit and that of those we care for.

Table 3.5 Examples of positive and negative selection, optimization and compensation strategies, based on Bajor and Baltes (2003)	
Positive	**Negative**
Selection When I think about what I want in life, I commit myself to one or two important goals	I just wait and see what happens instead of committing myself to just one or two particular goals
Optimization When things don't go as well as they used to, I keep trying other ways or seek help	When I don't succeed right away, I don't try other possibilities for very long
Compensation When I can no longer achieve what I used to be able to achieve, I look for something different or new to achieve	I give up OR keep trying to achieve the same goals OR just wait and see what happens
Loss-based selection When I can't do something important the way I did before, I look for a new goal	When things don't go as well as they have in the past, I still try to keep all my goals OR I just wait and see

Exercise

Evaluate your own approach to life by reflecting on your answers to the following questions:

• Do you have a long-term goal? If so, do you think you might be willing to review and modify it at a later stage?
• If you have more than one goal (e.g. career, children), how will you decide which should take priority?
• What new skills or resources will you need to achieve your goals? How will you acquire these?
• What setbacks might you envisage along the way and how hard are you likely to try to overcome these?

Life is full of unexpected challenges and setbacks. Some of these can be overcome. Others require a complete shift in expectation. Below, we describe a domestic situation of the sort faced by people who live in a shared space.

Adapting to life changes

Ted recently moved to live with his son Mark and Mark's wife Janice. He had always relied on his wife to do all the household chores and expected his daughter-in-law to do the same. Janice had worked hard to train Mark to assist with these, but now even he was starting to copy his father. Janice was working and also helped Sasha with child care, so this led to considerable tensions. Anna became aware of the reasons for these difficulties as a result of her nursing lectures and set up a family meeting to review roles and responsibilities. This resulted in an agreement that Ted would help with light housework and vegetable preparation, but would need help with cleaning the bathroom and floors, and changing bed linen. Mark would help with loading and unloading the washing machine and ironing.

It is always a good idea to plan ahead and work out agreements in advance when contemplating this sort of life change, rather than waiting to see what happens.

Development in later life

Old age has been categorized as a separate life stage since antiquity. For example, Falkner and de Luce (1992) noted that the Greeks and Romans characterized old age as a time of physical and mental deterioration, social marginalization and closeness of death. Nowadays, old age is usually defined in chronological terms with the age of retirement a convenient point of entry. But some people choose to retire relatively early while others never stop.

The physical and cognitive health of those aged over 50 is very variable. Some develop chronic diseases at a relatively young age for genetic, environmental, economic and lifestyle reasons, while others remain alert, fit and active well into late old age. Some feel old in their fifties, others never feel old. Therefore objective and subjective transition points are very variable and chronological age is not a particularly useful concept. Functional age may seem somewhat easier to define in terms of the activities that people are able to undertake. However, these activities are often limited by cultural, legal and economic constraints, as well as individual emotional, cognitive and physical limitations. Overall, old age remains difficult to define.

Theories of age and ageing

Traditionally, theories of old age focused on the notion of gradual decline and disengagement. It is inevitable that many people will experience some decline in physical strength and function as they grow older and some will experience cognitive decline. But disengagement is more likely to be a sociological issue, as a result of poverty and family fragmentation, than a psychological one.

The terms 'successful', 'healthy' and 'positive' are all terms used to describe an optimum state in later life. But what do these actually mean? Erikson (1980) characterized successful ageing in terms of the successful completion of previous life stages. In essence, these include:

- *sense of trust* developed in childhood;
- *sense of purpose* and *competence* gained through childhood experiences;
- *sense of identity* and *set of values* gained during adolescence;
- *ability to love and care* resulting from intimacy and relationships in adulthood;
- *wisdom* that enables people to maintain a positive sense of self in spite of a decline in bodily and mental function.

Hung *et al.* (2010: 1386) recommended the use of the term 'healthy ageing', in preference to successful or positive ageing, defining it as:

> older people who experience positive outcomes in old age, not only in maintaining good physical health and functioning, but also in coping and remaining in control of later life and to age well in accordance with the values of their own cultures.

Lay views of healthy ageing

Hung *et al.* (2010) conducted a systematic review of healthy ageing in the English and Chinese literature. Their findings showed that 73 per cent prioretized independence (being in control and responsible for their lives, maintaining good health and making their own decisions in daily life). Important issues identified in lay studies, but absent in professional studies, referred to 'family', 'adaptation', 'financial security', 'personal growth' and 'spirituality'. Family and financial security were particularly highly rated in Asian studies.

Contrary to earlier predictions, Coleman and O'Hanlon (2004) presented evidence that as people get older most are likely to be satisfied with their lives, feel positive about themselves, and are no more likely to be anxious, depressed or fearful. Reasons include the flexibility to adapt to changed circumstances and re-evaluate and, where necessary, modify personal goals. In fact, if you look back to Table 3.5, you will find that this is not different from successful adult adaptation to change. It would appear that the processes involved in successfully adapting to change are the same regardless of age. A more important issue may, as the Greeks noted, be the proximity of death.

Interventions recommended to maintain cognitive and emotional health in later life, reviewed by Depp *et al.* (2010), include:

- *exercise*: increases brain serotonin levels and increases activity and sense of mastery;
- *dietary restriction*: a limit on calorific intake appears to increase energy metabolism and improve memory;
- *mental stimulation*, based on the 'use it or lose it' hypothesis. Although studies have shown that cognitive training improves cognitive performance, Depp *et al.* found little evidence to support this type of training in terms of its relevance in everyday life;

- *social activity*: in order to encourage reciprocity and involve young people, Depp *et al.* describe an American initiative where older people help schoolchildren with things like maths and reading;

- *mindfulness*: meditation has been shown to improve cognitive and behavioural flexibility and reduce systolic blood pressure (see also Chapters 7 and 8).

Depp *et al.* noted that many of these processes share common biological mechanisms in terms of stimulating brain activity and reducing stress.

Approaching life's end

As people approach the end of their lives, whatever their age, they seem naturally to reflect on their accomplishments and their failures and try to find a sense of meaning to their lives. This was illustrated in the vignette at the start of this chapter where Margaret reflects on her inability to have more than one child.

People who approach the end of life with a sense of accomplishment or satisfaction at having achieved certain life goals are generally less anxious and depressed, while those who have a sense of regret report more anxiety, depression and anger (Walker and Sofaer 1998). Life goals may relate to things like holding down a job, rearing children to be independent, having grandchildren, or overcoming challenges.

Everyone experiences some failures, though, for most, life achievements are balanced against these. However, for a few, it can seem impossible to come to terms with past events. This explains why some people express feelings of despair, regret and even bitterness as they approach the end of their lives. These are often the patients or clients who seem to complain about everything. Their attitudes and behaviour lead staff to avoid them, thus reinforcing their feelings of isolation, resentment and despair. These 'unpopular patients' (see Chapter 2) can be very challenging to care for, but avoiding their emotional needs only makes matters worse (see the self-fulfilling prophecy in Chapter 2). Finding time to sit and listen is an important way to help a distressed individual face death with a sense of peace and closure.

Therapeutic value of listening

While on placement with the health visitor, Anna visited a lady, aged 90, who seemed very depressed. Anna encouraged her to tell her story. After a difficult childhood, she had married at an early age to someone who turned out to be married already. She left him, but never admitted the reason to others, even to her own mother, who had died at the age of 94. As a result, she never married or had children of her own. By the time Anna left, she seemed much more cheerful. Being able to talk this through with someone who was empathic and non-judgemental really seemed to help her to make sense of these experiences in the context of the time and culture in which they had happened.

Example

Life review therapy is part of a growing tradition of narrative psychology, which we relate to the 'narrative self' in Chapter 2. It is a structured intervention in which individuals are encouraged to review, reorganize and re-evaluate the overall picture of their life, and gain a sense of meaning and coherence. This has been confirmed as an effective therapy for improving life satisfaction and emotional well-being in older people (Bohlmeijer *et al.* 2003) and for younger people who have a life-threatening illness (Ando *et al.* 2008).

It can be emotionally painful remembering situations associated with shame or guilt, but Coleman (1999) has suggested that life review has a confessional and spiritual dimension that encourages reconciliation. It enables people to come to terms with losses, and facilitates a positive transition to the final phase of life.

Research

Life review in cancer patients (Ando *et al.* 2008)

This Japanese study tested the impact of two sessions of structured life review for terminally ill cancer patients. They found it resulted in a significant decrease in measurements of suffering, anxiety and depression, and increase in happiness. The prompts used encouraged a positive focus (we have slightly modified these to retain essential meaning for a wider English-speaking audience):

- What has been the most important thing in your life and why?
- What memory has left the greatest impression on you?
- In your life, which event or person has had the greatest impact?
- What has been the most important role in your life?
- Which has been the proudest moment of your life?
- Is there anything about you that you would like your family to know or remember, and are there things you would want them to tell you?
- What advice or word of guidance would you wish to pass on to the important people in your life or to the younger generation?

Exercise

Reflect on these questions and think about how you might answer them. Talk to an older friend or relative and see how they feel about answering these questions. If they share their responses with you, is there anything in particular you find interesting or surprising?

Everyone will die and end of life care is part of normal working experience for all health and social care professionals. Evidence-based approaches suggest that helping people who are dying to have optimal quality of life and a dignified death is rewarding for all involved. This means good symptom control and attention to psychological, social and spiritual support. Moreover, care needs to be directed towards family members, both during the process of end of life care and in bereavement (see Field *et al.* 2007). We address these issues in Chapter 8.

Further reading

Gott, M. and Ingleton, C. (eds) (2011) *Living with Ageing and Dying.* Oxford: Oxford University Press.

Payne, S., Seymour, J. and Ingleton, C. (eds) (2009) *Palliative Care Nursing: Principles and Evidence for Practice*, 2nd edition. Maidenhead: McGraw-Hill.

Rushforth, H. (2010) The dynamic child: children's psychological development and its application to the delivery of care, in E.A. Glasper and J. Richardson (eds) *A Textbook of Children and Young People's Nursing*, 2nd edition. Oxford: Elsevier.

Santrock, J.W. (2009) *Lifespan Development*, 12th edition. Boston, MA: McGraw-Hill.

Chapter 4

Improving memory, understanding and communication

Key topics

- Memory processes and information recall
- Improving verbal and written communication
- Talking about 'unwelcome news'
- Effects of ageing on memory and understanding

Introduction

In this chapter, we focus on the following issues:

- Why do people forget so much of what is said to them?
- How can we help to improve memory, understanding and information-giving?

You may recall from Vignette 1, which we used to introduce the first chapter, that both Anna and Mr Smythe felt under pressure to recall important information about diabetes and its treatment. The following vignette illustrates two other types of situation where it can be difficult to recall matters of importance.

Lisa was recently made local representative for her professional group. At her first quarterly meeting, she found it hard to follow the jargon, so she made detailed notes. At the next meeting, the official note-taker was absent and members struggled to recall what had been agreed. After some discussion, their conclusion was totally different to the one Lisa had noted. The others were initially nonplussed when she brought this to their attention.

Following the meeting, Lisa was invited to lunch with some of the other representatives. When meeting clients, she always referred to her notes to ensure she knew them by name. But on this occasion, she felt embarrassed because she could not recall any of their names from the meeting.

This vignette illustrates how difficult it is to recall verbal information. Similarly, your own experience of education will tell you that much of the information you are given is neither properly understood nor accurately remembered.

In this chapter, we consider how psychological research can be used to improve memory and understanding. You can apply these principles to assist you in practice and with your own learning. We have divided the chapter into two parts. The first part addresses basic principles of memory and verbal communication that apply to everyone. In the second part, we address some specific issues related to memory and communication.

Background

Effective verbal and written communication is crucial to good health and social care and essential for gaining informed consent to treatment or intervention. Health professionals rely heavily on verbal and written information to inform patients about their diagnosis, negotiate treatment plans and educate the public about ways to improve their health.

Thorne *et al.* (2008) interviewed a large number of people with cancer and found they believed that good communication was their right. Some believed that communication was likely to influence the outcome of their condition, either by affecting their attitude to their situation, or by affecting their willingness to engage with doctors and undergo treatment.

Against this background, Fallowfield and Jenkins (1999: 1592) observed that:

many patients leave consultations unsure about their diagnosis and prognosis, confused about the meaning of and need for further diagnostic tests, unclear about the management plan and uncertain about the true therapeutic intent of treatment.

Our recent observations in practice indicate that this sometimes remains true. Such confusions cause unnecessary anxiety and distress and can lead to huge amounts of unnecessary spending on health care because patients fail to follow treatment advice.

Exercise

Think about a good and a bad experience you have had with a public service or talk to your family or friends about their experiences. What happened? What were the consequences? Can any of you think of any ways these experiences might have been improved by better communication?

We start this chapter by exploring basic principles from memory research and their implications for verbal communication.

Retaining verbal information

Figure 4.1 gives a simplified illustration of the complex process of information processing.

We receive new information through our senses (sight, hearing, smell, touch). Information that is attended to goes into short-term or working memory where it quickly decays unless it passes to long-term memory where it stays indefinitely.

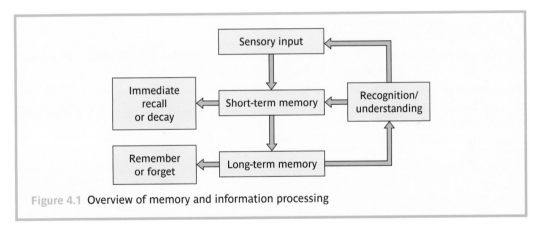

Figure 4.1 **Overview of memory and information processing**

How does information get from short-term to long-term memory?

Exercise

Just think about how you remember a new phone number. At first you can remember it for only a few seconds so you repeat it to yourself, often in small chunks, until you can write it down. But if you then dial the number regularly you no longer need to look it up – it is stored in your long-term memory.

'Information processing' is not a simple one-way process. This is because our existing knowledge and memories affect our recognition of the information, the attention we give to it and the way we interpret and understand it. To illustrate how principles of memory and understanding apply in practice, we use the following situation in which Lillian is being given the results of a biopsy she recently had taken from a lump in her neck.

Doctor: 'Well, Lillian, tests show that you have a type of cancerous growth called a lymphoma. This type of tumour normally responds well to treatment. We will get you into hospital next week to remove the lump and then organize some follow-up treatment in the form of chemotherapy.'

Sensory input

Many people find it hard to hear what is said to them, particularly amid the background noise of a busy environment. Patients or clients rarely admit to this because they are embarrassed or don't want to make a fuss. Similarly, students often don't complain if they find themselves unable to hear or concentrate if noise made by other students competes with the voice of the lecturer. In public situations, most people prefer to say nothing and so miss quite a bit.

Hearing unfamiliar terms

When people are introduced to new ideas, these are often expressed in language that is unfamiliar and therefore difficult to understand. In health and social care systems, people are given a lot of new information that is expressed in 'jargon'. Similarly, professionals are bombarded with new terms and concepts as part of their education. Students often say that the new terminology is what they find the most difficult.

Next time you attend a lecture, make a note of all the words you don't quite understand. Talk with a fellow student about the content of the lecture and see if they understood these terms.

Unfamiliar medical terms are frequently misheard by patients. Even if they are heard, they are often misunderstood. For example, when referring to test results, the patient may think the term 'positive' means 'good'. To them it implies there is nothing wrong, when in medicine it actually implies the presence of abnormal cells or organisms.

In our example, Lillian is unlikely to know what a lymphoma is, so the doctor has clearly identified it as a form of cancer. But she may or may not realise that cancer, lymphoma, tumour and lump all refer to the same thing.

Find the opportunity to talk with a patient or client about the information you have just heard them being given. Don't embarrass them by quizzing them – just ask them to tell you what they think about what they have just heard. How accurate is their recall and understanding?

It is always useful after giving essential information, or when gaining written consent, to ask the patient or client to tell you, in their own words, what they think it means. This allows you to correct misunderstandings at an early stage.

Arousal and attention

Cognitive performance, including learning and memory, is influenced by the arousal of the autonomic nervous system. This relationship follows an inverse U-shaped curve, known as the Yerkes–Dodson Law, as shown in Figure 4.2.

A low level of arousal reflects a state of boredom, apathy or disinterest in which attention is not properly focused on the issue being discussed. An extremely high level of arousal is associated with high anxiety or panic, which disrupts attention. In either of these states, Lillian would be unlikely to remember much of what was said.

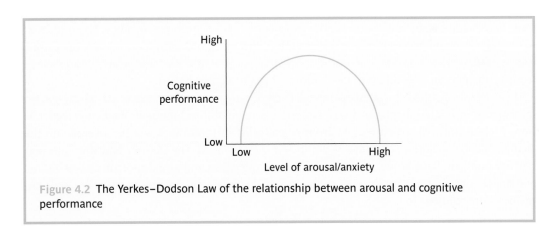

Figure 4.2 The Yerkes–Dodson Law of the relationship between arousal and cognitive performance

Take a little time to find out why someone seems to be very anxious. Don't feel under any pressure to solve their problems, just listen to them. How do they seem after you have listened to their concerns?

Listening to someone's worries or fears helps to gain their trust and reduce their anxiety. They are then more likely to be able to attend to what is said in a consultation (we give more examples in Chapter 10 on pain). Alternatively, if someone appears totally unconcerned when being given serious information or advice, increase their attention by emphasizing the importance of what is being said.

Familiarity, salience and selective attention

People tend to pay attention to what they already know about or expect to hear, and not necessarily to the things that health professionals see as important. In Lillian's case, the most salient aspects of information *for her* are highlighted in italics below:

Doctor: 'Well, Lillian, the tests show that you have a type of *cancer* called a lymphoma. This type of tumour normally responds well to treatment. We will get you into *hospital* next week for an *operation* to remove the lump and then organize some follow-up treatment in the form of *chemotherapy*.'

Lillian is most likely to hear the word 'cancer'. This may interfere with her ability to hear other important details which include the good news that 'the tumour normally responds well to treatment'. We all experience selective attention. Just as different students come away from a lecture with a different impression of the content, so patients or clients and relatives can emerge from a consultation with different ideas about what was said or meant.

Ley (1997) observed that information delivered in a systematic way is more effective than information given in a haphazard way. A particularly helpful technique is 'explicit categorization'. A clear and well structured lecture may use a list of topics that will be covered and the lecturer is likely to announce each new topic as it is introduced. The lecturer may then summarize key points or 'take home' messages, encourage questions and give opportunities to discuss and embed learning of key concepts at the end of the lecture. A similar structure is helpful in medical consultations too.

Anna sat in on a nurse-led wound management clinic. She noticed that at the start of each appointment, the nurse said: 'I am going to ask you how you have managed with the dressing since you have been home; then I will assess the wound and decide if there need to be any changes to the treatment; and lastly, if there are changes, we will discuss the best way to manage these. So, now tell me how you have been getting on . . .'

Quantity of information

There is a strict limit to how much information we are able to take in and remember at one time. In the nineteenth century, Ebbinghaus and Wundt asked people to recall a series of nonsense syllables and showed that people could normally repeat about seven of these. Miller (1956) confirmed that short-term (working) memory has a processing capacity limited to 7 +/−2 bits or chunks of information. The combination of seven letters and numbers in the British car number plate was determined by this research. But a 'chunk' is not the same thing as a letter or number. For example, an English speaker will find it much easier to remember the number plate LIM1T since this reduces five discrete digits to one meaningful chunk of information.

How many discrete chunks of information are commonly given to patients during a single consultation? In the short extract from Lillian's consultation, it is possible to identify at least nine separate bits of important information (in italics below).

Well, Lillian, the tests show that you have

1   a type of *cancerous* growth
2   called a *lymphoma.*
3   This type of *tumour*
4   normally responds well to *treatment.*
5   We will get you into *hospital*
6   *next week*
7   to *remove the lump*
8   and then organize some *follow-up treatment*
9   in the form of *chemotherapy.*

Example

This sort of information, delivered in quick succession, is very unlikely to be remembered accurately. Therefore it is better to give information in short meaningful chunks and ensure the person has understood each one before moving on to the next item.

Speed of delivery

Information held in short-term memory decays rapidly and is usually lost after about 20 or 30 seconds. The holding of new information in short-term memory and its transfer to long-term memory is facilitated by repetition or mental rehearsal. For example, if we wish to remember a new password, we repeat it to ourselves until it has 'sunk in'.

When we are given a series of important items of new information in a short space of time, there is no opportunity to repeat or reflect on each one. Therefore it is important to introduce frequent pauses. It is also important to help people consolidate the information that has been given in a consultation. This will be particularly helpful after a consultation such as Lillian's where the content may have come as a shock.

Distraction

Distraction disrupts thought processes. If we are distracted while we are trying to rehearse and absorb important information, we have to start all over again. This helps to explain why much of the information we are given is promptly lost. If Lillian's consultation is time-limited or her concentration disrupted, a lot of important information will never reach her long-term memory.

Style of communication

The way professionals use language, facial expression and intonation can all affect the meaning and interpretation of the message, often in ways that were not actually intended.

Research

Introducing subtle bias

Hall *et al.* (2003) reported that, following antenatal genetic testing, women who were given information about the presence of chromosomal abnormalities accompanied by negative statements were far more likely to undergo termination than those who were given information in a neutral or positive way. Thus the outcome was biased in favour of the attitudes of the staff giving the information.

Hall *et al.*'s study illustrates how information and choices are easily manipulated by the ways in which professionals communicate them.

Exercise

Imagine you are Lillian and are told one of the following.

1 'Well, Lillian, I'm afraid that we will have to get you into hospital right away.'
2 'Well, Lillian, we would like to get you into hospital right away.'

How does each of these make you feel?

It is worth remembering that subtle differences in the ways that information is conveyed will affect the way the information is interpreted and encoded and can have a big impact on the individual's emotional and behavioural responses.

Primacy and recency effects

When people are given several pieces of new information in sequence, they are inclined to remember the thing they hear first (the primacy effect) and the thing they hear last (the recency effect), and forget most of the rest. One reason is that they have more opportunity to mentally rehearse these items. Think about the way Lillian was told about her diagnosis and treatment:

Well, Lillian, the tests show that you have

1 a type of *cancerous* growth
2 called a lymphoma.
3 This type of tumour
4 normally responds well to treatment.
5 We will get you into hospital
6 next week
7 to remove the lump
8 and then organize some follow-up treatment in the form of *chemotherapy.*

Example

In this case, Lillian is most likely to remember the fact that she has cancer and will have to have chemotherapy. If the doctor really wishes to convey to Lillian the good news that her lump is likely to respond to treatment, it is better to reorder the sequence of the information given to Lillian:

Well, Lillian,

1 *Your tests indicate that you have something that is likely to respond well to treatment*
   . . . pause
2 You have a form of cancer
3 called a lymphoma
   . . . pause
4 We will need to bring you into hospital
5 next week
6 to remove the lump
   . . . pause
7 and then give you some further treatment
8 in the form of chemotherapy
   . . . pause
9 *Fortunately, the outcomes of this treatment are good*
   . . . longer pause
10 Now just repeat back what I have told you so I know that you have understood it properly.

Example

This way, Lillian is more likely to go away feeling positive about her results and the doctor can feel confident that she has not misunderstood anything. The consultation may take a little longer but in the long run this approach can save a lot of unnecessary time correcting misapprehensions and dealing with unnecessary anxiety.

Long-term memory

Long-term memory has been the subject of much research and theory development in psychology, assisted more recently by the introduction of brain imaging techniques. Once transferred from short-term to long-term memory, memories are stored in the brain according to a series of complex linkages between language, meanings, emotions, images, sounds and responses that are still not fully understood. Long-term memory is normally divided into three distinct types.

- *Procedural memory* is concerned with the learning of motor skills, rules, habits or sequences. For example, the route Lillian follows through the hospital will be stored as procedural memory. After the initial deliberate learning process, procedural memory translates into an automatic response that does not require conscious effort (see dual process in Chapter 1). Examples commonly used to illustrate this include riding a bike or driving a car.
- *Semantic memory* is concerned with knowledge of facts and is heavily dependent on language. The word 'semantic' means 'related to meaning'. This underpins the type of learning that occurs at school, college and university. If the *information* given to Lillian is to be remembered it will go into semantic memory.
- *Episodic or autobiographical memory* is concerned with memory for events. In particular it is associated with the storing of sensory images (including sights, sounds and smells) that relate to significant life events and have emotional significance. Lillian's memories of the *event* of being told she has cancer will be stored in this way.

In the following section, we focus on the ways in which long-term memory, particular semantic memory, is organized into what are called 'schemas'.

Semantic memory schemas

New information is encoded in relation to people's existing frameworks of understanding or patterns of belief which are referred to as 'schemas'. These enable us to organize and process large amounts of information. We can compare schemas to the organization of books in a library or files on your computer. If something completely new and unexpected arrives it requires extra effort to decide where to store this new information. But until reorganization has been achieved, books or information can go missing.

Some new information can require really major changes to the way that we think about the world in order to make sense. This type of information can be very hard to absorb, as illustrated below.

Making meaning

A classic experiment by Bartlett (1932) studied what happens when a complex and mysterious story is passed from one person to another in the same way as 'Chinese whispers'. He selected a North American folk tale, 'The War of the Ghosts', that contained a number of features that were difficult to make sense of for those in twentieth-century western cultures.

Bartlett found that the story changed in certain predictable ways as it was passed on. The story became shorter, more coherent, and more conventional in terms of cultural understanding.

This study is easy to replicate and demonstrates that while distinctive and familiar events are retained, less familiar information is altered to fit in with the frameworks of understanding of the individual. In other words, meaning is literally being made.

When a patient is given medical information by word of mouth, they tell their friends and relatives, framed in ways that both can understand. The facts and the events surrounding them become transformed in the telling. This is one reason why care professionals often find that a patient or client reports a completely different version of events from that recorded, or their understanding appears quite incorrect.

Joe's friend, Kris, had suffered from a painful back condition, ankylosing spondylitis, since he was a teenager. Although he had learned to cope quite well, his GP referred him to the local pain clinic where he was offered a course of acupuncture. While Kris was waiting for the doctor to place the needles, the nurse asked him what effect he thought acupuncture would have. He replied that the needles would untangle his nerves and cure his pain.

The exact mechanisms by which acupuncture can lead to therapeutic benefits are the subject of ongoing research (Zhao 2008). Explanations focus predominantly on the release of endogenous opioids. But while some people gain significant benefit from acupuncture, there is no evidence that it offers a curative solution to chronic pain.

When this was explained to Kris, he opted not to have any further treatment.

A patient's apparent failure to grasp what they were told may simply be caused by their instinct to incorporate it into their existing schemas. If you start by asking a patient or client what they already know or believe, as in the following example, it is possible to sort out misunderstandings and give correct information in a way that they are likely to understand. For example, when Lillian returned for further treatment, the nurse might check her understanding using the following approach:

Lillian, perhaps you would like to tell me what you understand about what is wrong and what the plan is for your treatment?

Disruption of a biographical schema

Mental schemas and autobiographical memories are gaining increasing attention within health and social care. Receiving important information is not just a matter of remembering a list of facts. For example, finding out that one has a disease or has lost a job changes an individual's life story or schema by confronting them with a different future to the one anticipated. This is often referred to as biographical disruption (see Chapter 3). As patients receive news about their disease and treatment, they try to make sense of it in the context of an unexpected and important change to their anticipated life story or schema.

When Lillian heard the doctor tell her she had cancer, she started thinking about the much longed-for holiday she was due to go on with a friend in two months' time. It was her first long-distance holiday and she had spent so much time planning and looking forward to it. Logically, her health was far more important, but why this and why now? All she could think about was that it could not possibly be happening to her. Perhaps she would wake up in the morning and find that it was all a bad dream. As she considered this, she realized that she had missed most of what the doctor was saying. She did not like to ask the doctor to repeat it, even when asked if she had understood everything, because the doctor was obviously very busy.

Finding out that one has a serious or chronic disease is a lot to take in during a single brief consultation, particularly when it involves learning a new medical language. It is hardly surprising that people fail to recall important details. It is a good idea to discuss the personal relevance of information, rather than just its general meaning, since this is more likely to ensure that material is understood and increases the amount likely to be remembered.

Recognition versus free recall

It is always easier to recognize a fact when presented with it again, than having to repeat it without prompt (free recall). Therefore, the way we ask questions can easily bias the response we get. In particular, a closed, directive question may prompt a response that should not be relied upon.

Ted was prescribed tablets for his heart condition, but was not yet in a routine and kept forgetting to take them. When Janice asked him if he had taken them, he lied and said 'yes', because he didn't want Janice to think he was forgetful. It took Janice quite some time to realize that he wasn't taking them properly. She then ensured that he used the special dispenser properly.

If we want to find out what someone has remembered, it is never a good idea to ask a closed question that requires a 'yes' or 'no' answer. Faced with this option, most people will tell us what they think we want to hear. Instead, ask an open question such as 'please remind me what we agreed last time'.

Context-specific memory

You may have had an experience where you completely forgot something that was said to you, but do recall it when you revisit the place where it was said. Certain semantic information is encoded into a schema that includes environmental information, which means it is strongly contextualized. The resulting memories may be context-specific, which implies they are facilitated by a return to the environment or emotional state in which the event or incident originally took place.

At one visit, Lillian was told about an ointment that might be helpful for her skin. She clean forgot about it until she entered the hospital the next time and something about the sight or smell in the clinic suddenly reminded her.

Example

Many traumatic memories are coded in the same way and may be triggered unexpectedly by sights or sounds that are associated at an unconscious level with the traumatic event (see Chapter 8).

False memories

False memories have attracted a lot of attention in relation to memories for childhood abuse and eyewitness memory. Loftus (2005: 361–6) gave a detailed analysis of this phenomenon, defining false memory as the impairment of memory for a past event as a result of exposure to subsequent misleading information. She concluded that it is possible for people to falsely believe details that were never actually experienced, but were suggested to them.

The mechanisms by which false memories are created remain a matter of debate. Possibly the original event was never properly encoded in long-term memory. Maybe the original schema becomes elaborated by new false information though automatic and unconscious thought processes or as part of routine updating of the memory system. It may come about because of an unconscious need to fill gaps during the retrieval of memories.

The fact that false memories can easily be formed is important to note. Loftus warns that they can arise through informal conversations with others or by being asked leading questions. The more distant the original event, the more prone they are to false additions or variation. This implies that childhood memories are vulnerable to false additions or distortions. Can we distinguish a false memory from a real one? It appears that false memories may initially be described using sentences that are longer and contain more uncertain language, for example phrases such as 'I think'. But once people have convinced themselves that the false memories are true, their accounts become indistinguishable from 'real' memories.

In the context of health and social care, the existence of convincing and detailed false memories has obvious implications for those who rely on information from patients or clients to make a diagnosis or other type of judgement. The people who describe false memories are not lying; they are convinced that they are telling the truth.

Lisa was involved in a child protection case and needed to interview Mrs Lake, a neighbour who claimed to have just witnessed an episode of abuse. When she arrived, she found that several neighbours had congregated to discuss what was going on.

Lisa hurried to take Mrs Lake on one side and ask her to describe the event in her own words. Lisa was careful not to ask any direct questions (for example, those that start with 'do you remember that . . .') since she was aware these could plant ideas in Mrs Lake's memory.

At this interview, Mrs Lake seemed hesitant and her story was rather sketchy in places. Later on when the case came to court, Mrs Lake gave confident details that were not present in the account she originally gave Lisa. Lisa wondered to what extent conversations with neighbours had elaborated Mrs Lake's memory for the events of that day.

In health care, it is common to try to speed up a consultation by saying to a patient 'Do you remember the last time you were here, we did . . . ?'. While this may seem a good way of jogging someone's memory, it is worth noting that this style of questioning is capable of introducing a memory for an event that did not actually take place at all. Likewise, when working with people who are emotionally vulnerable, it is possible for us to introduce our own assumptions about possible causes into their reality. This is how so-called 'recovered' memories may be constructed.

Table 4.1 contains a summary of key ideas from the chapter so far. The suggested ways of improving memory and understanding are applicable in all health care contexts.

Improving learning and study skills

1 When you attend a lecture, take the opportunity to observe the communication techniques used by the lecturer.

    a How successfully did the lecturer maintain your attention?

    b Could you read, hear and understand all of the lecture material?

    c Were there any distractions and, if so, how were these managed?

    d Did you have the opportunity to ask questions?

    e What might have improved your learning and your satisfaction with the lecture?

2 Now assess your own study methods.

    a Do you make adequate preparation so that your attention is fully focused on the task in hand without distractions?

    b Do you ensure that you properly understand the material by checking it with the lecturer and using recommended reading?

    c Do you assemble the information into meaningful chunks or categories under the heading of key points?

    d Do you pause frequently to reflect and allow the information to sink in?

    e Do you stop periodically to test your memory and understanding by writing out a summary of each key point?

    f Do you make sure that you don't overload yourself at each session?

Table 4.1 Summary of key memory processes, with practical implications

Process	Influences	Limiting factors/effects	Actions to improve outcomes
Sensory input	Sensory impairment	Poor vision and hearing	Check visual and hearing acuity Check aids are functioning
	Distracted attention	Limited by noisy environment and other worries	Limit environmental distractions Check out patient's concerns
	Level of arousal	Attention inhibited by disinterest and high anxiety	Alert attention if disinterested Find out cause of anxiety and calm the patient
Short-term (working) memory	Capacity	Limited to 7+/–2 chunks of information at one time	Give information in discrete meaningful chunks
	Duration	Limited to 20–30 seconds unless repeated or rehearsed	Keep pausing to check understanding and allow progression of information to long-term memory
Transfer to long-term memory	Sequence	First and last things remembered best	Give most important message first and repeat it last
	Distraction	Disruption	Avoid interruptions
Long-term memory, stored as schemas	Schemas are based on prior experiences that give meaning and understanding	Information that is not personally meaningful may be forgotten, or distorted, or reinterpreted in relation to existing framework of understanding	First elicit patient's understanding Stick to relevant information Give opportunity for questions Check understanding again after giving information Back up with appropriate and accessible sources of information Provide a structure for what you say through explicit categorization
Loss of information from memory	Other information blocks retrieval of items from long-term memory	Leads to confusion or inaccuracies	Reinforce messages to patients with written material or other prompts, as appropriate Record patient information before undertaking other tasks
Retrieval bias/false memories	Leading questions act as prompts	Accesses memories otherwise not available for recall	Ask questions in an open, inquiring way Avoid directive questions that include reminders
Evaluation of message	Emotional tone and content of delivery	Affects interpretation and decisions	Maintain a neutral stance when offering informational choices

Improving communication in practice

1 Observe a trained member of staff when they are giving health information to a patient or client. What changes to the interaction might you suggest in order to improve the patient's memory and understanding?

2 Under guidance from your mentor or line manager, select a patient or client who is willing and able to describe their medical condition, treatment or management. With permission from the patient or client, arrange to spend a fixed amount of time with them (say 10–15 minutes) and ask them to tell you what they understand about their condition or treatment. Then go and compare the patient's perception of facts, key events and their meaning with what is written in their health records.

  ● How closely does the patient's account match the details in their notes?

If you find discrepancies, discuss these with your mentor or line manager before deciding how to account for them and what to do about them.

In the following sections, we include the following issues: talking to patients or clients about unwelcome news, giving written information, the effects of ageing on memory, and memory loss.

Talking about 'unwelcome news'

The description of Lillian's experience of being told about having cancer highlights reasons why it is difficult for people to remember information when being given unwelcome news about their diagnosis. One possible response to this difficulty is to ask patients if they wish to have a friend with them for the consultation. The other person can help the patient by taking notes or, with the patient's agreement, asking questions. Hogbin and Fallowfield (1989) were the first to study the effects of offering patients a tape recording of the 'bad news consultation' in cancer care, so they could listen again at their leisure. This does not suit everybody, but those who elected to do so found it extremely helpful in gaining a better understanding of the whole situation, and in explaining it to close family or friends.

Having to deliver unwelcome news is very difficult, as illustrated in the research by Fallowfield and her colleagues.

Censoring unwelcome news

Fallowfield *et al.* (2002: 297) observed that health care professionals often censor information in an attempt to protect patients from potentially distressing information. However, she argued that the well-intentioned desire to shield patients from the reality of their situation usually creates even greater difficulties for patients, caregivers and members of the health care team, since it leads to a conspiracy of silence and heightened state of anxiety and confusion:

▶

▶ Ambiguous or deliberately misleading information may afford short-term benefits while things continue to go well, but denies individuals and their families opportunities to reorganize and adapt their lives towards the attainment of more achievable goals, realistic hopes and aspirations.

Gaston and Mitchell (2005) undertook a systematic review of the information needs of cancer patients and found that these changed over the course of the cancer journey. Desire for information was generally strong, but they found evidence of widespread misunderstanding of disease course, prognosis and treatment aims. Ambiguous information contributed to misunderstanding, for example 'response to treatment' could be interpreted as meaning cure.

Not wanting information

Leydon *et al.* (2000) described three reasons why patients may not want to know more than the basic facts regarding their condition: 'faith' (in the medical staff), 'hope' (avoiding information that might undermine their belief in the future) and 'charity' (not wanting to take the time of medical staff that might be helpful to others).

Given the variation in individual needs for information, a good way to find out what people want is to ask some 'what if' questions, as in the scenario below.

Before Lillian went for her first biopsy, her doctor explained that the results would show whether or not she had cancer. She was asked how she might feel if she did have cancer, and what sort of information she would wish to be told. When the results came through, the doctor reminded Lillian of what she had said and asked her if she had changed her mind. She was then given the sort of information that she felt able to cope with.

Improving written information

A good way to improve memory and understanding is to support verbal information with written information.

Verbal versus written instructions

Johnson and Sandford (2004) conducted a Cochrane review to compare verbal hospital discharge information with a combination of written and verbal information. Two trials met their inclusion criteria, both involving parental information regarding their children. One trial involved discharge from a burns unit; the other followed an episode of otitis media (ear infection). In both cases, parental knowledge was significantly improved if verbal information was combined with written information.

The main problem with giving written information is to ensure that the people for whom it is intended can read and understand it. For example, there are many people for whom English is not their first language or who have literacy problems. A review by Boulos (2005) concluded that even the most readable of the patient information on diabetes required a reading age of 11 to 13, while Lloyd (2010) reported that up to 12 million adults in the UK had a reading age of 11 years or less. Information about medications is particularly important because of the potential for overdose or underdose. Those with low levels of literacy are more likely to have health and social problems (Powers *et al.* 2010) and are therefore likely to be represented disproportionately in the health and social care systems.

Presenting information to adults

Wolf *et al.* (2007) investigated adults' understanding of drug dosage instructions, depending on the way the instructions were presented. The instruction 'Take one teaspoonful by mouth three times daily' was understood by 86 per cent of those with adequate literacy and 59 per cent with low literacy.

But when asked how many tablets per day would be needed if the instruction was 'Take two tablets by mouth twice daily', only 35 per cent of those with low levels of literacy were able to reply with the correct number (four tablets), compared to 80 per cent of those with adequate literacy.

When attempting to gain informed consent from a patient or client, it should not automatically be assumed that they will be able to read and understand written information in the form in which it is routinely presented. Having given them time to read it, it is important to ask the individual to tell you in their own words all that they think is about to happen.

Presenting information to children

Barnett *et al.* (2005) wanted to find out about children's understanding of the type of written information given to those invited to participate in a randomized controlled trial of a new drug. This included their understanding of randomization (whether they would get the real or the dummy drug) and safety and effectiveness (whether the drug would make them better). Participants were schoolchildren aged 9 to 11 of above average ability. Information was given in three different formats: question and answer, block text and story.

The children's overall understanding of the written information ranged from 54 per cent to 63 per cent. The story format improved understanding. The question-and-answer format was least well understood.

Houts *et al.* (2001) tested the use of 'pictographs', simple pictorial representations, sketches or cartoons, to illustrate health care instructions for patients with weak literacy skills. For example, a pictograph is able to illustrate a sequence of actions. They found that if these pictographs (or pictograms) were presented and discussed with the patient during the consultation, they were better able to read the simple message used to caption the pictograph and were therefore better able to understand it. The pictographs appear to encourage people to think about what has been said and serve as a reminder about what to do.

Exercise

Next time you are in a public waiting area, have a look at the leaflets on display, particularly those on topics you know little about. Do they tell you what you really want to know? How readable do you think these are likely to be? Try sharing them with members of your family of different ages and see what they think.

Table 4.2 Improving written information, from Horner *et al.* (2000: 19)

Improvement	Suggestion
Improve ease of reading	Increase font size (minimum of 12, but 14 to 18 is better)
	Use headings to highlight key concepts
Review the content	Substitute simple terms for multisyllabic terms
	Use direct language; avoid use of 'to be' verbs
	Present ideas in short, direct sentences
Improve comprehension	Define new or complex terms
	Add relevant illustrations to the text
	Use examples relevant to topic, identified population, or both
Evaluate the text	Determine reading level
	Field test patient education materials with identified population

The suggestions in Table 4.2 will help to improve written information for patients or clients.

We emphasize the last point by suggesting that the best advice for improving all types of written information is to involve representatives of user groups to develop and review the content and ensure it is produced in a form that is engaging, meaningful and accessible to the target group for which it is intended.

Osteoporosis – information for men

Research

Osteoporosis (weakening of the bones) is a common problem in men although it occurs, on average, 10 years later than in women. Raphael (2008) reviewed health education material in doctors' surgeries and found hardly any that contained an image of a man. Hardly surprising, therefore, that the men she interviewed were perplexed at being diagnosed with a 'woman's disease'.

Professionals and the public are increasingly turning to the media and the internet for information. Langille *et al.* (2010) conducted a systematic review, using Google, of information about inflammatory bowel disease and found that few sites provided good quality information. Overall, the median (mid-point) data quality score was 22 out of a possible total of 74. Many sites are commercial ones that have a vested interest in promoting or selling a product. Web 2.0 technology means that anybody can easily post information. Things like 'blogs' give interesting personal accounts but these are often very biased and should be treated with caution. Health professionals are obliged to provide evidence-based care based on information from credible sources. It is useful to be familiar with up-to-date web addresses for sites that provide high-quality, patient-centred and relevant information. At the time of writing, one of the best sites is: www.patient.co.uk/.

Effects of ageing on memory and understanding

It is often assumed that memory gets progressively poorer past the age of 60. But while there is some evidence that memory for recent events tends to deteriorate with age, semantic memory is unlikely to be seriously affected in the majority of people.

Cognitive function in older women

Barnes *et al.* (2007) conducted a prospective study of almost 10,000 women aged 65 or over in the USA. They measured cognitive function at the start (baseline) and again at 6, 8, 10 and 15 years using the modified Mini Mental State Examination* (MMSE). The following results were obtained at the end of follow-up (at average age 85 years) or death:

- 67 per cent showed either no decline or minimal cognitive decline of an average of 1 point out of a total of 26 points on the MMSE.
- The 33 per cent who were categorized as 'major decliners' showed an average cognitive decline of 3 points over the 15-year study period.

Cognitive decline was highest among those with health problems including diabetes, hypertension and stroke, and among those with high levels of smoking and alcohol consumption. Cognitive decline was also associated with lower levels of physical activity, smaller social networks and higher levels of depression.

*The Mini Mental State Examination (MMSE) is widely used to diagnose memory disorders and dementia. It tests for orientation in time and place, recognition, attention, recall and language – we refer to it again later in this chapter.

Many older people compensate for small changes by using strategies such as taking more time or writing memos.

Adherence to medications

Park *et al.* (1999) created an age-stratified profile of individuals with rheumatoid arthritis and studied factors that influenced whether they took their medications. They assessed cognitive function, disability, emotional state, lifestyle, and beliefs about the illness.

They found that older adults made the fewest errors while middle-aged adults made the most. A busy lifestyle was the strongest predictor of not taking medications in the way they had been asked to, and this was more likely to occur in middle life.

Hedden and Gabrieli (2004) summarized evidence-based ways to help maintain memory function in later life. These are consistent with the promotion of healthy ageing discussed in Chapter 3 on development in later life:

- stay engaged in mental activities;
- maintain cardiovascular physical activity;
- minimize chronic stressors (see Chapter 7);
- maintain a diet high in poly- and monounsaturated fats, including fish and olive oils, and vitamin E, polyphenols and antioxidants (for example dark-skinned fruits and vegetables).

Sudden memory loss

Sudden memory loss, confusion and disorientation in older people can be mistaken for signs of dementia, but are more commonly due to medical conditions such as respiratory or urinary tract infections, anaemia, or self-neglect associated with malnutrition or dehydration. In later life, confusion is also a relatively common response to drug or anaesthetic metabolism. Correctly assessing the cause of the problem and initiating appropriate action or treatment should restore memory function in most cases.

Ted's friend Violet, aged 81, described what had happened the day after an operation she'd had three months previously. She recalled seeing snakes crawling over the lady in the bed opposite and remembered trying to climb out of bed to remove them. She was aware of becoming more and more agitated as nurses kept bringing her back to bed, until one of them finally explained that these were hallucinations caused by the anaesthetic. She recalled her sense of relief at receiving this explanation.

Total memory loss (amnesia) is actually rare. Traumatic brain damage can occasionally cause complete loss of short-term memory and encoding, such that the individual fails to remember anything that has occurred since the onset of the disorder or trauma. More common are specific types of memory loss associated with damage to different parts of the brain. For example, it is fairly common following a stroke to find that the individual has unilateral neglect.

This means that patients 'forget' that they have a left or right side to their body until they are reminded. The arm or leg functions perfectly well when they make a conscious effort to move it, but in the course of trying to walk or feed themselves, they fail to attempt to use it. Some people actually fail to see objects on the left or right side. This may be caused by a breakdown in the ability to integrate visual, perceptual and motor information and may respond to a programme of re-education. These types of memory loss all require expert assessment, advice and management.

Understanding dementia

Dementia, including Alzheimer's disease, is associated with progressive brain disease that involves loss of memory, confusion, and problems with speech and understanding. Initial symptoms include problems with short-term memory, such as forgetting where the car was parked or turning off the cooker, and problems associated with semantic memory, such as forgetting the names of common objects. Progressive symptoms include the gradual loss of long-term memory including loss of procedural memory, such as how to park the car or how to turn on the cooker. Episodic memories retreat, though childhood memories usually remain intact, particularly those involving events that are emotionally significant. The number of people with dementia increases dramatically with age (Chapter 3), though people who have Down's syndrome have a higher risk of dementia at a much earlier age.

Dementia is diagnosed using the Mini Mental State Examination (MMSE, Folstein *et al.* 1975), to which we referred previously. It includes repetition of common words, naming of common objects and responding to a prior written instruction. The results require careful interpretation and supportive evidence. The test is not valid for use with those who are not entirely familiar with the language in which it is presented (Teresi *et al.* 2001), and responses may be compromised by a high level of anxiety. The onset of dementia is usually sufficiently gradual to allow people to adapt to early memory changes and the stigma associated with the disease often prevents people from seeking help at an early stage.

There is no cure for dementia, though some drugs have been developed that can delay progression and improve quality of life. In the early stages, simple memory aids such as writing reminders and making lists can help to overcome forgetfulness. Memory clinics offer cognitive retraining, which consists of learning new problem-solving strategies to cope with memory loss, and repetitive techniques to improve memory. This has been shown to improve learning, memory, activities of daily living, depression, and self-rated general functioning in the earlier stages of dementia (Sitzer *et al.* 2006). Depression and anxiety are commonly associated with dementia and require treatment (see Chapter 8).

A happy state

Anna had assumed that dementia was always distressing for those who suffered from it. But during her training, she visited one elderly care home resident who eagerly told her that she was aged 42, ran her own dancing school in London, and was currently enjoying a holiday in this lovely hotel where the food and the staff were wonderful. In fact, the lady was aged 84 and had been resident in the care home for two years.

Example

The caregivers of people with dementia are particularly at risk of stress-related illness (Chapter 7). Therefore an important aim is to enable patients and their families to manage and come to terms with problems that can include agitation and aggression as well as forgetfulness and confusion. Many caregivers experience great distress because the person they love no longer remembers who they are, or may mistake a spouse for a parent or a daughter or son for a deceased wife or husband.

In terms of therapeutic management, the best known psychological approaches are 'reality orientation' and 'validation therapy'. Reality orientation is intended to improve memory function by providing information and correct feedback about time, place and people (Spector *et al.* 2000). Tools include frequent reminders, display boards and group sessions. A review by Boccardi and Frisoni (2006) found modest improvements in cognitive and behavioural functioning using this approach.

Janice's friend Joan noticed that her 91-year-old grandmother was getting increasingly forgetful and tended to repeatedly ask her about her day. She found this very annoying and struggled not to be cross. Janice helped her to realize that her grandmother was not being deliberately difficult. She encouraged Joan to use contextual cues like clocks, printed notices and labels, which helped her grandmother to function better at home.

Aspects of autobiographical memory, particularly those related to emotionally salient events, usually remain intact until the very late stages of dementia. These memories provide important insights into the world the patient currently inhabits. Validation therapy focuses on giving empathy and respecting their reality (Ballard *et al.* 2009). It is a useful tool for communicating and building a therapeutic alliance with those who have severe dementia, once reality orientation is no longer possible or merely increases agitation.

Interpreting behaviour

Mills studied institutionalized older patients who had severe dementia by asking them about their past (Mills and Walker 1994). She presented a case study of Mr Fellows, who initially seemed very confused and depressed. But he described detailed episodes from his childhood which his wife confirmed as accurate. One day he described how he had once lost his school cap, which meant his mother had to buy another (they were very poor). This explained to staff why Mr Fellows would often wander round in an agitated state saying 'Where's my cap?'

Later, Mr Fellows confided how ashamed he was of being incontinent and how annoyed he was that the chiropodist had not attended to his feet. He actually had quite a lot of awareness of his current feelings and needs.

As the study progressed, Mr Fellows started to cheer up and became less agitated and depressed. The best explanation for this is that members of staff were better able to respond to him as an individual with an interesting life history.

As a result of her study, Mills recommended that a social history should accompany each older person in need of care. Recalling early memories, whether happy or sad, helps individuals to regain some sense of coherence within their lives (see Chapter 3). It also helps care providers to gain a sense of the individual as a person in his or her own right, rather than drawing on stereotypes.

Exercise

Find time to sit with someone who has been diagnosed with dementia (including Alzheimer's disease). Invite them to talk a bit about themselves. Find out what sorts of memories are most salient for them. Are these happy or sad? If the individual seems sad, place a hand on their arm and allow them to finish. How did they seem afterwards?

Touch is comforting and provides the human contact that many people with dementia lack. Other interventions that help to improve enjoyment and quality of life for people with dementia include reminiscence, music, singing and dancing that dates back to the time when they were young. Table 4.3 summarizes key points from the second section of this chapter.

Table 4.3 Summary of key points related to specific memory topics

Topic	Problem	Practical implication
Difficult topics	The shock of receiving unwelcome news can make it hard to take in what is said	Pre-warning, tape recording, having a companion and/or written notes can be helpful
	Information that is edited or distorted with euphemisms to 'protect' the listener can have serious negative consequences	Use plain language Check that the patient has understood both the meaning and implications
Written information	Visual impairment caused by inadequate or dirty spectacles is extremely common	Check the patient can read the print Offer alternative such as recording
	Poor level of literacy or learning difficulty	Check that all material can be understood by the target group
Language problems	There are now many adults whose English is functionally poor	Check level of understanding of the spoken and written word Use a translation service where possible
Ageing	Memory changes in later life are usually compensated for by memory-enhancing strategies	Don't assume that older people have poor memory. This is often incorrect and patronizing

Topic	Problem	Practical implication
Sudden memory loss	Common infections, self-neglect, dehydration and medications can cause sudden memory loss	Screen for acute medical problems and medication side-effects as a priority
	Confusion is often associated with agitation	Take time to attend to the patient's concerns. This usually has a calming effect
Dementias	Dementias affect short-term and semantic memory. In the later stages, procedural memory is affected and episodic memory recedes	Understanding the personal history of someone with a memory disorder can help health professionals, patients and their carers
		Close human contact is an important part of quality of life

Table 4.3 *Continued*

Further reading

Bauby, J-D. (1997) *The Diving-bell and the Butterfly*. London: Fourth Estate. A short personal story communicated through the blink of an eye. Also a film.

Thurman, S. (2011) *Communicating Effectively with People with a Learning Disability*. Exeter: Learning Matters.

Chapter 5

Learning and behaviour

Key topics

- Classical and operant conditioning: theory, applications and therapies
- Social learning, self-efficacy and locus of control
- Learned helplessness

Introduction

In Chapter 4, we explored the ways in which new information is learned through deliberate thought processes. In this chapter, we investigate learning that involves automatic ways of responding. Specifically, we focus on the following question:

- How do we learn to respond differently to different situations without awareness?

When Margaret went into hospital for investigation, her routine pain-relieving medication was changed from a red branded tablet to a white generic drug that contained exactly the same active ingredient. She complained that it was not the same and did not relieve her arthritis pain. No amount of explaining would persuade her that these tablets were any good.

Later, she was given a saline drip. The previous time she had been given one was after an operation and post-operative pain relief was delivered with it. This time, as soon as the saline drip was inserted, her pain started to decrease.

These episodes convinced some staff that Margaret's pain was purely psychological. Anna disagreed, but was not sure how to explain why.

By understanding the types of response described in the vignette in terms of learning processes, we are able to interpret behaviours which seem otherwise to be weird, unnecessary or inexplicable. We can also help ourselves and others to introduce effective strategies to change behaviours that are unhelpful.

Background

These learning processes were described in the twentieth century by a school of psychologists known as 'behaviourists'. They were so-called because they believed the only scientific way to study psychology was to measure changes in observable behaviour under different conditions. Hence, these types of learning became known as 'conditioning'. Behaviourists did not deny the existence of thoughts and emotions, but chose to ignore them because they could not be directly observed and objectively measured.

Behavioural research originally took place in laboratory conditions, using pigeons, rats and other animals. This led sceptics to doubt if these types of learning are applicable to humans. It is true that we live in complex environments and are capable of complex thought processes, whereas the experiments were limited to simple learning in restricted environmental conditions. Yet conditioning processes may provide useful insights into some predictable aspects of human behaviour.

Conditioning

Conditioning refers to an automatic process of learning by association. Two distinct types of conditioning were identified during the twentieth century: classical conditioning and operant (or instrumental) conditioning.

- *Classical conditioning* refers to the development of an automatic reflex response to an inert stimulus through a process of unconscious association. Examples of reflexive responses amenable to classical conditioning include fear, nausea, and changes in blood pressure.
- *Operant or instrumental conditioning* refers to changes to voluntary behaviours (those over which we normally have conscious control) as a result of the previous consequences of engaging in the behaviour. Types of voluntary behaviour that are subject to this type of learning include eating a healthy diet, smoking or studying for an exam.

Classical conditioning

Classical conditioning is the simplest form of associative learning. In the 1920s, Pavlov demonstrated that dogs salivated at the sound of a bell that signalled the impending delivery of food. While salivation to food is a natural physiological reflex response, salivation to the bell was a learned response which resulted from the association of the bell with food. This implicit 'learning by association' is termed classical conditioning.

Classical conditioning is one way that we learn to respond reflexively to certain stimuli (objects, events, situations or environments). In Figure 5.1, we illustrate how a child can 'learn' to be afraid of doctors or medical environments.

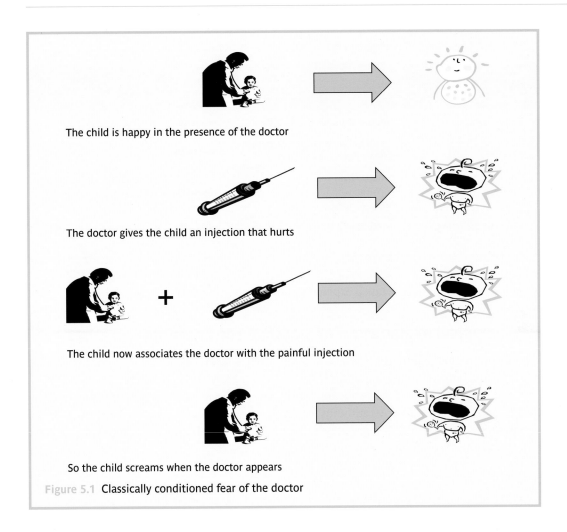

The child is happy in the presence of the doctor

The doctor gives the child an injection that hurts

The child now associates the doctor with the painful injection

So the child screams when the doctor appears

Figure 5.1 Classically conditioned fear of the doctor

When he went with his mother for his immunization, Lee had no reason to fear the doctor. But when the doctor gave Lee his injection, it came as a painful shock. The next time Lee was taken to see the doctor, he became very frightened and upset and struggled to escape. It made no difference how many times his mother explained that he was not due for another injection, the doctor was now firmly associated in Lee's mind with the painful injection. In fact, Lee had no control over his fear because it was a 'conditioned response'.

We explain this in Table 5.1.

Table 5.1 Classical conditioning of a fear response to a doctor

Timing	Stimulus 'object', 'event' or 'situation'		Response
Before conditioning	Neutral stimulus (NS): 'doctor'	⟶	Neutral response
	Unconditioned (active) stimulus (US): 'unexpected pain'	⟶	Unconditioned response (UR): 'fear'
During conditioning	'Doctor' (NS) is paired with 'unexpected pain' (US)	⟶	Unconditioned response (UR): 'fear'
After conditioning	Conditioned stimulus (CS): 'doctor'	⟶	Conditioned response (CR): 'fear'

Below, we offer a more detailed explanation for those who may find it helpful.

Psychological explanation of classical conditioning

The unconditioned stimulus (US) is something that triggers an automatic reflex response, known as the unconditioned response (UR).

Conditioning is a process of subconsciously pairing the neutral stimulus (in this case the doctor) with the unconditioned stimulus (US).

Following this pairing, the previously neutral stimulus (the doctor) produces the same response as the unconditioned stimulus (US).

In our example, the previously neutral stimulus, the doctor, is now referred to as the conditioned stimulus (CS) and the response, fear, is referred to as the conditioned response (CR).

What is important for those working in health and social care is the principle, rather than the terminology. The important thing to remember is that any body reflex can be conditioned to respond to a seemingly neutral or inert stimulus. Examples include the following:

- Conditioned fear or panic responses may be triggered by all sorts of people, objects, events, situations or environments, including doctors, dentists, clinics and hospitals.
- Conditioned physiological responses, such as asthma or nausea, may be triggered by the sight, sound or smell of a variety of objects, animals and environments.
- Conditioned intolerance to food stuffs may be triggered by their sight or smell.
- Placebo and nocebo responses may be triggered in response to inert substances or treatments. These responses are both illustrated in the vignette at the start of this chapter. We give more detail and further explanations for these responses in Chapter 10 on pain.

Exercise

Looking at the sorts of responses that might be classically conditioned, can you think of any reflexive, involuntary responses of your own that might have been caused by this process?

Explain the process to friends who are not familiar with the concept and see if they can think of any examples.

Many patients undergoing chemotherapy feel nauseous at the sight or smell of the hospital. This is a classically conditioned reflex response produced by the close association between post-chemotherapy nausea and the environment in which it was induced. It is difficult to gain conscious control over this type of reaction once it has become a conditioned response.

Example

Lillian had three sessions of chemotherapy at her local hospital. After each session, she felt very nauseous. On the fourth session, she started to feel sick as she entered the hospital and had a strong urge to turn round and go home. She told herself that this was silly – why should she feel sick before she even reached the treatment unit?

When she told the staff about her experience, they gave her anti-nausea tablets to take before setting off for the hospital. These eventually broke the association and she was able to come to appointments without feeling sick.

Another example of classical conditioning is the triggering of an asthmatic attack by an inert object. Recent research (e.g. Vits *et al.* 2011) has confirmed that the association between an allergen, such as dust mite or animal fur, and an inert object may be sufficient to produce a conditioned allergic response. For example, if someone is allergic to dog fur, the mere sight of a furry toy or picture of a dog may be sufficient to induce a conditioned asthma attack.

Example

For years, Joe believed that his hay fever-like symptoms were caused by allergy to cats. He experienced itchy eyes and a runny nose when a cat entered the room, so he rehomed his cat and avoided visiting people with cats.

More recently, he discovered from skin tests that he is actually allergic to house dust mites, but not cats. House dust mite cells are present in bedding and allergic responses are often worse on waking. The regular appearance of his cat in his bedroom first thing in the morning, when symptoms were at their worst, had produced a conditioned hay fever response to the sight of a cat (the conditioned stimulus), or even a picture of one.

All reflex responses (those that involve the arousal of the autonomic nervous system) are amenable to classical conditioning. They include anxiety, fear or panic, relaxation, urinary and anal sphincter control, hunger, thirst, sexual arousal, facial ticks or other involuntary body movements or mannerisms, and responses to foods and medicines. Whether positive or negative, the process of associative learning (classical conditioning) is the same.

Anna needed to study for her exams, but found that she got tense every time she got out her notes. She realized that the room she was studying in was causing the problem – it was small, dark, cluttered and noisy. So she tried taking her notes down to the local library where she could sit in a pleasant, light, quiet and relaxing environment. She was able to concentrate there and no longer tensed at the sight of her notes.

The most important point to remember about classical conditioning is that the conditioned response is reflex. It is not under conscious or voluntary control and is not amenable to rational argument or will-power.

Conditioned emotional responses

Watson and Raynor (1920) demonstrated that an 11-month-old child, known as 'Little Albert', was conditioned to show fear towards a white rat, after the sight of the rat was paired with the sound of a sudden loud bang. Albert subsequently showed fear of other white furry animal objects (Harris 1979) through a process known as 'generalization' (which we explain below).

Anxiety and fear involve autonomic responses that cause breathing, pulse rate and blood pressure to increase and muscles to tense. Because emotions such as fear and anxiety involve these autonomic responses, they are very susceptible to classical conditioning. In an extreme form, these responses give rise to what is termed a panic attack.

Margaret had never been in an aircraft but had what all of her friends thought was an irrational fear of flying. She was not certain how it had developed, but it seemed to date back to reading about a whole family killed in an accident. Now she only had to see a picture of a plane to bring back the mental image of that accident.

Margaret wanted to visit an old school friend in Australia, so went on a special course put on by the airline. They taught her a relaxation technique to use in simulated situations. This broke the association between aircraft and fear and she was able to make her trip.

Most associations take repeated experiences to develop. However, exposure to a single intense stimulus that leads to strong autonomic arousal can be sufficient to cause a conditioned fear response. For example, someone who has been in a rail accident may subsequently experience panic at the thought of travelling on a train, even though the probability of another accident is extremely low. This type of conditioning may be a contributory cause of post-traumatic stress disorder (PTSD) (see Chapter 6).

Positive emotions such as relaxation can also be conditioned.

Margaret sought complementary therapies for her arthritis pain. These were delivered by a friendly practitioner in a comfortable room surrounded by candles and gentle music. The treatment was probably not 'effective' in terms of evidence-based medicine, but Margaret contrasted it with her last hospital visit – an abrupt receptionist who failed to make eye contact; a long wait in a corridor on a hard chair; a brusque examination conducted amid an array of threatening instruments. The resulting treatment might have been evidence-based, but it took Margaret two days to recover and she now feels stressed at the thought of another hospital visit.

The importance of fear-reduction in hospital settings

Classically conditioned fear and anxiety responses are troublesome and difficult to treat. Therefore prevention is always better than cure. In hospital and other institutional settings, this can be promoted by a friendly and informative approach, and better preparation for planned procedures. Health professionals can help patients to anticipate potentially frightening or painful medical procedures so that they do not experience sudden or unexpected fear or pain. For example, music is still under investigation as one way of alleviating the physiological and psychological effects of anxiety in patients undergoing surgical procedures (Wang *et al.* 2002).

Lee needed to go to hospital for surgery. The staff in the unit recognized the importance of preparing Lee for this. They had a pre-op. clinic where Lee could see the surroundings, meet the staff and other children, and even watch a video showing what procedures he would experience. Staff encouraged Lee to rehearse his encounters using a doll. This reduced the likelihood of a fear response and also reduced Sasha's anxieties about Lee's operation.

Generalization

It is not uncommon for the conditioned stimulus to generalize, which means that the conditioned response extends from one specific object or environment to a whole class of objects or environments. For example, Lee's fear of the doctor who gave him the injection might generalize to all doctors or even all health care professionals. Likewise, Lillian's nausea might generalize to all hospital buildings and not just the one in which she received her chemotherapy. Lissek *et al.* (2008) provided psychophysiological and behavioural evidence that fear responses can generalize to non-threatening events and situations, as is often found in post-traumatic stress disorder (PTSD).

Extinction

Conditioned responses are not necessarily permanent. In the example we used earlier, Lee associated the doctor with the painful injection and this caused a conditioned fear of the doctor. Lee's conditioned fear response is likely to disappear if his subsequent visits to the doctor involve nothing unpleasant and are instead paired with nice experiences, such as playing with toys in the play area and choosing a reward sticker during or after the consultation. This process is known as 'extinction'. Extinction normally occurs once the individual has been exposed to the same conditioned stimulus in the absence of the conditioned response.

Reversing classically conditioned responses

Exposure

One way to eliminate a classically conditioned fear or panic response is a form of behaviour therapy where individuals are deliberately exposed to their feared stimulus in order to demonstrate that they actually have nothing to fear.

Research

Reducing fear-avoidance

Boersma *et al.* (2004) tested out exposure treatment with a small group of patients who had severe functional limitations as a result of back pain. These were patients who feared that particular movements would cause further damage to their backs and more pain. Working with each individual in turn, the researcher assessed which movements they feared, demonstrated that they could safely engage in these movements without causing any damage, and encouraged them to do exercises at home on a regular basis. They found that most patients no longer avoided activity for fear of causing more damage to their backs.

While exposure therapy can be successful in treating unnecessary fears, there are ethical reasons not to place people in frightening situations without their consent. However, exposure can sometimes happen naturally.

Example

Anna was terrified of spiders. But she moved into a house where there seemed to be a large one in the bath each morning. At first she panicked, ran out and screamed for help. But after a couple of weeks of exposure, she was able to capture it in a glass and throw it out of the window.

In psychological practice, a more gradual approach called systematic desensitization is used.

Systematic desensitization (Wolpe 1958)

Systematic desensitization has a long history of successfully treating a wide variety of incapacitating and long-standing conditioned fear and anxiety responses. It involves progressive exposure to the feared object, situation or environment while relaxing. Individuals are first taught techniques of relaxation and controlled breathing that oppose autonomic arousal. They then learn to apply these techniques when confronted with a 'hierarchical' series of situations that are graded in terms of threat, starting with the mildest stimulus. This ensures that any association between the feared stimulus and autonomic arousal is eliminated as the previously feared stimulus becomes paired relaxation. If Anna had sought treatment for her spider phobia, she would probably have received the following approach.

Overcoming fear of spiders

1   Anna learns to practise full relaxation.

    She then progresses through each of the following stages, while practising her relaxation skills, until all feelings of anxiety have subsided:

2   Anna confronts a picture of a spider.

3   She confronts a spider in a glass box.

4   The spider is introduced in an open container.

5   Anna handles the spider.

Systematic desensitization is an important component of cognitive behaviour therapy (CBT) for those with fears and phobias (see Chapter 8).

Spontaneous recovery of conditioned responses

A conditioned response that has been extinguished can recur spontaneously through lack of exposure to the conditioned stimulus. For example, although Anna overcame her fear of spiders in the bath, her fear might return if she did not see another spider for a few months.

Summary of classical conditioning

In classical conditioning, an individual unconsciously associates an inert stimulus (one that does not normally cause any response) with an active stimulus (one that gives rise to a reflex response). Subsequently, the individual responds to the inert stimulus AS IF it were the active stimulus. In Table 5.2, we give some more examples of classically conditioned responses and their consequences.

Table 5.2 **Examples of classical conditioning**

Neutral stimulus = conditioned stimulus (CS)	Active stimulus = unconditioned stimulus (US)	Unconditioned response (UR) = conditioned response (CR)	Result
Trip to the GP	GP's reassuring words	Patient less worried	Just visiting the GP makes a patient feel better
Sitting down to work	Unsuccessful work	Anxiety	Student feels anxious when studying
Sitting down to work	Successful work	Pleasure	Student feels good when studying
Smell of hay	Trip to the countryside	Pleasure and relaxation	The smell of hay produces feelings of pleasure and relaxation
Task	Negative feedback	Raised blood pressure	Thinking about the task increases blood pressure

Operant (instrumental) conditioning

During the mid-twentieth century, B.F. Skinner developed the principles of operant conditioning (Skinner 1953). The assumption of operant conditioning is that all behaviour serves a function for that individual, which means that it leads to a predictable consequence for that person. A behaviour that is followed by a positive consequence for that individual is more likely to be repeated. A behaviour that is followed by a negative consequence for that individual is less likely to be repeated.

Operant conditioning (also termed instrumental conditioning) applies to voluntary actions – those over which we are able to exert conscious control. Most health-related behaviours, including smoking, eating, exercising and having sex, are included in this category. But if we apply the principles of operant conditioning, choice and free will seem rather more constrained than we might imagine. According to the theory of operant conditioning, our voluntary behaviour is dependent on its immediate consequences.

Example

Behaviour	Consequence	Effect on behaviour
Eating strawberries	Pleasure	Eat more strawberries
Touch a hot iron	Burn	Never touch a hot iron
Work hard	Praise	Continue to work hard
Tackle a new task	Failure	Avoid tackling new tasks
Have a tantrum	Mother's attention	More tantrums

In operant conditioning, learning takes place as a result of reinforcement and punishment.

- *A reinforcer* increases the likelihood of the behaviour occurring in future. In the example, pleasure, praise and mother's attention are reinforcers because they maintain or increase the behaviour.
- *A punisher* decreases the likelihood of the behaviour occurring in future. In the example, burn and failure are both punishers.

Most of the time, we are aware of the relationship between our behaviour and its consequences and can control it. But if we want to change our behaviour, its immediate consequences can be very hard to resist.

The determinant of learning in operant conditioning is the association between the action and its immediate consequence, in a particular context.

Janice knows that eating doughnuts is making her fat and promises herself that she will never eat another. But the next time she is in the bakers, she finds the thought of them irresistible, so she buys and eats two. At the time of eating them, the smell, flavour and texture of the doughnut outweigh the feelings of guilt and annoyance she feels afterwards.

The subjective perception of reinforcement and punishment

Reinforcement is not necessarily the same thing as reward. Food is only reinforcing if someone is hungry and likes the food on offer. The child who receives little adult attention may behave badly to provoke a smack if they see this as a means of gaining attention.

When the new baby was born, Lee became much naughtier. Sasha scolded him, believing that this was a punishment. However, Lee viewed the scold as attention and kept repeating the naughty behaviour to gain more of his mother's attention. In behaviourist terms, the scold is defined as a reinforcer.

One person's punishment can be another person's reward.

Using the definitions above, list all of the sources of **reinforcement** and **punishment** you can think of that are associated with smoking. Talk to friends or relatives who smoke and see if you can extend your list. How many reinforcers and how many punishers can you identify?

Smoking seems a disgusting habit to a non-smoker and is often incomprehensible to health professionals who view it in terms of its long-term negative health consequences. But it actually has a lot of immediate and highly reinforcing consequences for the smoker, all of which need to be taken into account when planning a smoke-stop programme.

Why do women with families smoke?

Graham (1993) conducted a qualitative research study to find out why working-class women smoked when they could ill afford to. She found that smoking provided 'time out' from their difficult and demanding lives. One woman explained that when she lit her cigarette, it was a cue for the children to leave her alone. The cigarette provided a small oasis of personal time and space.

In cognitive terms, reinforcement and punishment are based on subjective perceptions. In other words, actions are influenced by perceived outcomes for the person who engages in them. As health or social care professionals, we need to be very careful not to assume that our own or our professional preferences and values are the same as those of a patient or client.

In the above example, the professional may see smoking as a dirty, dangerous and expensive habit, while the smoker sees it as offering a pleasurable refuge. In order to help the smoker give up smoking, it is necessary to explore all of the reinforcing effects of smoking *for them*. Only then is it possible to help them plan how to substitute for the effects of each of these.

Primary and secondary reinforcement

- A *primary reinforcer* is something that fulfils basic needs, such as food, drink or sex. Substances such as nicotine and crack cocaine may also be regarded as primary reinforcers because they satisfy basic psychological and physiological needs in the person who is addicted to them.

- A *secondary reinforcer* is one that can be used to acquire primary reinforcement. Money may be regarded as a form of secondary reinforcer because it allows the individual to buy food or other goods.

Primary reinforcers may have a stronger impact because their effects are more immediate. Secondary reinforcers in the form of tokens that have an exchange value are sometimes used in behaviour modification (we address this a little later in this chapter).

Schedules of reinforcement

The term 'schedule' refers to a pattern or sequence of reinforcement or punishment. For example, reinforcement may be continuous (occurs each time the behaviour takes place) or intermittent (occurs only occasionally). An occasional intense reward or punishment is capable of influencing behaviour more strongly than continuous but less intense ones. Gambling is a good example of how even a modest occasional win can motivate an individual to continue to play (Lin *et al.* 2009), whereas continuous reinforcement may lead to satiation. For example, if we always praise someone, this is eventually taken for granted and ceases to encourage further effort.

The immediacy of consequences

Generally, the more immediate the consequence, the more powerful is its effect. Small children will normally choose to have a small chocolate bar now, rather than wait for a large one later (assuming they like chocolate). As we grow older, we learn to delay gratification, but the effect of an immediate reward is still powerful.

The Stanford 'marshmallow' experiment (Mischel *et al.* 1972)

The format for this experiment is that the experimenter invites each child to choose a preferred treat (including marshmallows). The experimenter then leaves the room after instructing the child that they can choose to have one preferred treat right away, or they can receive it as soon as they ring the bell to bring the experimenter back. Alternatively, they can have two treats if they are able to wait for the experimenter to return without ringing the bell. The aim of the experiment is really to measure how long it is before the child opts to receive their treat.

Follow-up studies have demonstrated a significant association between pre-school willingness to delay gratification and a variety of long-term outcomes in adolescence and adulthood, including academic performance, self-worth, ablty to deal with stress and aggression (see review by Mischel *et al.* 2011). Other recent studies have confirmed that inability to delay gratification in childhood is associated with difficulties with impulse control in adolescence and adulthood, leading to behaviours such as binge-eating (Davis *et al.* 2010) and drug-taking (Romer *et al.* 2010).

Many health-related behaviours are hard to control because they have immediate positive consequences for the person engaged in them.

We earlier invited you to list all of the incentives and disincentives to smoke. Look at these again and rank them in order of immediacy.

You will probably notice that most of the incentives to smoke, for the smoker, are immediate while the disincentives, such as adverse health consequences, are delayed. This may be an important reason why smokers find it difficult to give up smoking unless or until they experience symptoms of illness. The same principle applies to other health-related behaviours, such as eating sugary foods, which have immediately satisfying consequences.

Punishment frequently fails to work because it is not administered immediately after the crime was committed. Chastising a pre-verbal child when a misdemeanour is discovered, rather than when it was committed, is very unlikely to have the desired effect because they may not understand what they got wrong. Even in older children, the main deterrent to bad behaviour is the likelihood of getting caught, as we noted when presenting Kohlberg's stages of moral development in Chapter 3. In the absence of a proper explanation, the child may interpret parental displeasure or punishment as meaning 'I am a bad person', rather than realizing that it is directed at their behaviour.

The certainty of the consequences

In order to have any impact on behaviour, the probability of receiving reinforcement or punishment must be perceived to be reasonably certain. For example, the threat of severe punishment may fail to eliminate or reduce crime if the chances of getting caught are believed to be small. Theoretically, the same applies to the perceived probability of getting ill.

Janice tried to persuade Joe to cut down on his smoking and drinking for health reasons. But the reinforcing consequences of smoking and drinking alcohol were all immediate, predictable and certain. In contrast, Joe could see no immediate benefit of cutting down, and it was by no means certain that he would get ill as a result of smoking or drinking. He cited the example of his uncle who smoke and drank heavily but had lived to a ripe old age.

Our example illustrates a common reason why healthy people are not persuaded to follow advice on health grounds. Many people fail to take action until symptoms actually occur and this may be too late. The perceived probability of getting ill becomes greater as one gets older and this may explain why people are more willing to take health advice and change their lifestyles as they grow older.

Environmental or situational cues

Individuals quickly learn that particular actions have certain consequences only in specific situations or contexts that act as cues.

Sasha scolded Lee when he attempted to go near the fire. This stopped him from approaching the fire in her presence so she assumed that it was now safe to leave him alone in the room when the fire was lit. However, as soon as Sasha left the room, Lee attempted to poke the fire. He had learned that he must not touch the fire when his mother was present, but he had not learned that he must not touch it when she was absent.

Many health-related behaviours are described as being under 'stimulus control'. That is to say, they involve voluntary responses that occur automatically in certain situations or in response to certain social and environmental cues (Marks 1993).

Joe lights up a cigarette automatically as soon as he picks up his newspaper or sits down to drink a cup of coffee. Lighting up a cigarette is normally considered to be a conscious or voluntary response, but has become an automatic response in these situations.

Health-related behaviours, such as smoking, fail to respond to health promotion or health education because in many situations they are not the product of conscious thought (Hoffman *et al.* 2009). Rather they are habits that involve automatic responses to particular environmental or internal cues. Once someone has expressed the desire to give up smoking, it is necessary to interrupt these habitual routines and bring the behaviour back under conscious control (see Chapter 9 on health beliefs and behaviour).

Phobias

Where classical and operant conditioning work together

Classical and operant conditioning are usually treated quite separately for the purposes of psychological theory. In many situations, they work together. For example, people often change their behaviour in order to avoid unpleasant reflex responses, such as fear and anxiety.

Janice's friend Carol has dental phobia, which may be explained by the following conditioning processes.
   Remember:

- Classical conditioning applies to reflex responses, such as fear.
- Operant conditioning applies to behaviours that are under voluntary control.

Carol had a very painful experience at the dentist and as a result she panicked	A visit to the dentist is paired with fear
At her next visit to the dentist she is very afraid	The dentist has become associated with fear due to classical conditioning
She is so afraid that she walks away from the door, feeling relieved that she doesn't have to face it	**Escape** behaviour is under voluntary control and is reinforced by immediate fear reduction (operant conditioning)
Next time Carol is sent a dental appointment, she feels anticipatory anxiety. She stops thinking about it as soon as she has torn up the letter	Tearing up the card is voluntary **avoidance** behaviour. It is reinforced by immediate fear reduction (operant conditioning)

Example

   Escape and avoidance behaviours are important in maintaining fears and phobias. So long as she does not have to face up to the thing she fears, Carol will never find out that the pain was a one-off situation and the dentist is not as scary as she thinks.

Lifestyle and behaviour

Behaviours such as smoking, eating, drinking and taking exercise play important roles in filling time in our lives. Behaviourists actually refer to these and other types of activities as 'time-filling behaviours'. If someone wishes to stop engaging in a problem behaviour, it is necessary to replace it with something else that is equally rewarding. This means that the reinforcing consequences of smoking, drinking or drug-taking need to be taken into account if a programme of lifestyle change is to be effective (DiClemente 1993). The following example illustrates some of the difficulties in trying to change young people's drinking behaviour in a binge-drinking culture.

Example

Joe enjoys drinking seven or eight pints of beer with his mates at the pub several nights a week. This is not because he is thirsty or addicted to alcohol, but because it is a relaxing social activity that occupies a pleasant evening out. Sasha wants him to cut down on his drinking. But if he wants to spend the same amount of time with his mates, he will need to find an alternative to drinking beer that provides similar sources of reinforcement. A low alcohol lager may seem a reasonable alternative, but is more expensive, does not taste the same, and does not have the social approval of his drinking companions.

Taking up a new health-related behaviour such as exercise requires extra time and space in an individual's life; therefore another activity will need to be displaced. For example, if exercise is to be maintained, it must be more reinforcing for the individual than alternative ways of using their time. People often prefer to engage in a group exercise programme because of the social, rather than the health consequences.

Explaining illness behaviours

The term illness behaviour was introduced by Mechanic in the early 1960s to describe the different ways that people perceive, evaluate and act on their illness. Illness behaviours include engaging in self-care activities. But the term 'illness behaviour' is usually used to describe abnormal or maladaptive ways of responding, such as excessive help-seeking or dependence.

Behavioural explanations for illness behaviours focus on reinforcement. Chronic pain provides a useful example. Pain produces expressive 'pain behaviours', such as crying, wincing and other non-verbal expressions of pain and distress. Craig (2004) described how these attract the attention of others who respond by offering help and protection. If this happens a lot, the person in pain gradually becomes less active and more dependent, the pain behaviours become more exaggerated and the pain gradually becomes chronic.

Research

The role of the spouse in maintaining pain

Pence *et al.* (2008) studied the pain behaviours of 64 married or cohabiting men and women who had chronic headache. They measured pain behaviours that included distorted walking, facial or audible expressions of distress, and avoidance of activity. Reported spouse behaviours included:

- facilitative responses to well behaviours;
- negative responses to well behaviours;
- solicitous responses to pain behaviours;
- negative responses to pain behaviours.

They found that negative spouse responses to well behaviours and solicitous responses to pain behaviours were the best predictors of exaggerated pain behaviours in these headache patients.

You might find it useful to think about these findings as you read our examples in Chapter 10 on pain.

Changing behaviour

Behaviour modification is a method used to change unwanted or undesirable behaviour by deliberately manipulating its context and/or consequences. It is based on all of the operant principles we have just considered.

During the 1970s, behaviour modification became a popular way to control socially undesirable or obsessive behaviours in long-stay institutions, using a 'token economy'. This meant that socially desirable behaviours were reinforced by immediately giving tokens that could be exchanged for primary reinforcers of the patient's choice (sadly, this often took the form of cigarettes). Behaviour modification fell from favour in the late twentieth century for the following reasons:

- It was considered unethical to try to change people's behaviour without their consent.
- It seemed to deny the existence of free will and was thought to devalue human beings by treating them like animals in a 'Skinner box' (B.F. Skinner's experimental conditions).
- It was believed that both punishment and reward were included in behaviour modification. In fact, punishment played no part in Skinner's approach. Undesirable behaviours were ignored while desirable behaviours were reinforced.

However, there remain some applications in common use, notably when applied to children and to self-modification. For example, the principles of classroom management are generally based on giving attention for good behaviour and ignoring bad behaviour. Star charts are often used to change some aspect of a child's behaviour. For example, this method has been shown to be one effective way of controlling nocturnal enuresis (bed-wetting) (Glazener and Evans 2002), assuming that the child is capable of achieving bladder control.

Sasha had difficulty persuading Lee, at the age of 3, to use the toilet for its intended purpose. So the health visitor suggested setting up a star chart system. They explained to Lee what they were going to do. He helped to design his own calendar and received a star each time he used the toilet properly. Once he had gained an agreed number of stars he received a gift of his choice up to a certain value. He soon got the hang of it and was trotting off to the toilet frequently in the hope of gaining stars. So Sasha had to change the exchange rate and use the incentive scheme to improve other behaviours.

Example

Similar approaches can be used to reduce temper tantrums or other challenging behaviours, provided the child is able to understand the process (see cognitive development in Chapter 3). But it is worth noting that behaviour modification does not always work as intended, as illustrated in the following example which really is based on a true story!

Example

Lee's star system was working so well that Janice recommended this approach to her friend whose 9-year-old child was refusing to eat his meals. His mother introduced a similar system with a financial reward for his collection of stars. The child quickly increased the tariff and, to his mother's dismay, saved enough money to buy a television set for his bedroom. But by that time he was refusing to eat at all unless he was paid to do so!

This cautionary tale highlights that before embarking on any programme of behaviour modification, it is worth considering the possibility of unintended adverse consequences.

Analysing the causes and consequences of behaviour

When attempting to use behavioural modification, it is essential to identify the specific behaviour that needs to change. Then it is important to measure the frequency with which the behaviour occurs, and record the context in which it occurs, any behavioural triggers (cues) and its immediate consequences. In psychology, this process is termed 'applied behaviour analysis' or 'functional analysis' of behaviour.

This approach can be applied to any behaviour and used by anyone who wants to change their own behaviour, manage their child's behaviour or change a challenging behaviour. For example, it is useful for someone planning to give up smoking, or a parent who wishes to eliminate their child's temper tantrums, or someone who wishes to improve their timekeeping. The process and the principles are illustrated here in relation to Lee's tantrums. It is essentially a systematic experimental approach.

Example

Reducing Lee's tantrums

Baseline measures
Sasha recorded exactly when each tantrum occurred during the course of a week.
    She noted the stimulus cues by recording what was happening at the time each tantrum started.
    She recorded what happened as an immediate consequence of each tantrum.

Analysis
Sasha realized that Lee's tantrums usually occurred when he was tired or when her attention was directed towards the baby or housework.

The intervention: behaviour change programme
Sasha planned ways of distracting Lee from situations likely to lead to a tantrum. She scheduled the housework while he was at nursery and saw to the baby when he was having a rest or otherwise occupied. If he had a tantrum, she used a system of 'time out' (from reinforcement) by removing him from the scene or ignoring him. Effectively, Lee gained more of her attention when he was being good and was ignored when he behaved badly.

Result
Within a few weeks, the tantrums were minimal. Sasha felt much more confident and other aspects of Lee's behaviour also improved.

One aspect of practice where this approach has been fairly widely applied is in the control of challenging behaviours.

Managing challenging behaviours

Research

Dixon *et al.* (2001) tested the use of functional analysis of behaviour in conjunction with behaviour modification in the case of a 25-year-old young man with a dual diagnosis of learning disability and psychosis, including auditory hallucinations. The aim was to reduce inappropriate or of-fensive talk. During assessment using functional analysis, it was observed that inappropriate talk was reinforced by attention. Behaviour modification involved ignoring inappropriate talk and attending to alternative appropriate talk and behaviours. As predicted, this led to a decrease in inappropriate talk and increase in appropriate behaviours.

These types of intervention are most appropriate where the therapist, caregiver or parent is in a position to manipulate the consequences of the challenging behaviour. It can identify some interesting and unforeseen issues.

Eliminating challenging behaviour

Example

Lisa visited a care home for people who had severe communication difficulties. One particular resident, Rose, tended to head-butt staff on a regular basis. Lisa suggested using behavioural analysis to identify the causes. With the exception of one occasion, this behaviour occurred every time Rose was given her toast at breakfast time. On the exceptional occasion, they had run out of white bread and gave her brown bread instead. Head-butting at breakfast time stopped completely when the staff started giving her brown toast.

Using this analysis, it became clear that Rose was trying to communicate her preferences by head-butting. Close attention to the cues and consequences of challenging behaviours led to a dramatic reduction in their occurrence.

Although the principles we have outlined undoubtedly work, it naturally raises ethical con-cerns in some situations. One problem is that these interventions can be very rewarding for the person using them. For example, every time Sasha sends Lee to his bedroom for 'time out', she gains a period of peace and quiet. The tendency then might be for Sasha to use 'time out' with increasing frequency for her own benefit. Fortunately Sasha knew that sending Lee from the room for a couple of minutes was sufficient to remove the reinforcing effect of the tantrum, and so this problem did not occur.

Self-modification

Although the supportive evidence is now quite old, the principles of functional analysis and behaviour modification may still help us change all sorts of aspects of our own behaviour – for example, being late for work or being short-tempered with our partner or spouse.

Lisa had put on weight and decided that the main cause was eating too many chocolate bars. She tried the following self-modification programme:

1   Her specific aim was to buy fewer chocolate bars from the machine at work.

2   She used a diary to record each chocolate bar she bought (to measure frequency). For each one, she recorded what prompted her to buy it (the cues) and how she felt afterwards (the consequences).

3   After a week of monitoring, she studied her pattern of chocolate buying and identified the cues and consequences surrounding it.

4   She altered her daily routine so that she could avoid the cue to buy chocolate.

5   She prepared fresh melon as a treat to eat instead.

6   She monitored the frequency with which she bought chocolate over the next few weeks so she could demonstrate the change.

By this time, she actually preferred fruit to chocolate bars and no longer needed to keep up her monitoring.

It is actually quite easy to apply the principles of self-modification to improve many aspects of daily life.

Try applying the principles of self-modification on an aspect of your own behaviour, using the approach we demonstrated above.

Anna used it when she found it difficult to get out of bed in the mornings. In fact, all she did was to arrange a special treat for breakfast and found that this was sufficient to tempt her out of bed.

Summary of operant conditioning

Assumptions

- All voluntary behaviour serves a function.
- A behaviour is reinforced (maintained) if it leads to positive consequences for that individual.
- A behaviour is less likely to occur if it leads to negative consequences for that individual.
- A reinforcer is something that maintains a behaviour.

Factors that reinforce behaviour (make it more likely that it will be repeated)

- Experience that the behaviour will lead to a positive consequence in a particular situation or context.

- The consequence is subjectively valuable to the person.
- The consequence predictably and reliably follows the behaviour.
- The consequence immediately follows the behaviour.

Behaviour analysis

- Identify the behaviour that needs to change.
- Monitor the frequency of the behaviour.
- Record the context and cues and immediate consequences of the behaviour.
- Analyse the pattern of causes and consequences.

Behaviour modification

- Make changes to the context and the cues that trigger the behaviour.
- Introduce incentives for changed behaviour.

Look at the following examples 1 to 5 and discuss them with a group of friends.
  What exactly are the **behaviours** in these examples?
  What sources of **reinforcement** are apparent in these examples?
  How likely is it that the behaviours will be maintained?
  What new reinforcers might encourage behaviour change in these examples?

1   Someone going out for an evening, with good friends.
2   Someone who is unfit, going to the gym.
3   A person who has a nicotine addiction, smoking a cigarette.
4   Someone who has a smoking habit, going without cigarettes for an evening.
5   A person eating a healthy meal of salad, rather than his usual burgers and chips.

Exercise

   The notion that our behaviour is solely controlled by external sources of reinforcement and punishment remains problematic. While there is little doubt that behavioural approaches do work in producing change, this is clearly not the whole story. In the next sections, we consider additional and alternative explanations. Whereas behaviourists focused predominantly on environmental determinants of behaviour, we will develop this by focusing on social and personal influences over behaviour and motivation.

Social learning

Observational learning

Albert Bandura started out as a behavioural psychologist but developed a special interest in social influences on behaviour, starting with his observations of how children imitate the behaviour of others.

Modelling and imitation

Bandura *et al.* (1961) conducted a series of classic experiments in the 1960s to study social influences on aggressive behaviour in children.

A group of children were allowed to play with a bobo doll (an inflatable doll designed to spring back up right after being knocked over) under different conditions. They then observed an adult mistreat the doll. When subsequently allowed back to play with the doll, they imitated the adult's aggressive behaviour without any prompting or incentive.

Bandura's experiments demonstrated that children don't just learn from the consequences of their own actions, but are capable of modelling their behaviour on that of important others.

Bandura's work on social learning started to fill important gaps in explaining the speed of human learning. It also highlighted the importance and influence of the social environment on behaviour. The following example illustrates how student nurses model their codes of dress and behaviour on those of experienced staff. (These changes are also influenced by pressures to conform; see Chapter 6.)

When Anna went on her first surgical ward placement, she had little idea what to expect. Almost without thinking, she observed what other members of staff were doing; the way they made beds, took observations, communicated with patients, responded to other members of staff, the way they wore their uniform and even the way they walked. She soon learned to copy what they did and how they looked.

The concept of modelling goes some way to explaining the process that sociologists refer to as socialization. It can be seen in the way that children and adults learn new social skills and competences. This is why practical learning is so important and why social or organizational behaviour patterns are particularly resistant to change.

In addition to imitation, Bandura's experiments introduced the notion of 'vicarious reinforcement'. He was able to demonstrate that children could judge the likely consequences of their own actions by observing what happens to others in similar circumstances. If others gained a reward, they also expected to receive one if they engaged in the same behaviour.

Self-efficacy and control

Bandura (1971) continued to develop the idea of imitation and vicarious experience. He acknowledged the importance of external influences on behaviour, but was critical of Skinner's assertions that human behaviour is passively driven by these forces. He proposed that once children have learned to imitate a new skill, they are capable of monitoring and adjusting their own performance through a process of self-regulation, by comparing their own performance with that of others. Through this active process, they achieve a sense of self-efficacy. Bandura has written extensively on the concept of self-efficacy, which has emerged as one of the most important concepts in health psychology. We refer to his self-regulatory theory in Chapter 9.

Bandura defined perceived self-efficacy as 'beliefs in one's capabilities to organize and execute the courses of action required to produce given attainments' (Bandura 1997: 3). Bandura argued that our sense of self-esteem is based primarily on our beliefs in our ability to achieve control, either individually or collectively, over our everyday lives. The failure to recognize and reward ourselves for good performance can lead to depression. He suggested that talented people often become depressed because they set themselves standards of achievement that are too high.

Bandura suggests that there are four main sources of information that can increase self-efficacy:

- the experience of gaining mastery over a task or situation;
- seeing others achieve mastery;
- having other people express the belief that mastery is possible;
- an absence of negative emotions (see Chapter 8 for a detailed explanation).

The opposite information has, of course, the effect of reducing the sense of self-efficacy.

Research in health psychology has demonstrated sense of self-efficacy to be an important determinant of health outcomes.

Self-efficacy and health

Cross *et al.* (2006) surveyed nearly 300 people with arthritis (a condition where pain control is difficult). They measured arthritis self-efficacy (the ability to manage pain and other symptoms) and health status. The findings showed that high reports of self-efficacy were associated with better control over pain, stiffness and function and better physical and mental health. Low self-efficacy was associated with more visits to the doctor and greater costs.

Korpershoek *et al.* (2011) systematically reviewed evidence from studies of self-efficacy in people recovering after a stroke. Seventeen studies were assessed and they found that higher levels of self-efficacy were positively associated with better functioning in terms of daily activities, mobility and quality of life.

Many care environments have the effect of reducing feelings of self-efficacy in patients, clients or resident, as in the following example.

Although Ted spent his old age living with his family, his friend Sid had moved to a rather poor residential home. The staff at the residential home did everything for Sid and his fellow residents, so the residents had little opportunity to experience mastery. It was clear to the residents that staff always assumed that they would not be able to do anything for themselves. After a while of living in the home, Sid lost all sense of self-efficacy and felt a sense of panic if he was asked to do anything for himself. This sense of panic reinforced his belief that he could achieve nothing. He stayed in his room and became very depressed.

Self-efficacy is not just an important predictor of health outcomes, but has been shown to be amenable to change. It has therefore become an important focus for intervention in health education and self-management programmes for people with chronic health problems (see Chapters 9 and 10).

Improving self-efficacy

Sid's care home was sold and the new owners, Mr and Mrs Jones, had a very different approach to care. They took an interest in him and encouraged him to take an interest in what was happening outside. They built a conservatory and transformed the garden with raised beds and a greenhouse. Residents were encouraged to grow tomatoes and plants for the garden. Sid soon made new friends and took up new interests. His pain control improved and he no longer experienced a sense of panic when asked to do things.

Self-efficacy remains one of the most important concepts in health psychology. Another familiar concept closely related to self-efficacy is locus of control.

Locus of control (LOC)

Whereas self-efficacy refers to belief in one's own ability to successfully execute a task, locus of control refers to the individual's beliefs about who or what is **responsible** for the outcome of the task. Although originally measured on a single dimension, internal versus external (Rotter 1966), Levenson (1974) subsequently proposed three possible attributions for who or what would determine the outcome of a particular task or situation:

- *Internal locus of control*: the outcome depends on my own actions.
- *External (powerful others) locus of control*: other people are responsible for the outcome.
- *External (chance) locus of control*: the outcome is a matter of luck, fate or chance.

Wallston *et al.* (1978) developed a multidimensional health locus of control measure which was used to predict the likelihood that an individual would take responsibility for their own health and manage their own illness. Studies tended to indicate that internal locus of control was associated with better health outcomes and external (chance) locus of control was associated with worse outcomes. However, most studies proved weak or inconclusive.

It became evident that control beliefs cannot be generalized to all situations. For example, I may believe that my headache is under my control, but my abdominal pain is a matter for the doctor and there is nothing anyone can do about my back pain. Therefore, a variety of condition-specific locus of control measures was devised for the purposes of research. Examples include addiction, diabetes, cancer, pain and heart disease locus of control (Walker 2001).

For the same reasons, it became evident that locus of control should not be regarded as a personality variable, but as a set of expectations that can and do change with experience.

Nevertheless, when applied in a specific situation, locus of control can be a useful concept since it gives some indication of the likelihood of people's wishes and intentions to take responsibility for managing their health, their illness or their situation. It can often be detected by observing what people do and the way they speak and react. An American psychology team found that people are most likely to respond to information if it matches their locus of control.

Responding to health advice

Williams-Piehota *et al.* (2004) were able to show that women with internal locus of control were more likely to respond to an invitation entitled 'The Best Thing You Can Do For Your Health – Mammography'. Women with external 'powerful other' beliefs were more likely to respond to one entitled 'The Best Thing Medical Science Has to Offer for Your Health – Mammography'.

It seems logical that internal locus of control is preferable in situations such as attending for mammography, where the individual has control over attendance. On the other hand, external powerful others locus of control is desirable in situations where medical help is essential for survival or future quality of life. Those with external chance locus of control have been shown to respond less well to health education, but may respond to tailored information that includes counter-arguments (Holt *et al.* 2000).

Consider each of the following individuals in relation to the three dimensions of health locus of control.

Margaret seeks medical advice whenever she feels poorly. She trusts the doctor and believes everything he tells her, but finds it difficult to adhere to medication or other treatments in the longer term.

Janice likes to be well informed and searches the internet for information before seeking medical treatment. She likes to know what she can do to help herself and feels quite angry if her needs for information and explanations are not being taken seriously by the doctor. She likes to take responsibility for self-managing her symptoms when she is ill and does not always follow the doctor's advice if she does not agree with it.

Mark tends to be fatalistic about his illnesses and believes that what will be will be. He consults the doctor as little as possible, never bothers with things like diet and exercise, and often doesn't bother to take his medication, even though he has a chronic health problem.

- What are the clues to their locus of control?
- Can you identify advantages and disadvantages for each dimension?
- If you had to design a 'healthy diet' health promotion leaflet for each of them, what sorts of information and arguments would you include?

Learned helplessness

While conducting early behavioural experiments on animals, researchers had noted that some experimental animals showed symptoms of what was termed experimental neurosis. Basically, they cowered in a corner and could not be persuaded to participate in further experiments. It turned out that this behaviour was caused by loss of control over what was happening to them. These experiments are upsetting and fortunately could not take place these days for ethical reasons. But they initiated a line of inquiry that might otherwise not have been thought of.

Learned helplessness (Seligman and Maier 1967)

Two dogs were administered a series of identical minor electric shocks. One (called the executive dog) was able to terminate the shock by pressing a panel with its muzzle. This also stopped the shock delivered to the other dog, so that both dogs received exactly the same intensity and duration of shock. The only difference was that one dog had control over the shock, while the other dog had no control.

Each dog was then transferred to a different experimental environment called a shuttle box. The dog was placed at one end and minor electric shocks were delivered through the floor, but the dog could easily escape by jumping over a low barrier to safety.

In this situation, the executive dog quickly learned to jump to safety while the other dog made no attempt to escape. The 'helpless' dog demonstrated what Seligman termed 'learned helplessness', which consisted of:

- a motivational deficit – it made no attempt to move;
- a cognitive deficit – it failed to recognize a simple escape route;
- an emotional deficit – it appeared very miserable.

Learned helplessness means learning that one's actions have no influence over outcomes. Seligman (1975) noted that the motivational, cognitive and emotional deficits he observed are all symptomatic of human depression, and proposed learned helplessness as a theory of human depression. The theory of learned helplessness predicts that people become depressed because of exposure to situations or events that they are unable to control. Subsequent researchers have applied this in different types of situations, including social settings.

Societal causes of learned helplessness (Mirowsky and Ross 2003)

Lack of control over important aspects of life has been suggested as a reason for the higher incidence of depression among people who are unemployed, those on low pay, those with less education, and women. Sociologists Mirowsky and Ross argued that depression among these groups is caused by their powerlessness in society and not by personal depressive tendencies that had brought them down the social scale.

Learned helplessness has much intuitive appeal. It highlights the dangers of depriving people of control, focuses on situational causes of depression, and implies that what has been learned can be unlearned. In contrast, cognitive theories of depression emphasize the importance of pessimistic belief sets that lead people to feel they have little control. These points of view are in fact complementary since what really matters is **perceived** control, not actual control. This explains why, in similar circumstances, some people become depressed while others do not.

Mark started feeling quite depressed after he retired from work due to ill health. He had experienced one previous bout of depression, which had lifted when he changed his job (see Chapters 7 and 8). Now, he felt that he had lost control over his life and felt helpless. Other people envied his freedom to do other things, but he could not be bothered. His symptoms were typical of learned helplessness. He demonstrated a motivational deficit (he made no effort to do anything), a cognitive deficit (he did not believe that he was capable of achieving anything more in his life) and an emotional deficit (he felt depressed).

Seligman *et al.* (1968) subsequently found that learned helplessness could be reversed if the experimenter physically dragged the helpless animal across the barrier on numerous occasions to demonstrate that it was possible to escape from the shock. This observation was used to develop behavioural interventions for depression.

Mark was referred to a clinical psychologist who invited him to review his skills and identify some achievable goals that would motivate him and restore his sense of control. Mark focused on cooking. Janice worked with him to identify suitable recipes and ingredients and soon Mark was preparing some lovely healthy meals. Success breeds success and Mark's depression decreased as he started to regain control over some aspects of his life and feel useful, rather than helpless.

Since the 1970s, learned helplessness has been subject to a number of critiques and reformulations but was ultimately challenged by the academic community as a theory of depression. This led Seligman to abandon the concept of helplessness and focus instead on positive psychology (see Chapter 8). Nevertheless, the concepts of perceived control, controllability and uncontrollability form important variables in applied research within health psychology and psychoneuroimmunology. You will find a reference to these concepts in Chapter 7. The principles we have outlined in this chapter have been incorporated into cognitive behaviour therapy (CBT), which is used in the management of stress (Chapter 7), anxiety and depression (Chapter 8), self-management of chronic illness (Chapter 9) and chronic pain (Chapter 10).

Table 5.3 Social learning: summary of key points

Concept	Explanation and implications
Modelling (Bandura *et al.* 1961)	We learn new skills by imitating others. This also applies to good and bad habits
Self-regulation (Bandura 1971)	We monitor and adjust our performance by comparing our own performance with that of others
Self-efficacy (Bandura 1977a)	The achievement of competent skill performance. A sense of self-efficacy increases self-esteem
Locus of control (LOC)	Beliefs about responsibility for outcomes: internal, external (others) and external (chance). Chance LOC tends to be associated with inaction and fatalism
Learned helplessness (Seligman 1975)	Learning that one's actions have no influence over outcomes. It is associated with lack of motivation, low self-belief and depression

Exercise

When you are in a care environment, always try to look for things that patients or clients could do for themselves and would probably want to do for themselves if they were given the choice, the time and the necessary assistance. You may notice that members of staff habitually do things that patients would benefit from doing for themselves because it is quicker to do so.

It would be useful if this 'exercise' became a habit that stayed with you for the rest of your working life. Even when given in a caring way, too much help or the wrong sort of help can have a disempowering effect on the patient or client.

Further reading

The principles of conditioning and social learning are covered in all general psychology text books (see suggestions at the end of Chapter 1).

Martin, G.L. and Pear, J. (2002) *Behaviour Modification: What It Is and How to Do It*, 7th edition. London: Prentice Hall.

Social influences and interactions

Key topics

- Persuasion
- Obedience, conformity, compliance and helping others
- Non-verbal behaviour and interpersonal skills
- Dealing with aggression and complaints
- Group behaviour and leadership

Introduction

In this chapter, we draw mainly from well-established research in social psychology to explore social influences on individual and group behaviours. In particular, we seek to address the following questions:

- What do we need to take into account when attempting to change the attitudes and behaviours of others?
- How does the presence of other people change the way we behave in various situations?
- How can we promote harmonious ways of working with others to improve our working lives and the care we provide?

The following vignette illustrates some of the issues we will be considering. It is based on some observations by Martin and Bull (2006).

Anna's friend Amy was training to become a midwife. She came from a large family and had always had a strong desire to support women and their partners during pregnancy and labour, and in looking after their newborn babies. Amy was attracted by the idea that part of a midwife's role is to act as an advocate for mothers so that, when it is clinically possible, the mother's wishes concerning the birth of her child can be followed.

She initially found the reality of maternity care difficult. Like others working in health and social care, she found herself working in a very hierarchical system in which she felt pressured to do things in accordance with rule-based protocols, rather than doing what the women themselves wanted.

Amy soon found herself complying with policies and conforming to standard practices, even when she initially expressed private doubts that they were in the women's best interests. She found herself able to justify these practices and procedures on grounds she might previously have rejected. Thankfully, the mentor on Amy's last placement was able to remind Amy of the reasons she had wanted to be a midwife in the first place.

This vignette provides a small example of how social influences have the power to change our beliefs as well as our behaviours, particularly as we are being socialized into a new occupation or profession.

Background

Much of western psychology tended in the past to focus rather narrowly on individual thought processes. We all like to think of ourselves as unique, yet our beliefs, emotions and behaviours are very strongly influenced by the attitudes and behaviour of those around us. In this chapter we explore how this social influence occurs. To do so, we have integrated research and theory from a variety of classic and original sources, together with information taken from texts devoted entirely to social psychology.

We start with the psychology of persuasion, since much of our lives, as professionals, is taken up with trying to persuade our clients or patients that it is in their best interests to change their beliefs or behaviours.

Persuasion

Persuasion is a process that involves encouraging others to change their beliefs and attitudes as a precursor to changing their behaviour. It forms the basis for much practice-based education and health promotion. Therefore it is useful to understand some of the principles that can be used to enhance persuasive techniques. A lot of research on this topic took place during the 1980s and the principles we set out in this section are substantially based on the models of persuasion developed by Chaiken, and Petty and Cacioppo, (Chaiken 1980; Petty and Cacioppo 1986). In line with the dual process model we set out in Chapter 1, these researchers distinguished between two routes to persuasion:

- *a deliberative and thoughtful process*, whereby the recipient of the persuasive message weighs up the available evidence;
- *a non-thoughtful response* based on simple peripheral cues, such as the authority or attractiveness of the message-giver.

In Chapter 4, we addressed ways of conveying personal information so that the individual is able understand and remember it. This section focuses primarily on mass communication, as in a health promotion campaign. The first step is to be quite clear who exactly the target audience is (those in greatest need or at highest risk). Then, in order to believe and act on health information, the target audience needs to engage with the following:

1 *See or hear the message.* The sender must select the medium (e.g. television or radio network, magazines, leaflets) most likely to reach the largest number of the target audience. Placing leaflets in a doctor's surgery, while cheap and convenient, may or may not achieve this.

2 *Pay attention to the message.* As we noted in Chapter 4, attention is selective, so the format of the message must be eye-catching and the audience must see it as relevant to them. For example, Raphael (2008) found in her study of osteoporosis that distributed leaflets featured only pictures of women. This incorrectly conveyed that osteoporosis is not of concern for men.

3 *Understand the message.* It is the responsibility of professionals to ensure that all those in the target audience will be able to understand the information given. For example, in Chapter 4 we draw attention to levels of literacy in the adult population.

4 *Accept the message's conclusion.* People are unlikely to accept a message if it conflicts with long-standing beliefs or personal experience (see Chapter 4), or if information gained from other sources is seen as more credible. We consider these issues below.

In order for the message to be accepted and persuasion to be successful, the following factors are important:

- the source (or giver) of the message;
- the nature of the message itself;
- the characteristics of the audience.

In successful persuasion these three elements are interlinked.

Petty and Cacioppo (1986) found that the interaction between the source, the message and the audience is influenced by educational level.

- Those who are well educated and think carefully about health and social issues are more likely to focus on the significance and content of the message.
- Those who are less well educated and motivated are more likely to be persuaded by superficial images such as the attractiveness of the presenter or eye-catching advertisement.

Their observations are captured in Figure 6.1.

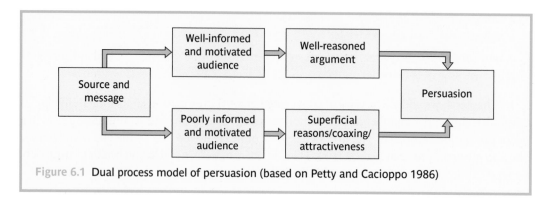

Figure 6.1 Dual process model of persuasion (based on Petty and Cacioppo 1986)

In practice, we need to remember that source, message and audience need to be compatible in order for persuasion to be successful, so we will now consider these three elements in turn.

The source or sender of the message

Several factors have been identified as influencing a recipient's judgements about the source or sender.

- *Perceived credibility of the message-giver.* This does not always equate to professional expertise. For example, nutritionists know most about diet, and physiotherapists about exercise, but lay members of the public may see the doctor as a more credible source of information on these topics, even though he or she knows far less about them.
- *Perceived trustworthiness of the message-giver.* Advice from professionals might be dismissed as untrustworthy if they are seen as having a financial or other vested interest. For example, a thoughtful mother might be less willing to take her child for vaccination if she thought the main reason for recommending it was to achieve a financially driven target.
- *Perceived attractiveness.* It appears that the attractiveness of the communicator is more influential for relatively trivial messages than for serious ones (Chaiken 1987). People may view the message-giver as a role model for the lifestyle being promoted and reject the message if they see that person as unattractive or not 'cool'.

Exercise

Think of something you purchased because of someone else's recommendation, but have since regretted buying.

- Why did you accept a recommendation from that particular person?
- Would you follow their recommendation again in future?

The nature of the message

There are two main types of approach used, whether trying to persuade an individual to change, or when designing campaigns to improve health or safety: emotional appeals and appeals to reason.

Emotional appeals

Television is a good medium for making emotional appeals because it combines sight, sound and movement. The persuasive power of leaflets can be increased by including pictures that have emotional impact. Many people prefer to relate to personal stories or examples that have strong emotional appeal, rather than statistical or epidemiological evidence that has strong rational appeal.

Many health and safety campaigns are designed to scare recipients into taking action; that is, they try to scare people into taking the required action. However, there are some notes of caution about the use of negative emotional appeals that induce a strong sense of pity or fear in the audience. Some charities have abandoned titles and advertisements that focus on victimhood because they have found that empowering images achieve a better result in terms of fundraising. Further, as we note in Chapter 9 on health and illness, increasing an individual's sense of vulnerability through fear can lead to avoidance of the issue altogether.

Appeals to fear

A meta-analysis by Witte and Allen (2000) indicated that high fear appeals are effective only if the recipient is confident that they are able to achieve the behaviour change recommended.

In those who are not confident of being able to take the preventive action recommended, high fear appeals result in avoidance rather than behaviour change (see fear-avoidance in Chapter 5).

The conclusion is that messages must be accompanied by clearly specified advice about simple and effective courses of action.

Research

Appeals to reason

When trying to appeal to reason when conveying a serious issue, it is worth considering if only one side of an argument should be presented, or if both sides should be considered. Research from social psychology indicates that a well-informed audience is more likely to be persuaded by two-sided arguments (Salmon and Atkin 2003) because they will be aware of the counter-arguments and will wish to see these addressed. A less well-informed audience is likely to be confused by two-sided arguments and it may be better to present them with a single point of view.

Before Mark was diagnosed as having diabetes and hypertension, Janice knew that he was in a high-risk group because of his weight and high carbohydrate intake. Janice gave him some leaflets she had picked up at the hospital and pointed out the risks. Mark discounted these as not relevant to him and refused to discuss it. Then he watched a television programme about a man who had lost his eyesight and a leg as a result of diabetes. The man pointed out that these consequences could have been avoided had he taken advice earlier. As a result, Mark went for a check and started taking more interest in his diet and lifestyle.

Example

The next section offers an explanation for why so many people avoid taking action in response to what seem to be reasonable and rational arguments.

Cognitive dissonance

Festinger (1957) observed that when individuals hold two or more beliefs that are inconsistent with each other, they experience a state of dissonance. For example, the belief that 'I am a healthy person' may conflict with the knowledge that 'I do not take enough exercise'. This state of conflict is called 'cognitive dissonance'. According to Festinger's theory of cognitive dissonance this state of dissonance is unsettling and needs to be resolved. When an individual is presented with a persuasive message that conflicts with his or her current beliefs and behaviour, this also creates a state of dissonance. The alternatives available to us when we are faced with new information that conflicts with our existing beliefs and behaviour are:

1 accept the new information and change our beliefs and our behaviour in accordance with it;
2 induce the communicator to change his or her beliefs;
3 seek support from others for our original beliefs and behaviour;
4 convince ourselves that the communicator is untrustworthy or uncreditworthy.

Example

When Joe was a teenager, he started using cannabis. He enjoyed being part of a social group of regular users.

Janice tried to persuade him of the potential dangers to mental health, particularly for teenagers. Joe discounted her argument on the grounds that none of his friends had experienced any ill effects. He argued that she was just trying to ruin his friendships and his fun.

The greater the discrepancy between the argument being presented and the individual's current attitudes, the less likely that attitude change will take place (see Wood 2000). This fits with the concept of the mental schema outlined in Chapters 3 and 4. Therefore, when preparing to give a persuasive argument, it is important to find out about the current beliefs of the target audience and try to work out a solution that they can understand and accommodate into their existing schema.

Exercise

Think of an occasion when you were faced with advice that you instinctively rejected. It might relate to your studies or to some aspect of your lifestyle.

- How did you feel when you had just received the advice?
- Which of the alternative responses listed previously did you eventually choose to take?
- Do you think your initial reaction was an emotional one or a rational one?
- Would you make the same response with the benefit of hindsight?

In the light of your reflection, how might you think about giving the same type of advice to someone else?

Before attempting to give advice or use persuasion, it is really important to take time to understand the beliefs and attitudes of the individual or group concerned. It is important to try to 'get inside their shoes' and use arguments that can be accommodated within their existing schemas.

It is always difficult to bring about change *en masse* if your arguments contradict the prevailing view. If the cause is a really important one, it is a good idea to start by approaching a group leader, trend-setter or role model who is open to the idea and engage their help in promoting change.

Keeping up the pressure

Change-promoting messages quickly lose their effect. The longer the gap between receiving the persuasive message and taking action, the more likely it is that other pressures will intervene. It also provides more opportunities to find justifications and counter-arguments. Therefore, it is helpful to encourage an immediate act of commitment. This is why the pressure salesman gets people to sign up to an immediate sale and why the law allows a cooling-off period.

When Mark was seen by the nutritionist, she reviewed his current diet and agreed a plan of change that would be achievable. He was asked to record his eating pattern and to see the diabetic nurse for a regular review. This made it more difficult for him to go home and forget or ignore what he had been told, or be tempted to cheat too drastically.

Once initiated, the new attitude must be sustained in order to preserve the behaviour change. It is important to keep up individual or public exposure to the persuasive message or media image over a long period of time. Mass campaigns are largely ineffectual unless the impetus is maintained. A systematic review by Fry and Neff (2009) supports the use of regular prompts, as part of health promotion, in order to maintain behaviour change.

In Mark's case, regular review was a way of maintaining his attention on his diet. Sadly, regular reviews are not normally offered for reasons of cost. However, a review by Powell and Gibson (2003) of self-management programmes for asthma showed that those who did not receive a regular review reported more health centre visits and days off sick.

Audience influences and effects

We have already mentioned the importance of attending to the knowledge and beliefs of the audience when preparing a persuasive argument. In this section, we consider a number of issues likely to influence success or otherwise.

Selective attention

It is well recognized that people tend to focus attention on issues that reflect their existing understanding or point of view (see Chapter 4). We illustrate this with an early but still relevant type of study.

Research

Kleinhesselink and Edwards (1975) asked university students to complete a questionnaire concerning their attitudes towards the legalization of cannabis. The students were then asked to listen to a broadcast, through headphones, that contained seven strong (irrefutable) arguments and seven weak (refutable) arguments in favour of legalization. Static noise through the headphones made listening difficult but, if they wanted to, students could press a button to reduce the level of noise.

The results showed that students who favoured legalization pushed the button to reduce noise significantly more often when strong arguments were presented. Students who opposed legalization pushed the button to reduce noise significantly more often when weak (refutable) arguments were presented.

The conclusion of this study was that individuals pay more attention to messages that support their own beliefs.

Festinger's social comparison theory (Festinger 1954; see Chapter 2) proposed that individuals deliberately seek validation of their own attitudes and beliefs by attending to those who hold ideas similar to their own and distancing themselves from those who hold different beliefs or attitudes. This means that some social groups, such as teenagers, may be difficult to penetrate by those seen as outsiders. Health educators need to find novel ways of gaining acceptance if health messages are to be received and taken seriously. Quite often, teenage habits change once they are able to take on adult roles and responsibilities.

Example

When Joe left school, he continued to take cannabis in spite of warnings from his parents. He spent less time at home and more with the friends who shared his own attitudes and his drug habit. But after Joe met Sasha, she expressed concern about the example he might be setting for Lee. Joe paid attention to her point of view and stopped using cannabis.

Self-esteem

It is predicted that, since people with low self-esteem do not place high value on their own ideas, they are more likely to conform to the views of their peer group (Cialdini and Goldstein 2004). Those who have high self-esteem are less likely to conform to peer pressure and more likely to be persuaded by rational argument.

This implies that those working at a professional level in trying to bring about lifestyle change need to use an approach that bolsters the self-esteem of the target individual or group. Attempts to denigrate the ideas held by other people are most unlikely to achieve the desired effect.

Summary of persuasive techniques

Table 6.1 provides a checklist of issues to bear in mind when attempting to use persuasive methods to change an individual's behaviour.

Table 6.1 **Persuasion checklist**

The source of the message

Will the audience perceive the source of the message as:
- credible, plausible, believable;
- trustworthy – acting without self-interest;
- attractive – suitable for the target audience?

The audience for the message

Who exactly is the target audience and how likely are they to:
- be exposed to the message for long enough;
- pay attention to it;
- understand it;
- accept it?

The nature of the message

Does the message appeal to emotion or reason in a way that is:
- appropriate to the topic;
- appropriate to the audience?

Examine a current campaign designed to promote health or safety, or even a product. Evaluate it against the checklist or persuasive techniques we have so far given.

- Can you identify the target audience?
- What assumptions do you think have been made about the knowledge and attitudes of that audience?
- What can you learn from the techniques they have used?

Now compare this with the persuasive techniques you have seen used in practice, either at an individual level or through posters or leaflets.

- Can you suggest ways of improving these in the light of the knowledge you have just gained?

Exercise

When using persuasive techniques, the persuader does so in the hope that members of the target audience will respond appropriately. In the next section we consider social factors likely to influence the response.

Obedience

Persuasion often appeals to reason, whereas obedience does not. Obedience means changing behaviour in order to follow the instructions of a perceived authority figure. Whereas persuasion implies a change of belief, people may change their behaviour, in order to be obedient, without first changing their beliefs. Obedience is an important topic in health and social care because the systems that deliver such care are often very hierarchical and 'demand' obedience.

At the same time there is an expectation that the professionals that work in these environments retain professional responsibility and have a degree of autonomy.

Our understanding of obedience owes much to Milgram, a psychologist in the 1960s, who wanted to understand what had enabled Hitler to induce mass obedience to engage in extreme acts of cruelty during the Second World War. Milgram set up a laboratory experiment that turned out to have implications far beyond his expectations.

Milgram's experiment on obedience

Milgram advertised for volunteers to take part in an educational experiment at a prestigious American university. On arrival, each volunteer was introduced to another participant and a draw took place to identify who would be the pupil and who the teacher in the experiment. In fact, the draw was fixed: the volunteer always took the part of the teacher while the other was a stooge who acted the part of pupil.

The 'teachers' were told by the experimenter to press a button to give their 'pupils' an electric shock as a punishment every time they made a mistake. Although the apparatus was in fact inactive, it appeared to the 'teachers' that the shocks they were required to administer in response to pupil errors gradually increased in intensity from 15 volts to 450 volts, the upper range clearly marked on the dial in red as 'danger'.

It startled Milgram and everybody else to find that 26 out of the 40 'teachers' continued, on instruction from the experimenter, to give up to 450 volts of shock even though their 'pupil' had progressed through protests and screams and by this time appeared to be unconscious. Nobody stopped at below 300 volts (the British household voltage is 240 volts and the American voltage 110 volts).

Can you think of reasons why people recruited into this experiment as a 'teacher' might be willing to inflict this level of electric shock on their 'pupil'?

The following features have subsequently been shown to influence obedience in this type of experimental situation:

- *The legitimacy or status of the authority figure.* When the experiment was repeated at a less well-known institution, obedience was less likely, although still occurred at an alarming level.
- *The proximity of the victim.* Obedience was less likely when the victim was in the same room, rather than behind a glass screen.
- *The proximity of the authority figure.* Obedience was less likely when the experimenter was in another room and gave instructions by telephone.
- *Personal characteristics.* Some volunteers appeared to be more conformist than others and more obedient to instruction.
- *Habit.* Some people appeared to respond automatically to authority cues.
- *Social rules of commitment.* Having agreed to participate in the experiment, the volunteers felt obliged to do as they were asked.

Professionals working in health and social care are trained to take responsibility for their actions, so you might doubt the relevance of this type of experiment. The results of the following experiment give pause for thought.

Obedience in practice

Hofling *et al.* (1966) conducted a hospital-based experiment in which a drug clearly marked 'Astroten 5 mg, maximum dose 10 mg' was planted in the drugs cabinet on a mental health care ward. The experimenter, purporting to be a psychiatrist, phoned the ward and told the nurse in charge to give a named patient 20 mg of Astroten. An observer intercepted the nurse before she (they were all female) reached the patient.

Twenty-one out of 22 nurses complied with the instruction even though:

- there was no written prescription;
- the drug exceeded the safe dose (11 claimed not to have noticed this);
- none of the nurses had ever heard of either the drug or the 'doctor' beforehand.

A subsequent experiment was carried out by Rank and Jacobson (1977), which showed rather different results, with fewer nurses complying with instructions. It is suggested that the reasons for this difference are as follows.

- The nurses in the Rank and Jacobson study were familiar with the medication they were asked to administer wrongly (Valium) while the nurses in the Hofling study had never heard of 'Astroten'.
- The nurses in the Rank and Jacobson study were able to talk to each other, which was not permitted in the Hofling study.

The differences between these two studies suggest that two factors may help care professionals resist inappropriate instructions and avoid mistakes. These are: a willingness to share uncertainties with colleagues and professional development that equips staff to judge for themselves whether an act is appropriate. Nevertheless, the following example illustrates how easy it is to fall into a trap of obedience.

As soon as Anna qualified, she worked on a unit that undertook invasive investigations for which there was a long waiting list. The procedure required the routine administration of a drug one hour beforehand. The drug was harmless in the dose normally given, but could be harmful in higher doses. The rules stated that she was not allowed to give a drug without a doctor's written prescription.

On this occasion, a new medical registrar, whom she had not previously met, had omitted to include the drug for one of the patients, as per the usual protocol. Anna bleeped him to ask what to do. He said he was with an emergency and asked Anna to administer the drug, which he would write up and sign for as soon as he arrived. The alternative was to curtail the list, which might cause delays to planned treatments.

- What should Anna do in this situation?
- What if the patient was a public figure likely to cause a scene at being kept waiting?
- What if the registrar expressed fear about the consultant's reaction to his mistake?

One of the main reasons for introducing degree-level training for care professionals is to raise awareness of these issues, encourage questioning and consider the potential consequences before accepting or giving orders. It would be easy to dismiss the findings of experiments on obedience in the light of educational and structural changes that have taken place over the last 30 years. Yet findings from a more recent study of midwives, by Martin and Bull (2006), suggest otherwise.

Obedience among midwives

Midwifery is a profession that takes great pride in its autonomous status. In the light of this, Martin and Bull conducted interviews with midwives from seven different units with the aim of identifying situational aspects within these maternity hospitals that promoted obedient behaviour from midwives.

Their findings showed that, aside from the requirement to follow unit policies and procedures and fear of litigation, the most common reason given for failure to act in accordance with what they would have wanted was fear of consequences from challenging senior staff:

'You are not making that decision for that lady, you are making that decision for the senior midwife's breathing down your neck.'

'Not many (midwives) do challenge them (senior staff) because they are frightening.'

'I wouldn't argue with the consultant . . . I wouldn't have any problem with this mum wanting a home confinement. But I think you could cause more friction by arguing in front of the consultant. I think you could lose that relationship.'

(Martin and Bull 2006: pe226–e228)

There is no reason to suppose that midwives are faced with different pressure from other care professionals. Levett-Jones and Lathlean (2009) provide examples from nursing practice, such as manual handling and injection-giving (see further reading at the end of the chapter). In order to understand our fear of engaging in confrontation, we need to understand a little more about the factors that influence conformity.

Conformity

In the previous sections, we referred to the importance of peer group pressure as well as pressure from authority figures. The tendency to conform to the beliefs and behaviours of significant others is an important source of social influence. These influences are the 'social norms' which form an important component of social cognition theories which predict behaviour (Chapter 9). Conformity, like obedience, can have serious implications for health and social care practice.

Experiment on conformity

The extent to which people feel under pressure to conform was demonstrated in a classic psychology experiment by Asch in the early 1950s.

Male college students volunteered to take part in an experiment which they were told involved visual judgement. They were shown a line on a card and asked to match it with the length of one of three lines shown on a separate card (as shown in Figure 6.2). This is an extremely straightforward and unambiguous task. However, each student was unknowingly placed in a room with confederates of the experimenter who deliberately selected the wrong line.

In this situation, one third of students consistently gave the same 'wrong' answer as the one given by the confederates. Seventy per cent of students conformed on at least one occasion. Only a minority remained independent in the face of this type of group pressure.

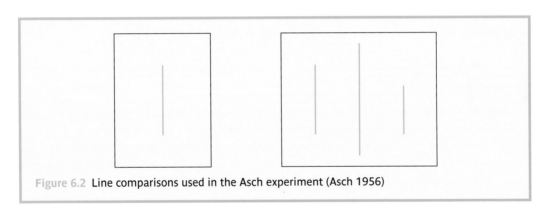

Figure 6.2 **Line comparisons used in the Asch experiment (Asch 1956)**

It would appear from Asch's experiment that people are prepared to deny the evidence of their own senses if this is contradicted by the confident beliefs or behaviour of others.

Imagine you are a student nurse, like Anna, working on a first clinical placement. You are asked to take a routine blood pressure. The automatic machine is temporarily out of commission, so you have to use an old-fashioned sphygmomanometer, as you were shown in a recent skills session. You are unable to detect meaningful sounds at the first attempt.

● What are you likely to do?

Research

Exercise ▶

> You try again, and this time you are reasonably confident with the result. However, it is much lower than the patient's previous recordings.

- What do you do?

The pressure is checked by a senior nurse who, having first checked the chart, confidently announces a pressure in line with previous recordings. You try again and obtain the same low recording.

- How do you feel?
- What do you do?

This sort of dilemma can arise in many different sorts of care situation. Conformity to the views and behaviour of other people has been shown to be more likely in certain circumstances:

- When the task is difficult or the information available is ambiguous or sparse. This is true of many situations in health and social care.
- When the desire for social approval overrides other aspects of judgement.
- When contradicting the judgement of someone else might appear rude or discourteous.
- If the others are perceived to have greater expertise. Novices may be correct, but it is the views of experts which normally prevail.
- If the confidence, self-esteem and self-efficacy of the individual is low.

Research

Conformity in practice

Hand hygiene remains a matter of great concern in care settings. Barrett and Randle (2008) carried out a study of the perceptions of nursing students regarding hand hygiene practices on wards. They found that one of the greatest influences on hand hygiene compliance was the desire to 'fit in' with what other health care workers were doing. This, of course, has the effect of perpetuating existing practice, both good and bad.

We can all think of occasions when we have done what we knew not to be right because we didn't want to stand out from the crowd. In this type of situation, management practices need to be in place to reduce pressures to conform to poor standards of care. Other examples of conformity can be found in relation to the effects of peer group pressure on risky health-related behaviours (see Chapter 9).

Developing a culture of good practice

Different workplaces are characterized by their own unique culture. We use the word 'culture' here to refer to patterns of behaviour and communication that become the norm among a group of people who regularly interact with each other. The cultures in different wards, clinics or offices can be strikingly different. In many health and social care workplaces the culture can be wonderfully positive, with staff supporting each other and all those that they work with, with energy and warmth. But while the norms within care environments are often positive, there are occasional examples of very poor practice, as typified by the following example.

Ted spent a few days on a planned investigation unit. He had little to do other than observe what was going on around him. He commented to Janice and Mark about the staff:

'They don't want to talk to the patients, they don't want to talk to the relatives, all they want to do is spend their time behind that desk talking to each other. They are masters at avoiding eye contact.'

Mark approached the nurse behind the main desk for information. The nurse listened to his request with ill-disguised impatience and said over her shoulder to her colleague 'Won't I ever get those bloods done?' before giving a very brief and uninformative answer.

Later, Ted was admitted to an intensive care unit. Here, in contrast, the culture was a positive one. There was clearly an expectation among all members of the team that care was focused on the needs of patients and their families and staff went out of their way to promote good communication with relatives. In spite of the obvious difficulties of working with such seriously ill patients there was a feeling of a single integrated body of staff working happily together and taking a pride in what they could achieve.

Janice, Anna and Lisa, all of whom work in caring roles, pondered the reasons for the differences between these two ward cultures.

Our example illustrates the worst, and the best, that a workplace culture can achieve. At the worst, a culture can be established within a unit where staff behave in ways that are not in the best interests of patients or clients. The nurse who spoke to her colleague about the bloods was not merely being rude to the patient's relative, she was happy to involve another nurse, secure in the knowledge that what she was doing was 'acceptable' within that ward's culture. When a deviant culture is established within a workplace it can be very difficult for managers to change, or for new members of staff to resist. It is difficult to deal with these types of situation alone, since 'whistleblowers' have in the past been discredited (see also Chapter 2 on stigma). Ideally it is best to gain support from others, as suggested by the Rank and Jacobson study. There are now clear guidelines on how a student or qualified nurse should raise and escalate any concerns swiftly and effectively (NMC 2010).

You might wonder why patients' relatives fail to complain about these sorts of situation but, of course, they are concerned about the future for their loved one in the care of those they are complaining about. Every so often one hears of accounts from the media of poor care, where the complaints of staff or relatives have been ignored in the face of collective disbelief unless or until irrefutable evidence from an independent source is brought to public attention.

If you are unlucky enough to encounter a workplace with a very poor culture, it may be helpful to patients or clients and others to draw that culture to the attention of senior staff outside of that workplace. If you are on placement from college you should bring the situation to the attention of college staff.

Social desirability

Social desirability refers to the tendency to conform to the views of others in order to give a good impression. We have just illustrated how conformity is strongly influenced by beliefs about what is socially acceptable. The term social desirability is most often used to refer to the tendency to answer questions in a way that people think the questioner wants to hear, in order to gain social approval. We have probably all told a lie at some time in our lives in order to put forward a good impression of ourselves. In survey-type research, researchers sometimes use the Crowne–Marlowe Social Desirability Scale (Crowne and Marlowe 1960) to identify those whose responses are strongly influenced by the wish to portray themselves in a positive light.

Example

Lisa's colleague, Tess, served on a research ethics committee. When presented with a study designed to detect improvements in sexual function following back surgery, Tess inquired of the (male) surgeon why the study included only female participants. He replied 'because men lie about sex'. The surgeon supported this statement with evidence from his own previous studies and the committee accepted the argument that men are less likely to give an accurate self-report if it is likely not to reflect well on their self-image.

In practice, it is important to be aware that social desirability is a significant reason why people do not always tell the truth about their lifestyle or their adherence to medications, or their cigarette or alcohol consumption.

Helping others

This book is written for those working, or training to work, in the caring professions. Many of us like to feel that people enter the caring professions for altruistic reasons. But what really drives people to want to help others?

There are both intrinsic and extrinsic rewards to be gained from helping others. Helping others may elicit social approval or praise and makes helpers feel good about themselves. Another explanation focuses on the notion of 'reciprocal altruism'. This reflects the belief that if I help someone else, they may help me if or when I need it. This applies to groups as well as to individuals. Self-help groups are often set up by people who have received help and wish to share their knowledge and experience in return.

Working with groups often seen as marginal in society

Omoto and Snyder (1995) studied why people volunteered to work with AIDS patients, at a time when AIDS was a strongly stigmatized condition. Based on their findings, there appear to be six reasons, aside from the need to earn a living:

1 *Humanitarian values*: wanting to help others.
2 *Curiosity*: the desire to learn more about illness or disability and to reduce personal fears and anxieties.
3 *Personal and social development*: meeting new people, making new friends; gaining experience of dealing with difficult topics.
4 *Social obligation*: out of particular concern for a particular underprivileged group in society.
5 *Esteem management*: the need to feel good and be seen as a caring person.
6 *Escape/avoidance*: to escape from other pressures, feel less lonely.

Most care professionals, if they are honest, will admit to coming into the profession for at least three of these reasons, quite apart from the important issue of pay and career prospects.

List all of the reasons why you decided to enter your chosen profession or work role. How many of these are altruistic and how many relate to your personal needs or aspirations?

The negative side of helping

We tend to see helping only in a positive light. But helping others is not always in their best interests. In Chapters 8 to 10, you will find references to the impact of different types of social support: emotional support (listening, caring), instrumental support (doing things for people) and informational support (giving information and advice). Research referred to in those chapters supports positive benefits from emotional and informational support, but demonstrates that doing things for people when they could or should be able to do them for themselves can, even when they want or accept the help, take away their autonomy and render them dependent or helpless. It is important when offering help to consider the potential for negative consequences. Sometimes it is better to be cruel to be kind, as illustrated in the following examples.

Margaret had two acquaintances, Sheila and Marjorie, both of whom had a stroke and were left with a left-sided weakness (both were right-handed).

Sheila's husband, Ron, encouraged her to do as much for herself as possible. When Margaret visited, she found Sheila struggling to peel the potatoes for lunch. She thought this rather cruel and offered to help. But Ron pointed out that Sheila felt better about herself when she could make a contribution.

When she visited Marjorie, the husband regaled her with all the things he now had to do for her. When he left them alone, Marjorie expressed the wish to die and it was clear that she was very depressed.

We discuss the virtue of 'giving' in Chapter 8 on emotional resilience. Ron was enhancing Sheila's resilience by encouraging her to help, whereas Marjorie felt completely disempowered.

Helping in an emergency

Why is it that not all individuals are willing to step forward and help in an emergency? Social psychologists became interested in studying the phenomenon of what they termed 'bystander apathy' following an incident in the USA when a young woman, Kitty Genovese, was brutally murdered outside a block of flats. Her cries for help over a half-hour period were heard by a large number of people, yet no one phoned for the police and the report of this shocked the nation.

Bystander apathy

Latané and Darley (1968) staged a series of 'emergencies' to explore the circumstances in which bystanders were more or less likely to intervene. A typical situation involved a man who had collapsed on a busy underground train. The following factors appear to determine willingness to help:

- People are more likely to act if there are cues to the seriousness of the situation from other bystanders. Once one person initiates action, others will follow.
- The larger the number of strangers present who do nothing, the less likely an individual is to intervene. Each individual assumes that someone else will take the necessary action.
- People fail to act if they perceive themselves incapable of doing anything to help. Conversely, they are more likely to act if they feel they can do something useful to help.
- People are less likely to act in ambiguous situations. For example, people are likely to ignore someone lying on the pavement if they think they may be drunk, rather than ill.
- People are more likely to take action if they first have the opportunity to discuss the situation with other people.
- Helping actions are influenced by the perceived 'deservedness' or culpability of the victim. This may relate to a 'just world' hypothesis in which people are presumed to get what they deserve in life.
- People who are facially, physically or behaviourally unattractive are less likely to receive sympathy or help.
- People are more likely to help if they are in a good mood.

Health care professionals are all trained to administer basic life support and are probably more likely to help in emergency situations. It is often puzzling why people do not immediately come to the rescue when someone collapses in a public place. But it is reassuring to know that, once you have initiated action, others are likely to follow and be supportive.

Table 6.2 **Summary: social influences on individual behaviour**	
Concept	**Implications**
Obedience	People have a tendency to obey a high-status authority figure, regardless of the consequences, particularly if they lack the opportunity to discuss uncertainty with others
Conformity	People will tend to support the incorrect judgements of the majority, or of those in senior positions, particularly when in an unfamiliar or uncertain situation
	A deviant workplace culture can lead staff to engage in unprofessional behaviour and accept poor standards of care
Social desirability	People may lie about their behaviour or lifestyle in order to present a good impression of themselves
Helping others	Helping others is influenced by a variety of personal motives and not just altruism
	Giving unnecessary help can have harmful consequences
Bystander apathy	In emergency situations, helpers are often reluctant to be the first to offer help

Non-verbal communication

Up to this point in this chapter, we have focused mainly on the social influences on what people say and do. But some of the social influences that have a strong impact on us involve subtle changes in expression or demeanour. This is particularly noticeable when it comes to caring. Studies of patient satisfaction with health care have repeatedly shown that interpersonal aspects of care are central to patients' perceptions of quality of care. But, as care workers, it is not just what we do or say that matters, it is our caring manner. This includes subtleties of tone of voice, eye contact, posture and facial expression.

Attitudes (see Chapter 2) are evaluative responses that commonly involve approval and disapproval. These are expressed most vividly through non-verbal communication. If we disapprove of someone, or if we are nervous or annoyed, we show it in our facial expression, eye contact (or lack of it) and posture, and it is very hard to cover up our feelings or suppress these responses. We reveal a lot about ourselves through non-verbal communication. For example, we signal confidence or nervousness through our body and hand movements, facial expression, tone of voice and speed of delivery. Empathy, understanding, caring, pain and distress all involve communication, and non-verbal behaviours are the main ways of communicating caring.

Positive and negative attitudes such as pleasure or annoyance, approval or disgust, are revealed through non-verbal signals. Eye contact with a friendly smile normally conveys interest and a willingness to engage. As we illustrated in an earlier example, staff can use the avoidance of eye contact to signal that they have no wish to engage in social interaction. This may be why nurses become adept at walking past patients without making eye contact. But while this enables them to concentrate on the task they have in hand, it can leave patients feeling ignored and frustrated.

Non-verbal communication with patients

Silverman and Kinnersley (2010: 76–8) highlighted the importance of non-verbal communication in their review of issues faced by busy care professionals who need to look up records and make notes during a consultation. They offered the following recommendations:

- deliberately postpone using the records until the patient has completed his or her opening statement;
- wait for opportune moments before looking at the notes;
- separate listening from note-reading by signposting your intention to look at the records and signalling when you have finished, so that the patient understands the process (structuring).

Making effective use of non-verbal communication can be extremely empowering for patients and clients, as illustrated in the next example.

Janice had experienced a very stressful time in her life, dealing with family economic crisis, illness, bereavement and demands. Just as she felt these were coming to an end, she developed influenza. After the initial infection, she continued to feel anxious and panicky, felt sick and was unable to eat.

She visited the doctor complaining of persistent feelings of nausea. The doctor put down his pen, turned to face her and looked her in the eye before inviting Janice to 'tell me what has been happening in your life'. Immediately, the burdens of the last months fell from her shoulders. She wept as she told him, but from that moment, she felt better.

The doctor in the last example was well known locally for his caring manner, but not all care professionals exhibit such good interpersonal skills.

Interpersonal skills

Interpersonal skills are essential for people to be able to engage in all aspects of life. Communication is often treated as synonymous with the use of language. But we only have to find ourselves in a foreign country where we do not speak the language to discover how relatively easy it is to get by with the use of non-verbal communication. Much can be learned from observing mothers interact with pre-verbal babies, or by watching children who do not share a common language develop friendship through play. It would appear that interpersonal skills are normally present or learned from a very young age. Some of this learning is taught by adults and the child reprimanded for breaches of etiquette. But most is learned informally by modelling (see Chapter 5).

Many of the rules of social engagement are implicit and difficult to learn through formal teaching. Children who find it difficult to learn by observation, for example those with learning difficulties or autism, are disadvantaged and socially excluded because of their poor interpersonal skills. The inability to communicate effectively can lead to frustration and inappropriate or challenging behaviours. The lowering of inhibitions (disinhibition), associated with alcohol misuse or serious mental health problems, can cause severe embarrassment or lead to violent attack. In all situations, poor social skills have the potential to lead to social isolation, which in turn contributes to mental health problems.

Key elements of interpersonal skills include:

- *Facial expression.* Facial expression indicates the emotional state of the individual, for example, joy, distress, fear are all normally discernible. Absence of facial expression may be interpreted as disinterest, or may generate discomfort because the observer is unable to 'read' the individual's emotions. The presence of facial tics is disconcerting not just because they appear odd but because they can mask expression. Loss of facial expression is an early sign of Parkinson's disease.

- *Reciprocity.* One of the earliest signs of language in children is the ability to take turns, as in a conversation. The small baby watches the mother's face intently while she talks, and then responds by mouthing similar sounds. In adult conversation, turn-taking signals interest and engagement, as opposed to self-absorption or disinterest.

- *Body posture and gesture.* These can signal a variety of intentions. For example, leaning forward signals interest and engagement. This does not always come naturally. For example, a research student who was about to conduct interviews with older people needed to be reminded that sitting back with arms folded did not express empathy or interest.

- *Respect for personal, social and public space.* It is normally perceived as uncomfortable or threatening when others get too close. Relatives and close friends are normally allowed closer than strangers. But it is important to recognize that personal space is largely determined by cultural rules of acceptability. Therefore people from other cultures may unwittingly breach social etiquette. Nurses normally gain the patient's permission, but may need to breach personal space in order to carry out necessary tasks. People who have dementia may not fully appreciate what is happening and protest at being approached by a 'stranger'. Similarly those under the influence of drugs or alcohol may 'misread' an approach as a sexual advance or threat.

- *Gaze.* In most western cultures, the avoidance of eye contact is interpreted as 'shifty'. It can also signal uncertainty or low self-esteem. But in other cultures, lowering of the gaze is a mark of respect. Fixed eye contact is uncomfortable or threatening. Non-friendly eye contact is seen in many cultures and subcultures as a mark of disrespect, or act of aggression, which can provoke attack.

Exercise

Next time you have the opportunity to observe a lengthy interaction between another professional and a patient or client, see if you can spot any discrepancies between what the patient or
client says and how they respond. See if the professional also observed these discrepancies.

● What do you think is the best way to deal with these sorts of situation?

We have found it helpful to point out, in a concerned way, when we think someone looks
uncomfortable or we think they might not have understood something. Most people appreciate
the act of concern and it can save a lot of time dealing with misunderstandings.

Some people who breach rules of social etiquette are unaware they are doing it. People with
Asperger's Syndrome have particular difficulties with communication and psychologists are
working to develop innovative 'virtual reality' techniques to improve these (Parsons *et al.* 2000).
They have also tried to develop programmes to assist with orientation into different cultures
(Bhawuk and Brislin 2000). Care workers need to be able to identify reasons for, and respond
appropriately to, inappropriate behaviours in order to avoid misunderstandings, conflict or
injury.

Managing conflict

Dealing with aggression

Aggression and violence by patients or their caregivers towards care staff appears to have been
on the increase, particularly in accident and emergency departments and mental health settings
(Chapman *et al.* 2010).

Research

The escalation of aggression

Chapman *et al.* (2010) point out that people who are mentally ill quite often experience mood
disturbances and display sudden, unexpected and ostensibly irrational behaviours which
threaten staff. The same applies to those under the influence of alcohol or drugs. They report
indications that these sorts of behaviours elicit defensive reactions from staff that, in turn, lead
to an increase in aggression from patients.

Clearly, we condemn the use of violence in all circumstances, but at the same time we recognize that an important way to avoid conflict is to try to understand the sort of situations likely
to prompt it, from the point of view of the other party. If someone comes to a hospital, clinic or
social services centre, they are normally trying to communicate a need. When someone com-
plains or gets annoyed or upset it is usually because they feel that their needs have not been

recognized or adequately responded to. The natural response to a complaint or criticism is to defend one's position and offer an explanation. But a defensive response, no matter how well intentioned, is almost always interpreted as counter-attack. People who have aggressive tendencies tend to expect and perceive hostility in others. In those who lack self-control, particularly if they are disinhibited by alcohol or drugs, this can easily trigger a violent response.

Joe and his friend, Dez, had been out for the evening. Dez drank rather too much, fell over and hit his head, which was bleeding, so Joe took him to the nearest hospital. After they had waited some time, Dez got upset. He wrongly thought he was being discriminated against, so he started to make a fuss. The triage nurse explained, unsympathetically, that the nurses and doctors were treating seriously ill patients and he would just have to wait his turn. Dez interpreted this to mean that he and his injury were unimportant and he started to get angry. Fortunately, Joe was able to intervene to calm him down.

Rules of reciprocity and civil conventions of communication break down under the influence of alcohol or drugs, particularly when people are aroused because of fear or anxiety. In these situations, it is necessary to avoid any verbal or non-verbal behaviour, such as eye contact, dominant posture and/or comments that might be interpreted, rightly or wrongly, as unsympathetic or confrontational. Similarly, touch can provoke attack if seen as an attempt to dominate or control. Hence, those working in situations where there is a high risk of attack, such as mental health units or accident and emergency departments, should receive special training in conflict avoidance and management.

When confronted with an individual who appears angry or upset, it is natural for the care worker to feel offended or upset. Thus both the individual and the care worker feel themselves to be the victims in the confrontation. If, instead, the care worker adopts the role of rescuer, rather than victim, any confrontation is usually quickly diffused. Here are some guidelines:

- Acknowledge, verbally, that you have seen that they are angry/upset. Look concerned.
- Ask them to tell you what the problem is. Look interested.
- Acknowledge their right to feel angry/upset in the situation as they perceived it (this is not the same as admitting responsibility). Look sympathetic.
- Try to negotiate a solution. Look sincere.
- The rules of reciprocity oblige the angry/upset party to listen to the reasons why you might have difficulty meeting their demands.

Further information about ways to de-escalate aggression in mental health settings is given by Cowin *et al.* (2003).

Not all patients or clients are able to engage in rational debate, but most remain sensitive to non-verbal cues. The following exercise was developed in response to students' complaints that they were frequently attacked or had objects thrown at them by older patients, on general wards, who were suffering from dementia.

This is best undertaken in the skills laboratory and involves role play. The individual who will learn most is the one taking the part of the patient, so it is a good idea to take this role in turns. The parts are as follows.

Scene 1

- The patient in bed is a fiercely independent old person who has been admitted reluctantly from home. He or she has soiled the bed and is attempting to conceal it from the nurse by wrapping the faeces in a tissue.
- The 'nurse' locates the source of the smell and signals obviously to her colleague as s/he approaches the patient, saying loudly that they will need to clean him/her up; starts to tug at the bedclothes.
- The patient responds to the encounter and is then asked to report how it made him/her feel.

Scene 2

- Once the 'patient' has discussed how this made them feel, a similar scene is enacted using a much more sympathetic and discrete approach, starting with a conversation about how the patient feels about being in hospital and leading later to the issue of the soiled bed.

None of the students who took part in this exercise wanted to play the part of the 'nasty nurse', although all said that they had seen this type of incident in practice! The 'patients' instinctively clutched at the bedclothes, said that they felt humiliated and had a strong urge to hit the 'nasty nurse'. Underlying this behaviour appears to be a strong urge to resist attempts by strangers to invade their personal space or violate their autonomy. Adhering to culturally accepted rules of social etiquette by establishing a relationship before attempting to engage in close physical contact is particularly important in these circumstances.

Dealing with complaints

Complaints managers within large organizations, such as NHS Trusts, have become adept at responding to patient complaints. But responses sometimes neglect the fact that most complainants are looking for assurances that the same thing won't happen again to others.

Dealing with complaints in the NHS

A detailed report on dealing with complaints in the NHS was issued by the Parliamentary and Health Service Ombudsman (2010). The main reasons for dissatisfaction with the ways complaints had been handled concerned inadequate or incomplete response. The second highest reason for complaint was the attitude of NHS staff. The report includes the following responses from complainants:

▶ *Before mediation*:

'I am not happy with the response I received from [the Trust]. I do not believe the questions and concerns I raised were fully answered at either the meeting or the final response letter I received a long time after the meeting' (p. 39).

After mediation:

'I have felt an enormous sense of relief that the findings acknowledge some of the truth of what really happened to me and this has been an important aid to me coming to terms with what happened and starting to get some closure' (p. 4).

Key points drawn from their recommendations are:

- Take the complaint seriously and investigate thoroughly.
- Demonstrate that attention has been given to the details of the complaint.
- Acknowledge responsibility for mistakes.
- Apologize.
- Give a full and thorough explanation for what happened.
- Undertake to ensure it will not happen again.
- Put things right quickly and effectively.

Dealing with interpersonal conflict

Conflict can often arise between work colleagues. Here we give an example and suggest ways of avoiding or dealing quickly and effectively with this type of situation.

Janice, in her new role as health care assistant, gave a patient some advice. The staff nurse told Janice off because it was for trained staff to deal with this. Janice believed that she was acting in the patient's best interest and responded defensively. This led to bad feeling between the two members of staff, each of whom saw themselves as the victim of the other's persecution.

Example

In line with our previous suggestion for diffusing conflict, this type of situation is easily resolved if one of the players stops defending his or her position and apologizes. The other, not wishing to be pushed into the role of persecutor by refusing to accept an apology, will normally respond in the role of rescuer by saying 'that's all right' or 'don't worry about it' or 'it wasn't really your fault'.

Janice acknowledged that she should have checked with the staff nurse and apologized. The staff nurse told Janice that she was only doing her best for the patient and to think no more about it.

Knowledge of these rules of engagement can help to diffuse all sorts of potentially confrontational situations.

Group interactions

Inter-group conflict

The potentially divisive nature of social groupings, in terms of inter-group discrimination and prejudice, was demonstrated by Tajfel (1982). Tajfel's work suggests that members of a social group generally work towards maximizing profits or rewards for members of their own group (the in-group), often at the expense of other groups (the out-group). We discussed this in relation to the perception of others in Chapter 2. Examples of inter-group prejudice are to be found in arguments between health and social services over the deployment of scarce resources for community-based care, and the apportioning of blame following the non-accidental death of a child.

Within health care, examples of in-group/out-group conflict can be found in the relationships between different professional groups, between hospital and community, private and public services, or between similar units in different localities.

During your work, study or placements, see if you can identify signs of inter-group prejudice. Consider the following:

- What is the impact (if any) of this on the working environment for staff?
- What is the impact (if any) on the care of patients or clients?

Inter-group conflict usually focuses on the self-interests of group members. Having a shared goal is a good starting point for removing inter-group prejudice. For those working in the caring professions, sharing the goal of providing good quality person-centred care is a sound basis for collaborative working.

Group decision-making

Group meetings are inevitable within all organizations, but do not always lead to sound decisions. Janis (1972) was prompted to study group decision-making processes as a result of mistakes that led to the Cuban missile crisis between America and the Soviet Union in 1962. Janis proposed that the politicians who precipitated this debacle had been victims of 'groupthink'. Some of the main symptoms of groupthink are identified below.

Groupthink

- Illusions of invulnerability. Positions of power can lead people to believe that they cannot be proved wrong.
- Collective rationalization. Unrealistic assessments are supported by 'rational' arguments and used to convince other group members.
- Belief in the inherent morality of the group. This reflects the belief that the group is in the right and good must triumph.
- Stereotypes of out-groups. Outsiders are often automatically classified as 'bad guys' or enemies who must therefore be in the wrong.
- Direct pressure on dissenters. Dissenters are silenced and this discourages critical evaluation. Certain group members may take the initiative to reduce dissent by persuasion or coercion, and foster an illusion of unanimity. Silence is interpreted as support.

Groupthink can affect any group of decision-makers. It leads to biased and often frankly wrong decisions that are not based on the best available evidence. Groups of no more than 12 people from different backgrounds, with different skills and viewpoints, are less vulnerable to groupthink. It is important that the chairperson plays an impartial role in encouraging all members to voice their opinions, and encourage the debate of any doubts.

Anna had the opportunity to sit in on multiprofessional case conferences held regularly to plan treatment and care for patients in an elderly care unit. It soon became clear that the group was not operating effectively. For example, the medical consultant persistently arrived late, put forward his point of view, and then left. Another group member always selected a higher chair than the others and tried to direct decisions.

Eventually, a senior nurse broached this with other members and found that nobody was satisfied with the meetings or the quality of the decisions reached. Group members identified that the room was too small and the furniture inappropriate to facilitate sharing; decisions were not fully agreed and not implemented. As a result of this investigation, a larger and more comfortable meeting room was found and a set of ground rules agreed. These included all professionals dedicating time to attend, having a rotating chairperson, a short presentation by the lead professional, limited time for discussion, and an agreed plan of action with named persons responsible for implementation.

Example

The Royal College of Nursing have published a useful self-assessment tool (RCN 2005) to help team members identify problems with effective team-working.

Group leadership

The rise of Hitler stimulated Lewin (1939) to study the effects of authoritarian, democratic and laissez-faire leadership styles. These styles of leadership are similar to the classification used to describe parenting styles (chapter 3). Lewin's observations revealed the following findings.

- *Democratic leadership* encourages participation, engenders a sense of ownership and commitment within the group and generally leads to higher morale, friendliness, cooperation and productivity. Democratic leaders facilitate change while recognizing resistance and seeking to work with dissenters.
- *Authoritarian or autocratic leadership* is based upon coercion and is generally associated with lower morale among the group or workforce. It can be useful in order to achieve an important task quickly, but may place undue stress upon some members of the group.

Most people prefer to work with strong but democratic leadership. Hoel *et al.* (2010) found that bullying and harassment in the workplace were most commonly associated with autocratic

Table 6.3 Summary: group processes	
Avoiding conflict	Show respect for individual personal space and autonomy
	Avoid provocative non-verbal expression, gaze and posture
	Respond to a confrontation in the role of sympathetic rescuer, not as defensive victim
	Acknowledge the individual's right to be angry
	Where necessary, provide information so they can complain to the appropriate source
Dealing with complaints	Similar principles to above:
	• Treat it seriously and investigate it
	• Apologize and explain
	• Undertake to ensure that it will not happen again
Inter-group conflict	Working towards a shared goal is likely to reduce conflict between professional groups
Within-group decision-making	Equality of status and democratic leadership increases member participation and satisfaction
	Small groups made up of members who bring different perspectives to a shared task are less likely to reach the wrong decision
Leadership	Democratic leadership that encourages participation and sense of individual ownership is associated with better working relationships and more effective work practices

leadership. However, they also observed that laissez-faire and unpredictable leadership played an important role in perceptions of bullying. We have included further reading on identifying and managing bullying at the end of this chapter.

Although psychological research has identified characteristics of good leaders, leadership also involves skills and techniques that do not come automatically. Therefore, management training is essential in the preparation of those who are appointed to take on leadership roles within health and social care services, particularly at a time of rapid change. One of the main challenges for leaders of these organizations is to break down barriers between different professional groups, promote interprofessional working and be prepared to work with representatives of patient and other voluntary organizations to ensure that services meet the needs of those they serve in the most efficient and effective way.

Further reading

Aronson, E. (2007) *The Social Animal*, 10th edition. London: Worth.

Brehm, S.S., Kassi, S.M. and Fein, S. (2007) *Social Psychology, 6th edition*. Boston, MA: Houghton Mifflin.

Cowin, L., Davies, R., Estall, G., Fitzerald, M. and Hoot, S. (2003) De-escallating aggression and violence in the mental health setting, *Journal of Mental Health Nursing*, 12(1): 64.

Levett-Jones, T. and Lathlean, J. (2009) 'Don't rock the boat': nursing students' experiences of conformity and compliance, *Nurse Education Today*, 29(3): 342–9.

NHS (National Health Service) (2006) *NHS Employers' Guidance: Bullying and Harassment*. London: NHS Confederation.

RCN (Royal College of Nursing) (2005) *Bullying and Harassment at Work*, revised edition. London: RCN.

Thompson, D.L., Dorsey, A., Miller, K.L. and Parrott, R. (eds) *Handbook of Health Communication*. Mahwah, NJ: Laurence Erlbaum Associates.

7

Stress and coping

Key topics

- Stress, coping and social support: theory, interactions and applications
- Stress-related illness and stress management
- Stress in daily life, the workplace and hospitalization

Introduction

In this chapter we help you to answer the following questions:

- How do we recognize symptoms of stress?
- What are the causes of stress?
- How can we help to reduce stress for ourselves as well as our patients and clients?

We all recognize what it feels like to be faced with a new or strange situation. We all get anxious from time to time, or describe ourselves as feeling 'stressed'. This term is often used in a vague way to describe a variety of unpleasant feelings in situations we find challenging or difficult. The following vignette captures a situation that we have all faced at some time when starting a new course or a new job.

When Anna started her nursing degree she had little idea of what was expected of her – where to go, what to do, when to be there, who to talk to. She felt sick and anxious and wished that she was back home with her family.

When Lillian was admitted to hospital for removal of her breast, she too felt sick and anxious for very much the same reasons. But Lillian faced many additional worries related to her operation and its aftermath, which would include coming to terms with her changed body and the continuing sense of threat associated with having cancer.

Vignette

People in need of medical or social care are very often under a lot of stress, which can cloud their judgement, alter their behaviour and impede their recovery or adaptation. Caring for people in these circumstances is emotionally demanding and can be very stressful.

Background

Stress is an important issue in health and social care because it is a cause and a consequence of health and social problems. For example, stress can give rise to behaviour changes, such as withdrawal or aggression, which tend to alienate people from friends, family or professionals who might otherwise provide the support they really need. In those who are ill, it can confound medical diagnosis by causing, mimicking or masking the symptoms of mental and physical disease.

Example

Stress or hypertension?

When Mark visited the doctor, his blood pressure was high and the doctor suspected that he would need treatment for hypertension (a disease that carries a high risk of heart attack and stroke). At the time, Mark had recently retired and he was looking after his father, Ted, following the death of Laura (Mark's mother). Once Mark had had time to adjust to retirement and Ted was less dependent on him, Mark's blood pressure returned to within normal limits without the need for medication.

Stress is not a straightforward concept. A situation that one person finds stressful is not necessarily perceived as stressful by someone else. Equally, a situation that an individual finds very stressful at one point in time causes them no stress at all at another point in time. We start by defining exactly what is meant by the term stress.

What is stress?

Many different definitions of stress are to be found in the literature. This is because stress is a concept that requires a theoretical explanation. One of the simplest and most commonly used definitions reflects the concept of imbalance: 'Stress refers to an imbalance between a perceived demand and the perceived ability of the individual to respond to it' (McGrath 1970: 17). Most theories of stress assume that there is:

- *a stressor*: this refers to a change in circumstance, or new event, or situational demand that requires a response;
- *a process of appraisal*: the individual evaluates the demand and the resources available to deal with it;
- *a response*: this includes emotional and physiological changes, and cognitive and behavioural coping responses.

It is helpful to be able to recognize when people are under stress, so we start by considering its symptoms.

Symptoms of stress

Symptoms of stress may be physiological, emotional, cognitive and/or behavioural. Table 7.1 summarizes some of the most common responses to stress.

Normally when we speak of something as being stressful we infer something negative or unpleasant. But as Table 7.1 illustrates, the ability to respond positively to new challenges, rather than seeing them as threats, confers important benefits.

Recognize your own patterns of stress

Think of a recent situation that made you feel really stressed.

- What do you think caused you to feel stressed?
- Was this typical of the sort of situation that you find stressful?
- What symptoms did you experience?
- How did you deal with the situation?
- Was this typical of the way you normally deal with this type of situation?
- Did you deal with it successfully?
- Can you think of a more effective way of dealing with this sort of situation?

Exercise

Table 7.1 **Common responses to stress**

	Physiological	Emotional	Cognitive	Behavioural
Negative responses to demanding situations	Difficulty sleeping Indigestion or nausea Loss or increase in appetite Need to urinate frequently Panic attacks Headaches and muscle tension Increase in pain Reduction in immune response: increased risk of infection and illness	Upset Irritable Anxious Sad Depressed Frightened Angry	Confused Loss of concentration Can't make decisions Worry a lot Feel a failure Feeling helpless or hopeless Loss of empathy	Crying Being unreasonable Not eating, or eating too much Take time off work with minor illness Self-medication with alcohol, tobacco or drugs Withdraw from usual activities
Effects of dealing positively with demanding situations	Increase in energy Increased immune response	Satisfaction Optimism Well-being	Increased confidence and motivation	Enhanced practical, self-care and social skills Increase in productivity

Negative symptoms associated with stress are commonplace. But if a combination of these symptoms occurs frequently or persistently it could indicate the presence of stress-related illness. Sometimes, we develop patterns of response that are unhelpful or maladaptive. It is useful to recognize these in order to find ways of reducing the stress in our lives.

Some stress is avoidable

Janice parked her car overnight in a municipal car park. She put the correct money into the machine, but the ticket failed to register the correct expiry time. Janice could not phone the helpline because she had forgotten to charge her mobile phone. She spent the night worrying that the car might be clamped. On her return the next day, she saw that she had failed to follow the correct instructions on the machine.

Janice reflected that her failure to read instructions properly and her failure to keep the phone charged were persistent, avoidable causes of stress in her life.

People who have worked in health or social care for some time may be vulnerable to a condition called 'burnout' (Maslach *et al.* 2001). It occurs when staff are no longer able to cope with the emotional demands of caring. The symptoms of burnout are low job satisfaction, poor performance and a lack of ability to empathize with patients. Burnout poses serious problems for patients, colleagues and employers, as well as the individual concerned. We address contributory causes later in this chapter under the heading of stress in the workplace.

Physiological responses to stress

Stress research takes place under the heading of psychoneuroimmunology. This is a branch of cognitive science that studies the relationship between external events, psychological reactions, physiological effects and health outcomes.

Stress involves neurological and biochemical, as well as psychological responses. This can make it difficult to distinguish symptoms of anxiety (e.g. heart racing, nausea, muscle pain) from those of a physical disease. Furthermore, stress really can make us ill. Therefore it is important for all those working in health and social care to have some understanding of the underlying physiology.

Selye (1956) described physiological responses to stress as part of what he called the 'general adaptation system' (GAS). When faced with a sudden or new demand or threat, there is an immediate arousal of the autonomic nervous system and release of adrenaline and endorphins. Selye called this the 'alarm response'. It prepares the body for action and was described by Cannon in the early twentieth century as the 'fight or flight' response. It causes the following bodily processes:

- release of glucose stored in the liver in readiness for muscular activity;
- increase in cardiovascular activity as indicated by increased heart rate and blood pressure;
- increase in the viscosity of the blood and rerouting of blood from the digestive organs and skin to the brain and muscles;
- increase in the rate and depth of breathing and enlargement in the pupils of the eyes.

If the individual is unable to address the demand or threat using his or her usual coping strategies (the timescale is variable), corticosteroids continue to be released into the bloodstream while coping attempts continue. Corticosteroids provide energy for adaptive reactions and stimulate the body's natural defence systems. Selye (1956) called this period of physiological response the 'stage of resistance'.

When faced with unremitting demands, the body's resistance mechanisms decline in strength, resulting in stress-related illness. Selye termed this the 'stage of exhaustion'. In extreme conditions, resistance to stress can decline very suddenly, resulting in collapse or death. This is most likely to occur in those who are already sick and those whose immune system is already compromised.

In order to reduce stress and its adverse consequences, it is important to recognize the cumulative nature of the effects of stress. A person who has been experiencing stress for some time may be overwhelmed by some small stressor that acts as the 'straw that broke the camel's back'. In the next section, we explain what is meant by a stressor.

What is a stressor?

A stressor is an event, situational demand or change that challenges or exceeds the ability of the individual to deal effectively with it. The threat may be physical, psychological, environmental or social.

- A physical threat is one that involves a threat to the body, such as trauma, disease or ageing process.
- A psychological threat is one that interrupts or prevents progress towards the achievement of an important goal, or threatens the individual's self-esteem.
- Environmental and social threats include hassles at work or home, life-changing events and relationship breakdown or loss. We explore these different types of situation later in this chapter.

Stressors demand attention and action. However, not all stressors are bad for us. Exposure to new situations gives us the opportunity to develop and demonstrate new skills. Dealing successfully with new situations enhances our self-esteem, prepares us to deal effectively with future challenges and boosts our immune system. Failure to face up to, or deal adequately with new situations has the opposite effect.

Certain events or situations, such as a life-threatening illness or bereavement, are very stressful for most people. However, there are many situations which are stressful for some people but represent a stimulating challenge for others. The transactional model of stress and coping is the only theoretical model that takes full account of these individual differences.

The transactional model of stress and coping

The transactional model of stress, sometimes referred to as the appraisal model, was proposed by Lazarus in the 1960s and later developed with Folkman. Designed to explain individual variations in responses to stress, it introduced cognitive appraisal as the mediator between the stressor and the individual coping response. We illustrate this in Figure 7.1, into which we have incorporated some examples of moderating influences on appraisals and coping responses.

In Figure 7.1 cognitive appraisal acts as a mediator between the stressor and the individual's response.

The internal and external moderators include many variables that influence the strength of the relationship between the stressor and the individual's response.

In Figure 7.2, we illustrate the difference between a mediator and a moderator (based on Baron and Kenny 1986). These words are used interchangeably in much of the literature on stress, largely because of lack of theoretical clarity. Strictly speaking, the mediator (appraisal) intervenes to modify or change the outcome or consequence of an event (the stressor). A moderator influences the strength of the relationship between the event and its outcomes.

Cognitive appraisal

Lazarus (1966) described appraisals as mediators between the situational demand or threat (the stressor) and the emotional and behavioural response (coping). Appraisal is part of the process of perception by which the individual evaluates the demands of the situation and the resources available to deal with these. It determines how the individual responds to the situation.

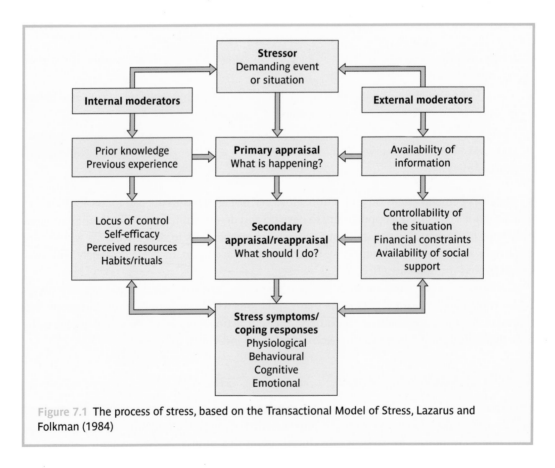

Figure 7.1 The process of stress, based on the Transactional Model of Stress, Lazarus and Folkman (1984)

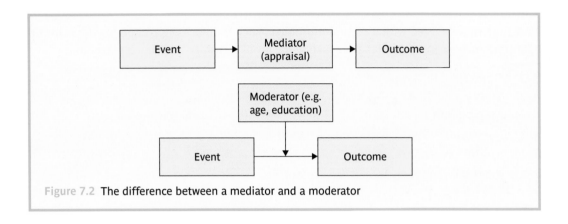

Figure 7.2 **The difference between a mediator and a moderator**

Contrasting illness appraisals and responses

Different people appraise the same disease or symptom in different ways, as illustrated by these responses to the diagnosis of osteoarthritis:

- Edith believed it was an inevitable consequence of ageing and adjusted her life accordingly.
- Marjorie saw it as a likely threat to her independence and became quite depressed.
- Joyce blamed herself for getting overweight. She felt both guilty and angry, which made her eat even more.
- Stan was relieved it was not something worse and took up more activities to make the most of his life.

A range of different appraisals can be found in response to any type of situation, be it a medical condition, social problem, the task of caring for a family member, dealing with death and dying, or any other demand. Different appraisals lead to different consequences.

Primary and secondary appraisal

Lazarus and Averill (1972: 243) proposed a three-stage model of appraisal:

- *Primary appraisal.* The individual determines whether or not this represents a threat.
- *Secondary appraisal.* The individual decides what, if anything, needs to be done about the perceived threat, based on the resources available to deal with it.
- *Reappraisal.* The individual decides whether or not to continue with the current strategy, or consider alternative options.

Next time you are faced with a common problem, such as managing competing demands on your time, invite a group of friends to analyse the problem using the following structure:

- What exactly is the problem?
- What are the alternatives for addressing this type of problem?
- How successfully do you normally deal with this type of problem?
- Did someone else have a better suggestion?
- Did you all have the same ideas? If not, how did they differ?
- Do you think you might benefit from adopting any of the suggestions made by others?

The exercise above should reveal interesting differences in the ways people perceive and deal with a common problem. The outcome of primary appraisal is determined largely by past experience. People who have previously coped successfully with a similar type of situation are more likely to ignore it, or perceive it as a challenge rather than a threat. Those who have no prior experience of similar situations are more likely to experience uncertainty and anxiety. People who have had difficulties coping with similar previous situations, or believe they lack the resources to deal with it, are more likely to view the situation as a threat and react with fear, anxiety or even a sense of hopelessness.

Secondary appraisal and reappraisal are likely to be influenced by a number of moderators (see Figure 7.1) including:

- knowledge about the situation or type of situation;
- beliefs about responsibility for dealing with it (locus of control);
- the availability of tangible resources believed necessary to deal with the situation (such as the money to buy essential goods and services, or social support to provide help);
- confidence in using relevant practical and problem-solving skills (self-efficacy).

Secondary appraisal is often influenced by habitual or automatic ways of responding which may be successful and adaptive, or unsuccessful and maladaptive.

Reducing stress for patients in hospital

When Mark heard he was to be admitted to hospital, he felt very anxious because he didn't know what to expect. Fortunately, he was sent an information booklet telling him what to expect, where to go, what to take with him, and what facilities were available to him.

He was greeted on the ward, shown round, introduced to other patients and informed about what would happen next, which was very reassuring.

The time spent on these preparations made for savings. Mark's vital signs on admission were within normal limits, he was more cooperative, and stress did not delay his recovery.

Many situations that professionals take for granted can be extremely stressful for people who are not familiar with hospital procedures or routines. It is important to be alert to signs of anxiety and to inquire about the cause. It is often quite simple to resolve.

Table 7.2 Coping strategies and coping responses		
Authors	**Types of coping strategy**	
Folkman and Lazarus (1985)	Problem-focused coping	Emotion-focused coping
Rosenstiel and Keefe (1983)	Active coping	Passive coping
Roth and Cohen (1986)	Approach strategies	Avoidant strategies
Coping responses	• Confronts reality • Seeks to mitigate or deal with the perceived threat • Engages in problem-solving • Seeks out appropriate resources to deal with the problem	• Seeks to reduce feelings of distress or fear without addressing the source of the problem (e.g. using alcohol) • Does nothing • Relies on others to sort things out • Distancing/denial: ignores the situation and avoids the likely consequences

Coping

The outcome of the appraisal process is referred to as the coping response. Lazarus and Folkman (1984) defined coping as the thoughts and behaviours used to manage perceived demands. Types of coping response have been given different names by different theorists, but can generally be grouped into two main types of coping strategy, as we have indicated in Table 7.2.

The strategy most likely to be successful in dealing with a problem depends on the nature of the problem and the resources available to deal with it. In general, some strategies are more likely to be effective than others.

Compare coping strategies

When it comes to preparing for an exam, different students cope in different ways. Analyse your own exam strategy:

- Do you approach revision systematically, for example by making lists and sticking to timetables?
- Do you try to avoid thinking about it and go out as usual?
- Do you rely on friends to help you out with revision material?
- Do you find a range of excuses for delaying revision or not doing well?

Now compare your strategies with those of your friends:

- Who seems most stressed before the exam? Which strategy did they use?
- Could you improve your own strategies in the light of this exercise?

Can you draw any lessons from this exercise that could be applied to help clients or patients cope with their situations?

Exercise

Problem-focused, active or approach coping strategies are likely to be most effective when a situation is controllable, which means that it is amenable to some kind of human intervention.

Emotion-focused, passive or avoidant coping strategies often reduce anxiety in the short term because they allow the individual to ignore or avoid the potential consequences in difficult situations. They may be adaptive in uncontrollable situations, such as a terminal illness (Taylor and Stanton 2007). But passive or avoidant strategies are rarely adaptive in the longer term because they prevent the individual from developing the skills necessary to deal with situations that are within their control. They may reduce feelings of stress in the short term, but increase stress in the long term, as illustrated in the following examples.

Examples

Avoidant coping

Joe is currently unemployed. He moved in with Sasha, who already has a small child, Lee, and they live on Sasha's social security benefits. Sasha is now pregnant and they have spent a lot of money on new baby equipment and treats. Their debts are mounting, but Joe destroys bills so as not to worry Sasha. They are now faced with an eviction order.

When Lillian first found a lump in her breast, she convinced herself that it could not be serious and would disappear in a week or two. When she eventually sought medical help, she needed more radical surgery than if she had reported it straight away.

The two distinct forms of coping we have identified are widely applied in stress research as a convenient classification. However, some coping strategies do not fall neatly into these categories and deserve special mention:

- *Confrontive coping* (Folkman and Lazarus 1985) involves aggressive efforts to alter the situation. We would comment that its effect is likely to depend on how, when and to what extent it is used. For example, a degree of assertiveness ensures that someone's needs are not overlooked, but too much forcefulness can lead the individual to be labelled as a 'difficult' client or patient (see Chapter 2).

- *Seeking social support*. Asking for advice or help is an active process. The receiving of information, emotional support and essential practical help provides an important buffer against stress. The giving and receiving of support is often a reciprocal and mutually satisfying process. However, persistently relying on other people to sort out problems leads to dependence and is associated with poor health outcomes. Thus social support can lead to either positive or negative outcomes, depending on the type of support and how it is received. In this way, social support can mediate the health outcome of the coping response.

The effects of different coping strategies

Penley *et al.* (2002) presented a meta-analysis of the relationship between coping strategies and physical and mental health outcomes.

- The use of problem-focused coping strategies was more likely to be associated with positive health outcomes.
- Confrontive coping and passive strategies such as distancing, seeking social support, avoidance and wishful thinking were more likely to be associated with negative health outcomes.

Research

Generally speaking, dealing with a problem by acknowledging it and trying to resolve it is better than ignoring it. But as Folkman and Moskowitz (2004) pointed out, the appropriate response depends on the problem the individual has to cope with and the context in which they are attempting to cope. A mismatch between the type of stressor and the coping strategy used can actually induce stress (Park *et al.* 2001). For example, Merritt *et al.* (2004) presented experimental data to suggest that those who put a lot of effort into coping without the financial resources necessary to achieve a successful outcome may be at greater risk of stress-induced cardiovascular disease.

Review of stress and coping theory

The transactional theory of stress is the most widely accepted theory of stress and coping, though it continues to attract critical comment, including some from the originators themselves:

> The transactional model of stress focuses exclusively on processes within the individual, ignoring the fact that much stress arises within families or communities. Social influences or needs can constrain or conflict with an individual's appraisal or coping strategy. On the other hand, a shared or group strategy for dealing with a problem may be more effective than an individual one.
>
> (Folkman 2009)

The transactional model initially gave little consideration to the nature of the stressor. However, the controllability of the event or situation, and congruence between stressor and coping strategy, is now considered to be an important determinant of the outcome (Folkman and Moskovitz 2004).

Research has confirmed that social support should be treated as a separate dimension of coping (Chesney *et al.* 2006). There is also evidence for further distinctions to be made between the positive effects of informational support and emotional support, and the negative effects of practical help when it involves too much reliance on others.

Some emotion-focused coping strategies, such as smoking, help to relieve anxiety but pose significant risks to long-term physical health. In this case, psychological needs conflict with health needs to determine coping responses and health outcomes.

Health risks associated with stress

Research from psychoneuroimmunology has shown that both acute and chronic stress compromise health and increase the risks caused by disease (Dünser and Hasibeder 2009). Stress can cause chronic illness, trigger an acute episode of illness, exacerbate existing symptoms, or delay recovery, including wound healing. Diseases caused or exacerbated by stress-induced physiological changes can potentially affect every body system. Stress-related influences on the immune system are of particular importance in determining health outcomes (Kiecolt-Glaser *et al.* 2002). They include:

- physiological changes in the endocrine system, including the release of pituitary and adrenal hormones, which affect the immune system in multiple ways;
- the effects of stress-related behaviours, including tobacco, alcohol and drug use, poor nutrition and insufficient exercise;
- disruption of sleep pattern;
- anxiety and depression, which appear to be directly related to changes in immune response.

We have illustrated these associations in Figure 7.3.

Those most at risk (Kiecolt-Glaser *et al.* 2002) and in need of care to reduce stress include:

- babies whose immune function is yet to be fully developed;
- people with immune deficiency or other diseases where the immune system is already compromised;
- older people whose immune function has declined naturally with age;
- critically ill patients;
- those who are malnourished.

In the next sections, we examine two key factors, control and support, that influence stress appraisals, coping responses and outcomes.

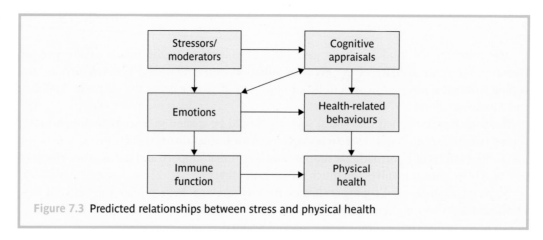

Figure 7.3 Predicted relationships between stress and physical health

Controllability

Controllability refers to the extent to which it is humanly possible to determine or influence the outcome of an event or situation. The ability to gain or maintain control depends on the following:

- The desired outcome must be realistic and achievable. If not, it is important to modify or change it, rather than persevere in trying to achieve the impossible.
- The resources essential to achieve the desired outcome (e.g. knowledge, skills, money) must be available.

Not all situations are controllable although most have some aspects that are amenable to control, depending on the individual's willingness to compromise or shift their desired goals (see Chapter 3 on adult development). Therapeutic interventions are often targeted at helping people to develop alternative means of achieving desired goals, or change their goals.

Promoting control

When Ted went to live with Janice and Mark, he had nothing to do and became quite depressed. His real love had been growing vegetables but he could no longer do heavy gardening, so they bought him a greenhouse where he could sit and grow tomatoes and strawberries. This gave him back a sense of control over his life and something to aim for.

Example

An uncontrollable situation refers to one where the individual is, in reality, unable to influence the outcome. In these situations, problem-focused coping strategies are of little use and may actually increase stress as a result of failure to achieve a satisfactory or desired outcome. Thus, Park *et al.* (2001) suggested that emotion-focused coping strategies may be adaptive for people who have a life-limiting illness. But even in these situations, it is usually possible to focus on small achievable goals, such as recording one's life story.

Coping with a chronic illness

Sanders-Dewey *et al.* (2001) examined the use of coping strategies in individuals with Parkinson's disease and their caregivers. They found that emotion-focused coping, such as avoidance strategies, were associated with increased psychological distress for both patients and caregivers, possibly because they inhibited communication.

Interestingly, they found that the use of problem-focused coping by the patient was associated with a higher level of distress in the caregiver. This may be because attempts by patients to manage their own condition conflicted with caregivers' instincts to care and protect.

Research

The caregivers of older people with dementia have been shown to be at high risk of stress-related health problems due to changes in immune function (Gouin *et al.* 2008). There are many reasons why caregiving in this situation is so stressful. These include the need to respond to constant need demands, the unpredictability and uncontrollability of the dementia sufferer's behaviour, difficulties in obtaining necessary support from caring services, and social isolation. This all gives rise to mixed feelings of anxiety, fear, guilt, shame, anger, loneliness and depression which are similar to the effects of bereavement loss (see Chapter 8). Many caregivers are themselves approaching old age, so these stressors arise at a time when immune function is already somewhat compromised, meaning that they are particularly at risk of stress-related illness.

Exercise

It is always helpful to know what patients or clients and their relatives find stressful, since it can often be easily rectified.

- Negotiate time (at least half an hour) to spend talking to a patient or client, or to the person most closely involved in caring for them.
- Ask them to tell you what they find most stressful about their present situation.

What have you learned? Might you be able to suggest or initiate an action that would reduce their stress?

Perceived control and mental well-being

Positive emotions are generally associated with working towards the achievement of desired goals or having successfully addressed a challenge. The experience of gaining personal mastery over new or difficult situations leads to increased self-confidence and self-esteem. For a long time psychologists have recognized personal mastery as an important source of personal satisfaction, motivation and positive mental well-being (Walker 2001). In fact, there is good evidence that our cognitive processes normally have a positive bias towards perceptions of control and optimism. Perhaps this helps to explain why most of us feel fairly positive most of the time, even when faced with adversity.

Perceived uncontrollability leads to learned helplessness (Chapter 5), which is an important cause of stress-related mental and physical illness. It has cognitive and behavioural dimensions, which may be interpreted as:

- perceived uncertainty: 'I don't understand what is happening';
- perceived unpredictability: 'I don't know what is going to happen';
- perceived uncontrollability: 'I don't know what can be done' or 'there is nothing that can be done'.

Because humans are social beings, there are two sources available to achieve desired outcomes or goals: personal action or help from others. Figure 7.4 illustrates the interaction between perceived control, perceived support and cognitive/emotional state.

The following scenario illustrates the relationship between perceived control, perceived support and emotional outcomes, and analyses what happens when someone develops a persistent symptom or illness, in this case headache.

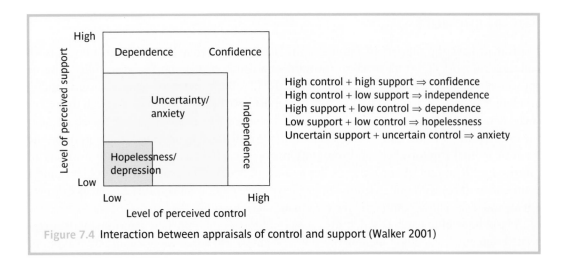

Figure 7.4 Interaction between appraisals of control and support (Walker 2001)

Situational analysis based on control/support

Janice has developed frequent severe headaches. With reference to Figure 7.4, the following analysis illustrates the relationship between Janice's control beliefs and her emotional response, given different levels of personal control (self-management) and/or social support in the form of medical help.

- *High control, low support.* Janice successfully treats the headaches without help using a combination of tablets and meditation. This strengthens her sense of self-efficacy and internal locus of control with respect to headache pain.
- *Low control, high support.* Janice cannot relieve it herself, so she seeks advice from an osteopath who treats it successfully with neck manipulation. She has no personal control over the pain, but is confident that she can depend on him to relieve it if it happens again. This reinforces external (powerful other) locus of control.
- *High control, high support.* As well as treating the headache, the osteopath gives Janice exercises to deal with future episodes. Janice now has confidence in her own actions (internal control) and the assurance of help (external powerful other control), should that ever fail.
- *Uncertain control, uncertain support.* The headaches recur unpredictably and often fail to respond to medication or painkillers. Janice feels helpless and very anxious. This is typical of patients waiting for treatment and strengthens external (chance) locus of control.
- *Low control, low support.* If nothing Janice or anyone else does can relieve her headaches, she is left feeling hopeless and depressed.

Example

Survey data collected by Ross and Mirowsky (1989) confirm that perceived control and perceived support complement each other as determinants of mental and physical well-being.

Social support

Most of us have the support of families and friends in everyday life. We gain support from colleagues at work and from social organizations to which we belong. The availability of some sources of support have declined over recent decades with increased geographical mobility and family fragmentation. But new forms of support have become available through the use of social networking. All of these forms of support are referred to as social capital. Social capital is the total resources, actual and virtual, available to the individual to provide social support in the form of mutual comfort, help and recognition. Social capital has been linked to a variety of positive health and social outcomes (Adler and Kwon 2002). When faced with problems, most people share these with others from whom they receive emotional comfort as well as practical advice and help. This is commonly referred to as 'social support'.

A large body of research has identified social support as an important determinant of stress-related outcomes, including mental and physical illness. However, there are different types of social support; some have positive effects on health, while others can have negative effects:

- *Informational support* refers to the giving or receiving of information or advice that supports problem-focused coping and has been shown to have a positive effect on health outcomes. Examples include the advice given by a grandmother to a new mother about child care, or the information sheet given to a patient.

- *Emotional support* refers to interaction that leads individuals to feel cared for, loved and valued. Emotional support provides reassurance and encouragement. It facilitates the individual's sense of self-confidence and self-esteem and is associated with positive health. It is often associated with having secure attachment relationships (see Chapter 3).

- *Instrumental support* refers to the giving of practical help to deal with problems, including financial support. It is essential at the beginning and often the end of the lifespan, or where people are unable to look after themselves. It is beneficial so long as the help provided is essential and does not take over from tasks the individual could and should do for themselves. Practical help beyond this leads to dependence (see section on chronic pain in Chapter 10).

- *Social affiliation* refers to a sense of belonging. It usually involves a system of mutual obligations and reciprocal informational, emotional and instrumental social support. Family, friendship networks, communities and organizations such as church and self-help groups all help to provide this.

Social vulnerability and stress

Janssen *et al.* (2002) reviewed studies of stress, coping and attachment in people with an intellectual disability (*sic*). They reported evidence that intellectually disabled people were more vulnerable to stress and use less effective coping strategies. Studies of attachment indicate that people with intellectual disability are at risk of developing insecure or disorganized attachment. This may put them at risk for developing challenging behaviours, particularly when faced with stressful situations or life change.

Research

Social support and health outcomes

Sephton *et al.* (2001) reported growing evidence of links between social support, stress, emotional state, endocrine and immune function. Social support, particularly emotional support (Uchino 2006), has been shown to moderate the relationship between stressors and immune function. This explains why bereavement may be associated with physical illness. The loss of a loved one not only has a direct emotional effect on the immune system, but can deprive the individual of the person who previously provided the emotional support they now urgently need. A wide range of face-to-face and online support groups offer information and support, tailored to meet the needs of a particular group of people.

Support groups, stress reduction and health

Andersen *et al.* (2004) set up a clinical trial to see if a support group for women following surgery for breast cancer had any impact on their health and well-being. In total, 227 women attended one session a week for four months, completing questionnaires and giving blood samples before and after. Compared to a control group who received the usual care, they showed significant improvements in perceived social support, less anxiety, better dietary habits, smoking reduction and stable or increased T-cell activity (that promotes immune response), compared to the control group.

Emotional support is essential for children in early life, which is why Bowlby (1969) identified attachment relationships as important (Chapter 3). Secure attachments have been shown to act as a buffer against stress (Fox and Card 1999). In addition, these early relationships may provide a template for future relationships. The lack of secure attachments reduces close social affiliations and networks in the long term, leaving people more vulnerable to mental and physical stress-related illnesses throughout their lives.

Positive and negative aspects of social support

Early research into social support tried to measure availability in terms of the number of close contacts. This proved to be of little value in understanding the relationship of social support to stress-related illness since the size of a social network does not indicate its quality. However, there are benefits from having a close social network. Hobfoll (1988) suggested that it provides people who will recognize when the individual is under stress or ill, and persuade them to consult a doctor, take a holiday or other appropriate form of coping action. He proposed that effort put into maintaining a social network acts as a kind of insurance policy in case help is needed in the future.

On the other hand a person's social network can provide a source of peer group pressure to engage in unhealthy lifestyles or come into contact with possible disease-causing factors, for example illegal drug use, excessive alcohol intake and sexually transmitted diseases. Relationships that involve conflict or seek to undermine the individual can have harmful effects on physical and mental health. The development of online social networking provides many benefits, but can lead to the avoidance of real life relationships and social support. It may also be a source of bullying and alienation.

There are some surprising negative effects from well-intentioned supportive actions. Ross and Mirowsky (1989) identified from survey data that, contrary to their predictions, the more people used talking to others as a strategy for coping with stressful situations, the more depressed they tended to be. The cause and effect relationship is unclear, but these findings may suggest that when talking involves grumbling or aims to elicit sympathy (gripe sessions), rather than problem-solving, it is not beneficial. Similarly, too much instrumental support (practical help) creates passive dependence, which can lead to negative health outcomes (we give an example of this in Chapter 10). Overall, support groups and social networks work well if they encourage and facilitate personal control, but not if they encourage people to focus on the awfulness of their situations.

The spiritual dimension of support

Spiritual support can offer a lifeline for those who feel helpless or hopeless including:

- those unable to find meaning or purpose in their lives;
- those who lack an established network of social support;
- those faced with a life crisis.

Spiritual or religious beliefs have been shown to be associated with increased psychological well-being and better health (Koenig and Cohen 2002). Having a spiritual faith provides existential meaning and coherence (Levin 2003; see also Chapters 2 and 3). Religious activities, such as praying or reading religious texts, provide active, effortful coping strategies. Attendance at religious meetings provides access to a supportive social network that provides reassurance and help in times of need.

Spiritual support and immune function

Sephton *et al.* (2001) studied the impact of spiritual belief on immune function in women with stage IV metastatic (advanced) breast carcinoma. They found that higher expression of spiritual belief was associated with higher levels of cells that promote immune response, including white blood cells, lymphocyte count, helper T-cells, cytotoxic T-cells and NK (natural killer) cells. Attendance at religious meetings was associated with higher lymphocyte count and immunity against infection.

There is, however, potential for psychological harm in those who expect protection in exchange for religious activity or affiliation. People are sometimes heard to say 'What have I done to deserve this?' or 'Why is God punishing me?'. People faced with these conflicting beliefs need special help to deal with them. In recognition of its importance, guidance on providing spiritual care is available online from the NHS Wales (2010).

Other moderators of appraisal and coping

Demographic influences

Demographic factors, including age, gender, education and socio-economic status, affect the type and availability of coping resources. Those who lack knowledge, skills, support networks or money are clearly disadvantaged when appraising and coping with many of life's demands.

- *Age.* As people grow older, they have a wider range of cognitive strategies they can draw on to compensate for declining physical strength. Younger people often perceive less danger while some actively seek out the challenge of dangerous activities, particularly in response to peer group pressure, thereby exposing themselves to increased health risks.
- *Gender.* Men and women are often exposed to different types of challenge or danger during their lifetimes, acquire different skills, and demonstrate different ways of coping, and may therefore respond differently. For example, it appears that women are more likely than men to seek and provide social support (Matthews *et al.* 1999).
- *Education.* People of different levels of educational attainment and job experience are likely to vary in the knowledge and skills they bring to different types of situation.
- *Socio-economic status (SES).* People with very limited resources and those who experience social exclusion are among those least likely to be able to cope successfully with the demands and challenges of life. Those who can afford to pay for goods and services when they need them are clearly advantaged over those who cannot.

Poverty, social exclusion and stress

Krueger and Chang (2008) analysed American health survey data to identify demographic influences on mortality. Their results support the social vulnerability hypothesis that individuals in the lowest socio-economic groups are disadvantaged by the combination of high-risk health behaviours, such as smoking and drinking, and high levels of perceived stress, largely because they have fewer resources to maintain their health or cope effectively with stress.

Research

Coping style

It has long been recognized that many diseases associated with stress, including heart disease, are influenced by family history. Genetic susceptibility is likely to be an important factor (Marsland *et al.* 2002). However, some of this influence may be accounted for by maladaptive family patterns of coping behaviour passed on during childhood.

Psychologists are naturally interested to identify stable dispositional factors or coping styles that account for why some people are more vulnerable to stress-related illness than others. There is little evidence that general measures of personality predict stress-related health outcomes. Past interest focused on the identification of Type A behaviour pattern (coronary-prone personality) and Type C behaviour pattern (cancer-prone personality). More recent interest has focused on Type D (distressed) personality (Mols and Denollet 2010), although this appears, in large part, to measure depression. Current interest focuses on other factors related to stress vulnerability and resilience (for more on this, see Chapter 8), including the following:

- *Hardiness* (Kobasa 1979) consists of three dimensions of resilience: *Commitment* (active involvement in life activities), *Control* (belief in autonomy and the ability to influence life events) and *Challenge* (belief that change is normal and growth-enhancing). This concept continues to attract positive results, for example, Garossa *et al.* (2010) reported that it was one of a number of factors associated with a lower risk of burnout in nurses.

- *Optimism and pessimism.* A number of studies have indicated that optimists have better psychological adjustment and immune responses (Rasmussen *et al.* 2009), possibly because they have more effective coping strategies and more supportive social networks (Brissette *et al.* 2002). In Chapter 8 on emotions we review some of the steps that individuals can take to maximize their resilience, including 'learned optimism' and doing all that is possible to increase well-being in daily life.

- *Hostility and anger.* General cynicism and interpersonal mistrust is robustly associated with depression (Nabi *et al.* 2010). Chida and Steptoe (2009) reviewed evidence that anger and hostility exert harmful effects on coronary heart disease (CHD) outcomes in healthy populations and those with CHD, particularly men.

- *Sense of coherence.* Antonovsky (1985) was concerned with how to create, enhance and improve health (salutogenesis) and identified sense of coherence (seeing the world as rational, predictable, controllable and meaningful) as a key source of resilience. A systematic review by Eriksson and Lindstrom (2006) confirmed that sense of coherence is strongly predictive of mental and physical health, in conjunction with other moderators, such as age, social support, and education.

It is clear from all the research that dispositional vulnerability and resilience factors play a modest role in determining outcomes and must be viewed in the context of the nature of the demands and the supports available. In Table 7.3, we list moderators that need to be taken into account when attempting to predict stress-related outcomes.

Table 7.3 Moderators of stress-related outcomes

Moderator	Influencing factors
Task demands	Controllability
Social capital	Availability of social support/support networks and resources
Demographic	Age (experience), gender, education, socio-economic status, poverty, deprivation
Health risk behaviours	Smoking, drinking, eating an unhealthy diet
Personal vulnerability	Type D: Negative affectivity + social inhibition Hostility
Personal resilience	Hardy personality (commitment, control, challenge) Optimism Sense of coherence

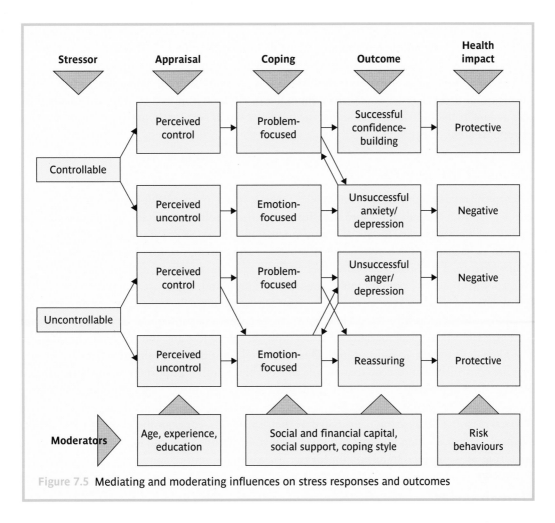

Figure 7.5 Mediating and moderating influences on stress responses and outcomes

In Figure 7.5, we have illustrated how mediating and moderating variables exert influence at each stage of the stress process.

Stress in specific contexts

In this section, we examine the practical implications of stress theory and research in specific contexts.

Illness and hospitalization

When people are ill or in hospital, they are often experiencing stress at a time when their immune systems are already compromised or under strain. It is therefore particularly important to reduce uncertainty and unpredictability and help them to find ways to enhance personal control. Emotional support and patient education are essential parts of this.

Health and social care professionals can do much to reduce stress for patients and clients, including keeping them adequately informed, assessing their needs and negotiating realistic goals, identifying appropriate coping resources, providing appropriate advice and offering suitable referrals for support, as necessary. The first aim of stress management should be to help the individual assess the number, nature and controllability of the stressors they face, help them to prioritize realistic goals and encourage effective ways of coping to achieve those goals.

Listening to people's problems is important, but does not imply an obligation to solve their problems for them. The act of offering a sympathetic ear is an important part of the caring process. Asking if the individual would like further help and, if so, identifying appropriate sources of support are the next steps.

Stressful life events

In Chapter 3 on development, we mentioned the need to adapt to stressful life events. Some life events are clearly more difficult and more stressful than others. Holmes and Rahe (1967) developed a measure of life events called the Social Readjustment Rating Scale (SRRS). It consisted of 43 common positive and negative life-changing events, ranked in order of importance. Marriage was given an arbitrary score of 50. Loss of a spouse was presumed to be most stressful and was given a score of 100. The SRRS proved a popular tool because it was simple and easy to use. But it is now seriously out of date and fails to take account of the many cultural changes that affect perceptions of stress.

Some evidence has supported a link between life events and subsequent illness, but generally the correlation (statistical measure of association) has been low and the results disappointing. The SRRS fails to take account of individual appraisals, nor does it distinguish between events that are controllable and those that are uncontrollable. Another important factor is that many stress-related illnesses are caused by maladaptive coping responses, such as smoking, drinking excess alcohol or comfort eating. Life events can never predict an individual's emotional or physical response because this is mediated by their appraisals. For example, events such as death, sickness or job loss often involve both loss of control over one's life and loss of emotional support from those we used to rely on for love or friendship.

Daily hassles

People who have had relatively little exposure to major life events may nevertheless experience stress. 'Daily hassles' refers to the accumulation of minor annoying things like missing the bus, being late for work or spilling the coffee. A considerable volume of research suggests that daily hassles are indeed associated with depression.

People who are disadvantaged through poverty, illness or disability are likely to experience a much greater number of what Hewison (1997) observed to be cumulative hassles and recurrent crises. These include negotiating with benefits agencies and hospital systems while attempting to deal with financial and various other losses and relationship problems (Walker *et al.* 1999).

Hassles in care situations

Exercise

Try to find out about the sorts of hassles that people experience in care settings. Ask patients or clients what they find most troublesome about the environment. Are there some minor hassles, such as noise at night, that can easily be reduced or eliminated to diminish levels of stress?

Traumatic events and post-traumatic stress disorder (PTSD)

In the context of stress, PTSD may be seen as a response to a single catastrophic uncontrollable event, which is associated with high uncertainty and unpredictability and therefore high physiological arousal and anxiety. We refer you to Chapter 8, where we review PTSD and its management in some detail.

Stress in the workplace

Much of our life is spent at work and the working environment has proved an interesting source of research into stress and stress-related illness. It used to be thought that stress was a result of work pressure and was therefore associated with the high-flying executive or senior management. But findings from the Whitehall studies of all grades of civil servants indicate that in fact those in the lower grades are more susceptible to work-based stress (Ferri *et al.* 2004).

Two models of explanation for work-based stress have been tested as part of the Whitehall studies:

- '*Demand–control–support*' refers to the influence on stress of three key moderating variables: the level of demand associated with the job task, the degree of autonomy or control the individual worker has to do the job, and the level of support available when needed.
- '*Effort–reward imbalance*' is an important determinant of job satisfaction. It reflects the extent to which people feel they get the remuneration and recognition they deserve for the job they do.

Findings show that effort–reward imbalance and low job control are related to the incidence of coronary heart disease (Marmot *et al.* 1999). Family life, social support and leisure activities are important buffers against the effects of work-related stress.

Example of job-related stress

A few years ago, Mark was working as a regional sales representative for a firm selling office supplies, working from home. But he had become increasingly anxious and depressed and was eventually signed off sick with 'depression'. He received help from a counsellor. A brief initial analysis revealed that his stress was probably job-related. His pay depended on sales and he invested a high level of effort for relatively little return. He felt he had little control over the management of his work schedule and was swamped with paperwork. He had no colleague or supervisor support since the office base was 50 miles away. High effort and low reward, plus high demand, low job control and low job support equals high stress. Mark resigned from the job and his depression lifted almost immediately. When he obtained a more autonomous job, working as a groundsman, the rewards were less, but so were the demands and Mark felt well supported within a team of others.

The caring services are subject to financial constraints and targets that expose employees at all levels to high levels of demand. In these situations, those who are dealing with private stress may be particularly vulnerable to 'burnout'. Professional caring requires what has been defined as 'emotional labour' (Smith 1992). Emotional labour may be defined as the self-regulation of emotional feelings and behaviours that make other people feel cared for and comfortable. Emotional labour involves demands that are additional to the physical tasks of caring. Burnout may reflect the withdrawal of emotional labour as a way of coping with a high level of workload and job demands, particularly where care staff are inadequately supported by colleagues and managers.

Identifying burnout

This is really for those who have been working in the caring sector for some time. Use the following chart to test your own risk of burnout. Tick each of the following (high or low):

Predictors of work-related stress	High	Low
Workload		
Emotional job demands		
Control over own work practice		
Management and colleague support		
Effort put into work		
Rewards from the work		
Overall job satisfaction		

 Suppose you face a high level of work-related demands, including emotional demands, and put in a high level of effort to address these:

- If you have little work-related control, a low level of support and feel poorly rewarded or acknowledged for the effort you put in, you are most likely to experience work-related stress or burnout.
- If you have a high level of autonomy, good support from management, good relationships with colleagues and receive what you consider to be a reasonable level of reward and acknowledgement for the work you do, you are very unlikely to be suffering from work-related stress or burnout.

Where would you place yourself in terms of risk of burnout?
Do you recognize burnout in any of your friends or colleagues?

The prevention and management of stress

In terms of stress reduction, prevention is better than cure. Those working in the public services can do much to reduce the stress levels of clients by informing them about what is happening, what to expect and what is likely to be expected of them.

People who are personally or socially vulnerable are likely to be more susceptible to stress. It is often therapeutic just to have someone who is willing to take an interest and listen to their concerns. The type of help and support needed depends on the main problem, whether it be making a difficult decision, facing up to a serious illness, dealing with a relationship breakdown, coping with bereavement or managing a financial crisis. Care workers should not attempt to involve themselves in issues that are beyond their knowledge or competence. Appropriate recommendations might involve anything from referral to a counsellor or chaplain to advising the individual to contact a benefits or debt adviser.

The workplace is a common source of stress. In this context, treating individuals for their symptoms of stress reflects an inadequate management response. A systematic review of work-based stress (Lamontagne *et al.* 2007) confirmed that the primary concern should be to prevent potential stressors at their source by focusing on the organization of work and work conditions. For example, participative management strategies are needed to focus on improving employee autonomy and support through job redesign and workload management and improved communication and conflict resolution. Based on findings from the Whitehall studies, Stansfield (1999) observed that since social support plays such an important role in preventing physical and psychological morbidity, interventions to improve social cohesion at work are of real value (we refer to building resilience through social connectedness in Chapter 8 on emotions).

Individuals should also take responsibility for protecting their own well-being at study and at work (see Palmer *et al.* 2003) by the following:

- develop the skills of prioritizing
- improve time management
- seek help and support when necessary
- be assertive in standing up for one's needs where necessary.

Personal counselling may help individuals to review their goals and consider ways to achieve them. For those with more severe anxiety or depression, cognitive behaviour therapy (CBT) uses psychological principles to improve the ability of the individual to be able to confront and deal successfully with life stresses (see Chapter 8 for more details about CBT). In Chapter 10, we illustrate how psychological principles can be used to improve ways of coping for someone with chronic pain and disability.

Further reading

Brosen, L. and Todd, G. (2009) *Overcoming Stress: A Self-help Guide Using Cognitive Behavioral Techniques*. London: Constable and Robinson

Mirowsky, J. and Ross, C.E. (2003) *Social Causes of Psychological Distress*, 2nd edition. New York: Aldine de Gruyter.

Palmer, S., Cooper, C.L. and Thomas, K. (2003) *Creating a Balance: Managing Stress*. London: British Library Publishing.

The second two remain in print and are not out of date.

Chapter 8

Emotional well-being

Key topics

- Promoting emotional resilience
- Explaining anxiety and depression
- Cognitive behavioural and mindfulness therapies
- Loss, grief and bereavement

Introduction

In this chapter we give further consideration to the causes and the consequences of positive and negative emotions in everyday life and in caring situations. In particular, we focus on answers to the following question:

- What can be done to maximize emotional well-being and increase the resilience that we all have when faced with difficult life events?

This question is relevant in our private lives and our working lives, and is particularly relevant for patients or clients who are faced with difficult or challenging situations. The chapter addresses two themes: first, the promotion of emotional well-being and resilience; second we focus on ways of helping those who experience emotional distress.

We start by introducing a vignette that contrasts two responses to the same situation.

Anna visited a stroke unit, where she met two patients, Les and Fred, both of whom had a stroke at about the same time. For Les and Fred, the physical event of the stroke had been very similar; at the outset, the two of them had a similar loss of physical function. But Les and Fred were now in very different situations. Les was regaining his abilities more rapidly than Fred. Les was keen to talk about his rehabilitation programme and what he was doing to get well again. He appeared to be reasonably happy in spite of having had the stroke. In contrast, Fred's conversation was focused on what he had lost because of his stroke; he was very low in mood and did not appear interested in rehabilitation.

Vignette

In the vignette, Les and Fred exhibit very different responses to the same difficult situation. In Chapter 7, we addressed the way people respond to negative live events in terms of stress and coping. In this chapter, we focus on the inner resources people have to deal with these types of situation as they arise. We start by examining in more detail what we mean when we talk about an emotion.

The nature of emotions

An emotion reflects a state of being that involves each of the following elements:

- *An experience*: an event or situation that impinges on us. In the case of Les and Fred, a whole range of new experiences have impinged on them as a result of their stroke.
- *Physiological responses* mediated in the short term by the autonomic nervous system and in the longer term by the endocrine system (for more details, see Chapter 7).
- *Cognitive appraisal*: the individual's interpretation of these events (see theoretical explanation in Chapter 7). Differences in individual appraisals help to explain why Les and Fred have responded so differently to their stroke.
- *Behavioural responses*. immediate responses, such as withdraw, remove or reduce the sense of threat, are involuntary (see the fight or flight response in Chapter 7). Subsequent responses, such as crying, result from cognitive appraisals of the situation.
- *Affect*: feelings, mood.

These responses all come together under the heading of 'emotional response'.

Les and Fred

It is evident that Les and Fred responded very differently to stroke.

- Les has a positive outlook and positive affect and is striving to overcome his difficulties. We would describe Les's response 'resilient'.
- Fred has a negative outlook and negative affect and is making little attempt to get well. Evidence discussed in Chapter 7 suggests that he may, as a result, have little resilience against stress-related illnesses such as infection or even further stroke.

Using the example in the vignette, Les is doing well, but why? The possible explanations include the following:

- Les is happier because he is doing well.
- Les is doing well because he is happier.
- Les's positive emotions encourage good progress, and his good progress encourages positive emotions. This is the virtuous cycle hypothesis.
- Because Les is a happier person, he has attracted a network of supportive friends who encourage his recovery.

The reverse might be true for Fred, for whom there is likely to be a 'vicious cycle' or downward spiral of negative emotions and poor progress. We recognize that positive and negative emotions are not mutually exclusive – it is possible to be happy and sad at the same time. We often remark that we don't know whether to laugh or cry in certain situations and it is very unlikely that Les would not have experienced this during his recovery from his stroke. What is important is to find ways to promote positive emotions and limit negative ones.

As we illustrated in Figure 7.3, emotions reflect the individual's cognitive state of well-being, but also play a causal role in maintaining their well-being. From an evolutionary perspective, emotional processes serve an adaptive function. For example, feelings of fear signal that a situation is threatening and needs immediate attention. On the other hand, the curiosity and vitality associated with positive emotions drive new initiatives and help people adapt and change when faced with new circumstances and challenging situations. Positive emotions enhance immune function, which leads to better physical health and faster recovery from illness. People who exhibit a positive outlook and positive emotions find it easier to attract and maintain a strong network of social support. This gives them more 'social capital' to draw on when things to wrong. The implication is that fostering positive emotions has an important role to play in the promotion of good mental health (Kobau *et al.* 2011).

Resilience

People in need of health or social care are often experiencing very difficult situations and many will experience negative emotions, including fear, anxiety, anger and depression. There are many people, such as Les, who respond well to serious adverse events in their lives. These are people who bounce back positively from setbacks and traumatic events and are thus described as having 'resilience'. Resilience is a quality that is not only important for patients; it is also important for staff who work in challenging care environments (Jackson *et al.* 2007; McAllister and McKinnon 2009) and who may be at risk of burnout (see Chapter 7). Attention to concepts such as resilience has shifted some of the focus of psychology away from what 'goes wrong' for people towards research designed to understand what is 'right' with people. What is termed 'positive psychology' seeks to find ways of building on people's strengths and enhancing their positive emotions.

People who have a positive outlook on life are usually described as optimists. Optimists generally do better in life; they are more confident, more likely to use problem-solving coping strategies (see Chapter 7) and more persistent in the face of difficulties. The advantages of optimism led Carver *et al.* (2010: 886) to suggest: 'The key would appear to be to train oneself to think in the ways optimists think and act in the ways optimists act.' This involves focusing on what can be achieved, rather than what can't be achieved (see Chapter 10 on living with chronic pain), and what positive outcomes might arise from the present situation. Because optimists have positive expectations when faced with difficulties, they have a greater sense of well-being and are less likely to experience negative emotions, such as anxiety and guilt.

Ways to well-being

In Chapter 3, we highlighted the reciprocal virtuous or vicious cycle that can occur after birth between the baby's expressiveness and the mother's response. A baby that cries a lot upsets the mother, whereas a baby who smiles a lot calms and delights the mother. Similarly, a baby whose mother is calm and happy tends to be more contented, whereas the baby whose mother is anxious or suffering from postnatal depression is likely to pick up these feelings. Thus, as we noted in relation to the nature/nurture debate, an individual's capacity for positive and negative emotions is partially determined by genetics but is transformed by life experiences. In Chapter 3, we also focused on early influences likely to build resilience in the growing child, including the formation of secure attachment relationships and authoritative parenting. Vulnerability to negative emotions can start early in life in those exposed to a depressed mother, poor parenting or childhood abuse. However, the plasticity or flexibility of human emotional growth and development provides opportunities for change. Therefore, the aim of positive psychology is to promote mental health for everyone by increasing emotional resilience.

Against this background, Frederickson (2001: 224) has put forward a 'broaden-and-build' theory that positive emotions serve as 'vehicles for individual growth and social connection'. A useful framework for achieving this is a government-supported initiative entitled 'five ways to well-being' which mirrors the 'five portions of fruit and vegetables a day' that became a cornerstone for physical health promotion. The five ways to well-being (Aked and Thompson 2011) are:

- be active;
- keep learning;
- give – be kind, help others;
- take notice – be mindful of what is going around you;
- connect with others – build a strong social network.

We consider each aspect in turn.

- *Be active.* There is now a body of evidence that physical activity is associated with good mental and physical health. Even small amounts of exercise can improve a person's mood and regular exercise is associated with better mental health and recovery from mental disorder.

- *Keep learning.* Engaging in learning has much to offer in terms of enhancing well-being (Feinstein and Hammond 2004). It exposes people to new ideas and activities and involves forward looking. It also provides a sense of mastery and competence and provides opportunities to connect with other learners. It is noticeable that those in the workplace who take an active and reflective interest in what they do are usually the most positive. McAllister and McKinnon (2009) recommend reflection on practice with a clinical supervisor as an important resource for resilience for people working in the caring services.

- *Give.* Seligman (2003) gave students two tasks: to do something pleasurable, and to do something to help others. The findings showed that helping others had a longer lasting impact on well-being and, for some, engagement in the helping task was a life-changing experience. It seems that engaging in random acts of kindness increase our happiness (Lyubomirsky *et al.* 2005). Seligman told of a ward orderly who made his rather dull work fulfilling by brightening up the environment for his patients.

- *Take notice.* A lot of the time, we are so preoccupied with what has happened to us, or what is likely to happen next, that we fail to appreciate the immediate simple pleasures afforded by the sensations of sight, sound, taste and touch. 'Taking notice' can be the appreciation of the place we are in, the company of a friend, or it can be a conscious effort to be grateful for the good things in our lives. We address this in more detail under the heading of 'mindfulness'.

- *Connect with others.* In Chapter 7, we refer to what is termed 'social capital', which relates to having a network of supportive resources. In particular, we identified that the availability of emotional support is associated with positive emotions and protection against the negative consequences of stress. Therefore, the building and maintaining of friendships should be regarded as a good investment.

These days, many older people live a long way from family and become increasingly isolated as friends die. Poor physical or mental health can make the maintenance of relationships even more difficult and can leave individuals and their carers feeling isolated. In these circumstances, support groups can play a vital role in reducing isolation, gaining friends and having fun.

During her community placement, Anna visited Ray, aged 90, who had been housebound with multiple health problems for many years. He was a pleasure to visit because he always looked on the bright side and had retained a wicked sense of humour. He and Doris, his wife of nearly 40 years, were completely devoted to each other. But Doris, in her mid-seventies, had little opportunity to connect with others, as family and neighbours had moved away and friends had died.

Lisa told Anna about a new local carer's group, so Anna introduced Doris to it. Their regular meetings gave Doris a new lease of life and lots to talk about with Ray. When Ray died, Doris found herself supported by her new friends and with lots of new interests to look forward to.

Example

At a personal level, it is tempting to neglect family and friends when we are busy, and avoid meeting up with friends when we are in a close relationship with one person. But in terms of self-care it is essential to take time to build a supportive social network. Young people increasingly rely on online social networking to connect with others and, as with all forms of social connection, others will be very wary of people who fail to adhere to rules of social etiquette. So it would seem that there are certain aspects of resilience that need to be learned.

Building resilience

The following recommendations are based on the 'The Comprehensive Soldier Fitness Program', which was designed for the US army to build the resilience of servicemen and their families.

Nine personal resources that foster social resilience (adapted from Cacioppo *et al.* (2011)

1 Perceive others accurately and empathetically and

2 communicate care and respect to others.

As we noted in Chapter 6, misreading social cues and responding inappropriately upsets others and can drive them away.

3 Feeling a connection with other individuals as part of a social group.

Having common interests is a good way to establish a relationship.

4 Not over-estimating one's social worth.

People who brag about themselves are often unpopular. Conservatively estimating one's worth has a self-protective function.

5 Have concern for the needs and welfare of others.

6 Respond appropriately and collaboratively to collective tasks or demands.

Have a look at the effect of different leadership styles in Chapter 6

7 Express social emotions, such as gratitude, respect or a plea for help, appropriately and effectively.

8 Trust others to act fairly and appropriately.

9 Be tolerant and open to diverse people, experiences and views.

A well-being audit for yourself

Consider the 'five ways to well-being' (be active, keep learning, give, take notice and connect with others) in relation to your own life:

- What have you done in the last month that relates to each of the 'five ways'?
- Which of the 'five ways' could you increase or change, so as to increase your own well-being?
- What are the barriers to increasing your use of the five ways? How might you overcome these?

Beware of the thought that 'this is not a good time' – it is very easy to make a habit of putting things off and this does not promote well-being.

Exercise

▶ **A well-being audit for others**

Think of someone you encountered recently who is ill or disabled and seemed to have predominantly negative moods.

- Applying the five ways, can you identify obvious deficits in their lives?
- Do illness and disability necessarily act as barriers to the 'five ways' and with what consequences?
- What might be done to facilitate activity related to the 'five ways' for them and for other patients or clients?

When considering the last point, try to think how this could be achieved with as little staff involvement as possible.

While we have a duty to ourselves and others to promote resilience, it takes time, thought and effort to achieve.

Mindfulness

The importance of taking notice in the present, of having immediate awareness, has long been part of the Buddhist tradition of what is termed 'mindfulness'. Mindfulness was introduced into western psychology by Kabat-Zinn *et al.* (1983) as a method of pain management and has now become an important tool within psychology for stress management. A good way to understand how it works is to think back to the coffee or tea breaks you take at work. You probably spent most of the time thinking about what had already happened and what was going to happen next in your work. If so, the break is not really a break at all – in a sense you were 'absent' from your own tea break. Mindfulness enriches our experience of these ordinary events so that a tea or coffee break can be a small but real holiday from your working day. The best way to illustrate this is in the form of an exercise.

Taking notice, being mindful

The next time you sit down to have a drink, do the following:

- Each time you pick up the cup of tea, notice the sensation of it in your hand.
- Notice the temperature, the weight and the texture of the cup.
- Concentrate on the movement of lifting the cup to your mouth and on each of the many sensations of drinking.
- Notice the tilting of the cup to drink and the swallowing of the tea.
- Notice the temperature of the tea and its flavour.
- Notice the tea enter your mouth and leave it again as you swallow.
- Notice the act of putting down the cup in the same way that you noticed picking it up.

Exercise ▶

> ▶ • If you become a bit more expert at mindfulness you might like to notice the absence of the heat of the cup on your hand and the absence of the cup's weight once you have put it down.
> • Notice emotions or physical sensations, such as tension or relaxation that arise as you sit there.
>
> Whatever arises during this exercise, the response is the same – just notice what is there and move your attention back to what you are doing.

Usually we think of drinking tea as being a simple act, not worthy of note, so we are likely to miss most of the sensations associated with it. It is surprising how hard it is to maintain awareness of what is happening NOW, for more than a few moments, particularly once the novelty has worn off. So as soon as you notice that you are not present, bring your attention back to what is happening in the moment.

It takes a lot of time and effort to be able to be mindful for longer periods in everyday life, for example while preparing the drink and washing up afterwards. If you are able to do this, you may notice that we normally focus on the end point of each activity rather than on the moment we are experiencing: in other words, we are goal-oriented.

For example, when washing up we are concerned about having clean cups, rather than the sensation of the warm water on our hands. In a goal-oriented state, we experience movement towards our goal as success and any interruption as a failure or frustration. The mindful state, in contrast, reduces the relative importance of goals. When we are mindful we are in a state of 'being' rather than a state of 'doing'. In this state, the sensations of washing up become the centre of our attention. Progress towards the goal still takes place but an interruption becomes another thing to experience, rather than a source of frustration. This helps to explain its therapeutic value in reducing stress. The distinction between the doing state and the being state is an important one in Mindfulness Based Stress Reduction (MBSR), also known as Mindfulness Based Cognitive Therapy, which we describe later in this chapter. Nowadays this has a particularly important role in the prevention of relapse for people who have been depressed.

Dealing with negative emotions

Many of the patients or clients we meet in practice find it difficult to 'bounce back' from the difficult or traumatic experiences they have been through, or are facing. We all encounter people who are anxious and some who have become depressed. It is no good telling them to 'pull themselves together' or 'get a grip' if they have not acquired the skills or resources to be able do this. So it is really important to understand something about the nature and causes of these emotional states and have some idea how best to advise those who experience them.

We start from the premise that some degree of anxiety and depression is a normal, if not universal, response to difficult conditions, particularly those that involve loss. These responses may, in some cases, develop into a mental health problem. However, this chapter is directed primarily at generalist care professionals who need to be able to recognize and respond to common emotional problems and offer immediate reassurance and advice to those they suspect might benefit from further mental health advice.

What do we mean by anxiety and how can it be managed?

Anxiety is a normal response to a situation that poses a potential threat (see Chapter 7). It can be summarized as follows:

Table 8.1 **Anxiety**	
Key factors	**Signs and symptoms**
Cognitive appraisal	Uncertainty about what is happening or what to do
Physiological changes	Symptoms associated with arousal of the autonomic nervous system including increased heart rate and systolic blood pressure, gastrointestinal upset, urinary urgency, breathing difficulties, loss of concentration
Behavioural responses	Agitation, obsessive checking and rituals, avoidance of anxiety-provoking situations, seeking help or support
Affect (mood)	Tense, nervous, worried

These are all normal responses to stress. In the extreme, they may be experienced as a panic attack. Most people seek help if any or all of these symptoms become sufficiently persistent or incapacitating as to have a serious negative impact on their quality of life.

Explanations of anxiety and psychological approaches to its management vary depending on the approach to psychology used. Consider the following scenario involving Anna:

In the first year of her nursing degree, Anna had to give a presentation to her tutor group. Although other students seemed nervous, they all delivered their presentations without too much fuss. Anna delayed until last, but as the day approached, she became panic-stricken and felt physically sick. She was even thinking about giving up her course because she could not face doing this. At this point, she sought help from the university counselling service.

Example

Counselling and psychology services offer different types of therapeutic approach, often depending on the training and preference of the therapist. Therefore Anna might have encountered any of the approaches summarized in Table 8.2.

Anna's anxiety about making presentations does not mean that she is 'ill', but simply that she finds certain situations difficult. However, some people experience extreme symptoms. Obsessive-compulsive disorder which involves endless ritualistic checking or handwashing is one example. Others experience generalized feelings of tension and panic which intrude on their daily lives and become debilitating. At this point, they may be diagnosed with 'generalized anxiety disorder'. There is often a fine line between normal anxiety and an 'anxiety disorder', as identified in the diagnostic manuals for mental health (APA 2000; WHO 2010). Much depends on not just how debilitating individuals find their symptoms, but where they seek help and who they consult. Each time a new edition of the manual is published, it contain new 'diagnoses'.

Table 8.2 Anxiety: explanations and therapeutic approaches

	Psychological approach	Possible explanation	Possible therapeutic approach
1	Cognitive	Anna's appraisal of the situation is distorted and dysfunctional. She underestimates her ability or sets too high a standard for herself	Challenge automatic negative (can't do) thoughts Replace with realistic thoughts: 'This is difficult because it is the first time I have done it'
2	Behavioural	Anna had a humiliating experience of public presentation at school	Learn relaxation skills and apply while rehearsing her presentation with a few friends to gain positive feedback
3	Psychodynamic	Anna was brought up according to strict standards, creating pressure to succeed	Help Anna to understand the origins of her feelings so that she is released from her own internal pressure
4	Humanistic	Anna has low self-esteem	Encourage Anna to talk about her fears and discover her own solutions
5	Social psychology	Anna is not confident in her self-presentation	Focus on dress, posture, voice and rehearse in front of the mirror and friends
6	Social cognitive	Anna lacks self-efficacy in terms of her presentation skills	See 1,2,5 and 6 above, and advise Anna to seek practical advice and help from her tutor

Exercise

You see a diagnosis of 'social anxiety disorder' written in someone's notes before you are introduced to them.

- What do you think this means?
- What impression do you form of the individual before you meet him or her?
- How do you expect the individual to respond to you?
- Are you likely to approach that person differently than if this had not been written in the notes?

Until recently, social anxiety was referred to as 'shyness', something many people experience to a greater or a lesser degree. The diagnosis might provide a route to treatment. But, once labelled as having a 'mental health problem', individuals can find themselves stigmatized, in health and social care, in the workplace and even when applying for insurance. This can lead to further damage to their self-concept and their self-esteem. Therefore we need to be very cautious about jumping to any conclusions when seeing in their notes that someone has 'history of mental health problems'.

Responding to a patient or client who is anxious

The reduction of anxiety for people faced with difficult or challenging situations is an important part of the caring role. People who are anxious tend to be hyper-vigilant (looking for problems), which makes them even more worried. This leads to them requesting more investigations and need more staff time. Anxiety places further strain on the patient's body and has been implicated in poor outcomes for heart problems. Anxiety increases perceptions of pain.

In Chapter 4 we discuss the importance of keeping people well informed and showing an empathetic and approachable manner. People faced with a health or social problem are often very worried about its implications for their ability to work, maintain personal relationships or meet obligations in their daily lives. For some, what might seem to others a relatively trivial event can be 'the straw that breaks the camel's back' in an already troubled life.

When Mark received a speeding fine, Janice could not understand why he seemed to go to pieces. But this happened at a time when he had recently lost his job, was worried about the family finances, his mother had recently died and he had been diagnosed with Type 2 diabetes. Against the background of cumulative stress the fine was just too much for him to cope with.

Some people appear to have a level of anxiety out of all proportion to the problems they face because of inadequate or maladaptive coping skills. For example, they may have role-modelled anxious responses from a parent, or never learned effective ways of dealing with the type of situation they find themselves in. Some have literacy or communication difficulties or inadequate social skills that make it difficult to deal with situations outside the confines of their home and family, or gain help from others when they need it.

The next time Mark attended for his routine check, the nurse noticed how tense he appeared. So she shut the door and said: 'You seem rather tense at the moment. Is there anything special worrying you?'

Mark told the nurse it was nothing (he knew she was busy, so didn't want to take up too much time). But the nurse placed a hand on his shoulder and said: 'I can see that you are worried. I have 10 minutes to spare – is there anything you would like to share?'

Mark was able to give a brief summary, which helped to put it all in perspective. Before he left, the nurse said: 'Is there anything you would like us to do to help?' This placed the decision-making back with Mark, who replied 'No thanks, you have already been a great help.'

In this scenario, the patient's response is typical, but the nurse's approach is not. Many, if not most, nurses admit to avoiding asking these types of question, or even avoiding contact with anxious patients because they say:

1   There is insufficient time to engage with patients about their problems.

2   There is no privacy to discuss personal issues.

3   They fear 'opening the flood gates' because it might increase the individual's distress.

4   They fear an obligation to 'do something' about the problem disclosed.

5   They fear they lack the skills required to facilitate and then close successfully this kind of conversation.

With respect to points 3, 4 and 5, health care professionals (in contrast to social care professionals) need to be reminded that by inviting patients to share their feelings or emotions the primary task of the professional is to *listen*, not to solve the individual's problems for them. No patient could or would reasonably expect a busy hospital nurse to sort out their employment difficulties, resolve their marital disharmony or offer bereavement counselling because this is not what they are trained to do. But patients do have a right to expect empathy and understanding and are usually very grateful that someone was sufficiently concerned to listen to them. For those who experience severe and recurrent anxiety problems, the first line of treatment recommended by the National Institute for Health and Clinical Excellence (NICE 2011) in the UK is the social cognitive approach in the form of 'cognitive behaviour therapy' (CBT). This form of therapy can be very effective and we discuss it in more detail later in this chapter.

Some people find that their persistent state of anxiety gives way to depression. In fact, it is quite common for people who have bouts of depression to experience a lot of anxiety as well.

What do we mean by depression and how can it be managed?

Depression can be described using a similar framework as that used above to describe anxiety:

Table 8.3 Depression

Key factors	Signs and symptoms
Cognitive	Sense of hopelessness, which may be accompanied by suicidal thoughts
Motivational	Loss of interest
Physiological changes	Fatigue, poor sleep quality, loss of concentration, poor appetite with weight loss, or compulsive eating and weight gain
Behavioural	Self-neglect
Affect (mood)	Negativity, lack of positive mood, irritability

Depression is very common and most episodes of depression resolve without intervention. It is normal to feel emotionally low and hopeless when we experience a loss or when things go badly wrong. But when these feelings become persistent and are accompanied by other symptoms from those listed above, it may be classified as 'major depression' (clinical depression) and diagnosed as a mental disorder. Severe depression can be totally incapacitating and in a minority of cases leads to suicide. It is important to note that suicide is the third most common cause of death among adolescent males worldwide (Wasserman 2006), while suicide among the general population is often associated with untreated depression. Therefore it should not be minimized or ignored.

Consider what action you suggest Lisa should take in the following example:

During her second year at university, an acquaintance of Lisa's, Marie, became progressively unable to sleep or eat properly, could not concentrate on her academic work, and lost interest in social events and activities such as swimming that she previously enjoyed. Lisa noticed that she was becoming withdrawn and uncommunicative and made frequent excuses to avoid social contact. During the first term of that academic year, Marie stopped wearing make-up, took little care of her hair and clothes, did not join friends for meals in the refectory and appeared to have lost weight. She appeared to spend more and more time in bed, but was irritable with others when challenged about this. Lecturers noticed that her attendance at seminars was increasingly poor and she failed to hand in her assignments on time.

Example

Vulnerability, triggering and maintaining factors in depression

Vulnerability factors are those that predispose people to becoming depressed. They include:

- *Biological vulnerabilities*:
  1 genetic predisposition;
  2 hormone disruption, for example thyroid dysfunction;
  3 drug and alcohol use;
  4 seasonal affective disorder (SAD);
  5 poor sleep;
  6 disease processes.
- *Psychological vulnerabilities*:
  7 inability to connect with others (see above);
  8 low self-worth and self-esteem.
- *Social vulnerabilities*:
  9 social problems and uncontrollable life events;
  10 absence of emotional support.

Trigger factors, such as a life event, can precipitate depression but, unless overwhelming, require vulnerability factors to do so – for example, not everyone who loses their job becomes depressed.

Maintaining factors include poverty, poor coping skills and/or lack of social support that conspire to maintain depression. Different ways of explaining depression and approaches to its management are given in Table 8.4.

Table 8.4 Depression: explanations and therapeutic approaches

	Psychological approach	Psychological explanation	Therapeutic approach
1	Cognitive	Depression results from unduly pessimistic interpretation of events and the ability to deal with them	Identify and challenge automatic negative (can't do) thoughts and core beliefs (I am no good) Replace with realistic thoughts: 'I am as good as anyone else'
2	Behavioural	Seligman (1975) learned helplessness – nothing I nor anyone else does can make any difference Lewinsohn (1974) lack of positive reinforcement in their lives	Start with simple tasks and demonstrate positive achievements Rehearse social skills that enable the individual to engage more effectively with others individually and in groups
3	Psychodynamic	Depression starts with unsuccessful early relationships, leading to low self-esteem	Help the individual to understand the origins of their feelings so they can release themselves from self-blame
4	Humanistic	Depression, low self-esteem	Person-centred counselling, based on positive regard to raise confidence levels

In terms of critique, the therapy used really needs to address issues raised during the assessment of vulnerability and maintaining factors. For example, psychological therapies cannot alter bereavement, joblessness or poverty, but can provide the individual with resources that will help him or her adopt a more resilient approach to dealing with these sorts of problem.

Those working in health care need to be aware that raised rates of depression are associated with a range of medical conditions, for example myocardial infarction, diabetes and cancer. Depression among people who are ill is often overlooked because there is a view that 'people are bound to be unhappy when bad things happen to them'. It is important that this depression is treated, not only because depression is unpleasant for patients or clients but also because of its impact on health outcomes, with poorer quality of life, higher morbidity (they are sicker) and higher mortality rates. Not only is immune function more likely to be compromised (see Chapter 7), but people who are depressed are less likely to adhere to the treatment plans, for example to take their medications.

The National Institute for Health and Clinical Excellence (NICE 2009) guidelines regarding depression suggest two screening questions to establish whether a person might have depression:

During the last month, have you often been bothered by:

- feeling down, depressed or hopeless;
- having little interest or pleasure in doing things?

We recommend that everybody working in health and social care should be aware of them. If, on asking these two screening questions, you find that a patient or client may be depressed, it is sensible to draw this to the attention of somebody who can refer them for further assessment.

The NICE guidelines recommend a stepped care approach to the management and treatment of depression, depending on the severity and persistence of the symptoms, in which psychological interventions play a central role. Currently, two of the most effective psychological interventions for depression and other disorders are cognitive behaviour therapy (CBT) and mindfulness-based cognitive therapy or stress reduction.

Psychological therapies

In this section, we focus on two psychological therapies that have been shown to be effective in the management of depression and anxiety-related disorders as well as the management of many chronic physical illnesses.

Cognitive behaviour therapy (CBT)

CBT has become the most popular psychological intervention for anxiety disorders, depression and chronic medical conditions, such as chronic pain, that have a psychological component. CBT is a social cognitive approach to therapy which, as the name suggests, combines cognitive and behavioural management strategies to recognize, interrupt and change dysfunctional automatic negative thoughts and maladaptive ways of responding in everyday life. CBT assessment is based on its own version of 'ABC' (Lam and Gale 2000), which is quite different from the ABC of behaviour modification (Chapter 5):

A refers to activating or triggering event(s);

B is the individual's beliefs about or interpretations of the event(s);

C represents the individual's emotional or behavioural responses or consequences.

According to cognitive principles:

A does not cause C: events are not responsible for emotional responses.

B is largely responsible for C: emotions are a consequence of the individual's beliefs about the events (see appraisals, Chapter 7).

When Marie became depressed, she blamed it all on her parents' recent divorce. But during her sessions of CBT, she came to realize that the real problem was her need to overcome these negative thoughts about her parents and her sense of blame and anger.

Example

CBT is typically a brief intervention that involves six to ten sessions, each of one to two hours of problem-focused interventions. With appropriate training, it can be delivered, often in groups, in a limited number of sessions, by a variety of professionals. Group therapy using CBT was shown to be more cost-effective than other forms of group psychotherapy or even individual therapy (McDermut *et al.* 2001). Butler *et al.* (2006) report large effect sizes (a statistical measure of effectiveness) for CBT for depression and a wide range of anxiety-related disorders in adults and children, including post-traumatic stress disorder (PTSD), panic disorder, agoraphobia and social phobia. It has also been shown to be effective in the management of a range of disorders and conditions such as asthma, chronic fatigue and chronic pain (Chapter 10). There is good evidence that it can be used effectively with all age groups, including older people (Hendriks *et al.* 2008) and adolescents and children (Christie and Wilson 2005). There is also increasing evidence that computer-based applications of CBT offer a cost-effective and acceptable alternative for those with depression (Kaltenthaler *et al.* 2006, 2008). For those with pain-related problems, such as headache, the results appear to be as good as face-to-face treatments (Cuijpers *et al.* 2008). Nevertheless, Butler *et al.* (2006) cautioned that some of the reported effects of CBT may be inflated by publication bias, including the failure to report long-term effects at follow-up.

Mindfulness-based stress reduction (MBSR)

We reviewed the technique of mindfulness earlier in this chapter. Being mindful forms the basis for Mindfulness-based Stress Reduction (MBSR) which, like CBT, is concerned with bringing cognitions into awareness. But unlike CBT, MBSR aims to bring about 'acceptance of' rather than 'manipulation of' thoughts and feelings. One of the key ideas in MBSR is that people who have experienced an episode of depression want to avoid relapsing back into a depressed state, so they try hard to avoid negative thoughts and emotions. It is very difficult to avoid thinking something.

Exercise

Spend a few minutes thinking of images of white bears.
   Now *Try hard* NOT to think about 'white bears' for a few minutes.

When people try to suppress negative thoughts and emotions, it is inevitable that those thoughts and feelings will intrude on their consciousness at some point. The inability to control them may be seen as a failure and this perception leads to more negativity. The desire to avoid negative thoughts and emotions can therefore lead to a downward emotional spiral and relapse into depression. MBSR encourages participants to simply 'be' with what is what is experienced, in the moment, including any negativity that arises.

The key to mindfulness

Mindfulness means taking a dispassionate or 'decentred' perspective on whatever thoughts and feelings arise. This is typified by sentences such as 'my thoughts are not facts' and 'I am not my thoughts'. This ability to 'be with' thoughts and feelings, while retaining a sense of perspective, allows those same thoughts and feelings to abate naturally and this prevents the situation spiralling out of control.

Of course it is not easy to 'be with' negativity, especially for people who have had previous experience of depression. MBSR provides a series of exercises in which participants learn to be mindful in different circumstances, starting off with being mindful of the experience of eating (appreciating each mouthful), then with various other physical sensations, and then with thoughts and feelings.

MBSR has been used to prevent relapse into depression and has also been used as an intervention to enhance well-being in non-clinical populations (Kaviani *et al.* 2011). It has been shown to be an effective intervention for anxiety and mood disorders (Hofmann *et al.* 2010). It has been shown to help people deal with sexual difficulties and improve immune function among patients with cancer (Shennan *et al.* 2011).

In the final sections of this chapter, we look at some specific situations in which negative emotions play a dominant role.

Post-traumatic stress disorder (PTSD)

PTSD is an anxiety disorder that can occur in the following circumstances:

- The individual has been exposed to a traumatic event.
- He or she experienced, witnessed, or was confronted with an event that involved actual or threatened death or serious injury, or a threat to the physical integrity of self or others.
- He or she responded with intense fear, helplessness, or horror.

PTSD has been recorded in response to a variety of events including assault, accident, disaster and medical treatment. Symptoms of PTSD include:

- Recurrent and intrusive distressing recollections of the event, including images, thoughts, and/or perceptions.
  - In young children, repetitive play may occur in which these or other aspects of the trauma are expressed.
- Recurrent distressing dreams of the event.
  - In young children, there may be frightening dreams without recognizable content.
- Sense of reliving the experience, illusions, hallucinations, and/or flashbacks, including those that occur on awakening or when intoxicated.
  - In young children, trauma-specific re-enactment may occur.
- Intense psychological distress and/or physiological reactivity on exposure to internal or external cues that symbolize or resemble an aspect of the traumatic event.
- Persistent avoidance of stimuli (images or situations) associated with the trauma, and general emotional numbing. For example, some people suffering from PTSD use alcohol or other substances as self-medication in an attempt to avoid or eliminate intrusive memories.

Other anxiety-related symptoms include at least two of the following:

- difficulty falling or staying asleep;
- irritability or outbursts of anger;
- difficulty concentrating;
- hypervigilance (constant wariness);
- exaggerated startle response (reacting to the slightest noise or disturbance).

Symptoms may occur immediately following the trauma, or may be delayed. Most people recover within a few weeks or months without treatment, particularly if there is good family support.

The literature indicates that PTSD can occur following a wide range of events including cardiac surgery in children (Connolly 2004) and childbirth (Walker 2000). Based on a review of available studies, Robertson and Perry estimated that between 10 and 20 per cent of staff working in emergency services demonstrated the symptoms of PTSD. It is commonly assumed that PTSD results from exceptionally threatening or catastrophic incidents, but the following example illustrates the subjective nature of the threat.

Example

Janice felt ill in the night and went to the bathroom where she suffered a severe attack of vomiting and diarrhoea. Mark found her unconscious on the bathroom floor in a dreadful mess and called an ambulance. Janice came round in hospital, unwashed in the same night clothes. Mark told her what had happened.

For several months after this, she suffered flashbacks and nightmares based on mental images of her experience. She constantly monitored herself for feelings of nausea and never went anywhere without checking out the availability of toilets. She experienced panic attacks when she tried to go out alone and was afraid to be left in the house on her own. It was several months before she felt able to return to work.

The trauma in Janice's case was the total unexpected loss of bodily control and subsequent fear that her own body would let her down again. Professionals need to be alert to this and recommend that anyone with manifest symptoms of PTSD ask for help from a specialist psychologist. It is also worth noting that there are some indications in the literature (Sinclair and Hamill 2007) that nurses and other health professionals who work empathically with people who are experiencing traumatic situations, such as cancer and domestic violence, may be at risk of vicarious traumatization. Supportive strategies, such as clinical supervision, are strongly recommended for those working in these types of situation.

Treatment of post-traumatic stress disorder (PTSD)

It was originally believed that immediate counselling was important in the prevention of PTSD. However, a meta-analysis of all studies of psychological debriefing indicated that debriefing *increased* the risk of PTSD nearly threefold (Rose *et al.* 2002). Therefore the current advice is that compulsory debriefing after trauma should stop. That is not to say that people should be discouraged from talking about the event to family, friends or confidants if they wish to do so. Those most likely to benefit from intervention soon after a traumatic event are those who have experienced previous traumas or lack emotional support (Litz *et al.* 2002).

It is advisable to warn people who have experienced a traumatic incident that it is possible they may at some time in the future experience flashbacks associated with feelings of panic. If so, they can be reassured that most of the symptoms will disappear within three months, but if they don't, their doctor should refer them for treatment to a clinical psychologist who specializes in PTSD. They are likely to use one of the following psychological interventions.

Trauma-focused CBT

The most effective early intervention for those with acute psychological distress is trauma-focused cognitive behavioural therapy (CBT; Roberts *et al.* 2010). The National Institute for Health and Clinical Excellence guidelines (NICE 2005) recommend trauma-focused CBT as the primary method of treatment for all age groups, including children. Systematic desensitization (see Chapter 5) is likely to be a component. This requires patients to consciously hold images of the trauma in their minds until sympathetic arousal has subsided and they feel calm. When done repeatedly, the fear response associated with traumatic memories is eliminated.

Trauma-focused eye movement desensitization and reprocessing (EMDR)

This is an alternative psychological treatment, based on a Cochrane review by Bisson and Andrew (2007). As in systematic desensitization, the individual is asked to hold traumatic images, but in this case while watching the therapist's finger move back and forth. After a series of repeats over several sessions, the individual is no longer able to visualize the traumatic image and the flashback images disappear.

How does this work? Psychologists are not entirely sure, but it may be that memories of a traumatic event are inadequately processed at the time and are incorrectly stored in memory schema (see Chapter 3). The goal of EMDR therapy is to reprocess these distressing memories into a coherent framework that enables the individual to cope better.

Does it matter how long ago the event occurred? Some people continue to experience PTSD long after the event; for example, there are many examples in the literature of World War II veterans who still manifest symptoms. Both CBT and EMDR are effective no matter how long after the traumatic event they are offered. As with all trauma therapies, it is helpful for people to talk about the event after treatment, in order to prevent recurrence.

The experience of loss

Experiencing losses is an inevitable part of life. When we make choices about careers, relationships, or places and ways to live, choosing one inevitably involves loss of the other. Transitions like marriage, promotion at work, or having a baby, bring both gains and losses. Some losses occur as part of a traumatic event. Other losses may be not of actual things or people, but of potential experiences, roles or relationships, and it is therefore possible to lose something that you have never had. This type of loss is experienced by many infertile couples, for whom the role of parent cannot be realized. Certain experiences such as unemployment, homelessness or loss of a body part or function are associated with multiple actual and potential losses.

Can you think of a loss that you have experienced at some point in your life? It might be the loss of person, a pet or an object that meant a lot to you.

- How did it make you feel and how did these feelings change over time?
- How did you express your loss, for example did you share your feelings with others or keep it to yourself?
- What (if anything) most helped you to come to terms with your loss?

The death of someone we love is generally recognized as one of the most serious adverse life events, yet loss of a pet or other attachment object can be almost as traumatic. Attachment bonds are important throughout our lives. The disruption or breakdown of these relationships is an important source of loss, leading to stress-related illness (Chapter 7), delayed recovery from illness, substance abuse, depression and other forms of psychopathology (Maunder and Hunter 2008).

Nursing staff encounter death more frequently than most other people, but many still have a high level of anxiety about it. Payne *et al.* (1998) found that those working in emergency care settings had higher levels of death anxiety than those working in palliative care settings, possibly because they had less opportunity to discuss their feelings. The next sections consider theories that account for people's responses to loss. In so doing, we use the following definitions:

- *Bereavement* is the process surrounding loss.
- *Grief* is the reaction associated with loss.
- *Mourning* is the behavioural and emotional expression of grief.

Mourning is strongly influenced by cultural norms. For example, the rituals that occur after a death, such as laying out the body, the type of funeral, and type of clothing worn by mourners, are all very much dependent upon cultural norms and these tend to change over time. At one time in the UK, funeral services were usually religious, whereas now the secular funeral is quite common. The funeral is often followed by a family or community gathering where the deceased person is remembered and aspects of his or her life celebrated. It is probably helpful to have well-accepted rituals because they direct people how to behave and how to respond to each other during a time when it is difficult to make informed decisions. Rituals, such as state funerals, both contain and allow public expression of feelings. Rituals also mark the status change of individuals, such as a wife becoming a widow. They provide an opportunity to demonstrate emotional support, and enable grieving people to derive comfort from others.

Explaining grief

Traditional theories of loss, like attachment, originally derived from psychoanalysis and focused on the concept of 'ego defence'. This means that some things are so threatening that the conscious mind (the ego) cannot cope with them. Freud introduced the notion of defence mechanisms, which are seen as unconscious ways of allowing us to continue functioning in very stressful situations, so that we can 'work through' problems at a later stage. Freud suggested that in order to recover from loss, we need to confront our fears and feelings in a conscious process that he called 'grief work'. Freud and Bowlby (Chapter 3) both suggested that failure to do this might lead to prolonged or pathological types of grief, though there is actually little evidence to support this.

Possibly the most widely known model of bereavement is that of Kübler-Ross (1969) who proposed that grief follows a series of fixed stages which need to be worked through. Once again, there is little evidence to support this as reactions to loss are very variable. Parkes (1972) noted a number of common responses to loss, most of which are similar to those noted by Kübler-Ross. Some of these are similar to the manifestations of depression, perhaps because both tend to involve perceptions of loss.

Table 8.5 Responses to loss

Component	Response
Initial reaction	Numbness, disbelief, unreality or denial
	Alarm reaction (Chapter 7): experienced as anxiety, restlessness and fear
Emotional response	Feelings of failure, regret or guilt
	Feeling alone or abandoned
	Anger
	Sorrow, despair, pessimism, rumination
Psychosocial and motivational responses	Yearning and pining for the lost one
	Continuing to interact with the deceased, for example feeling their presence and talking to them as though they were still there
	Loss of purpose, feelings of loss of the self, loss of enjoyment, sense of worthlessness
	Difficulty in maintaining social relationships
Physical symptoms	Insomnia
	Feelings of fatigue, lethargy, reduction in activity
	Slowed thinking, poor concentration
	Loss of appetite

Stroebe and Schut (1998) proposed a 'dual process' model of grief, illustrated in Figure 8.1. Instead of proposing a linear trajectory towards resolution, this identifies a process of oscillation between the feelings of grief and thoughts, feelings and behaviours directed towards restoration. Over time, grief experiences diminish while restoration activities increase. Restoration experiences include doing new things, finding sources of distraction and eventually finding new roles, identities and relationships. The rate at which this occurs is very variable. Some people orient themselves towards restoration at an early stage, such as undertaking activities in memory of the person who has died. Examples include fundraising in aid of a charity associated with the illness experienced by the person who died, or involvement in a self-help group for those who have experienced similar losses.

Grief is a normal process, not a state, and does not involve a series of stages. Grief is painful and affects almost all aspects of the person. Many people describe grief as physically painful and may need reassurance that they are not ill. Some people cope with grief by increasing their use

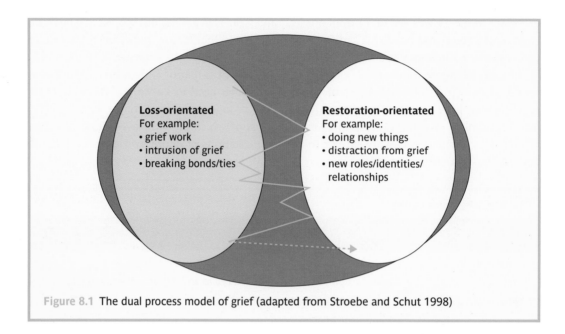

Loss-orientated
For example:
• grief work
• intrusion of grief
• breaking bonds/ties

Restoration-orientated
For example:
• doing new things
• distraction from grief
• new roles/identities/
  relationships

Figure 8.1 The dual process model of grief (adapted from Stroebe and Schut 1998)

of mood-altering substances like alcohol, tobacco or drugs. Drugs or alcohol use may (as in PTSD) begin as a form of self-medication to blot out memories of the loss. This impedes successful adaptation and increases risk to health. Loss leads to immunological suppression and increased susceptibility to infections and stress-related diseases (see Chapter 7). This helps to explain the increased risk of death in the first few years after the death of a spouse. In a minority who are vulnerable, depression following bereavement leads to increased risk of suicide. Bereavement support needs therefore to be seen as an important role for care workers. However, a study of district nurses found that only a small proportion felt it their responsibility to provide bereavement support for relatives after a cancer patient had died (Birtwistle *et al.* 2002).

Challenging assumptions about bereavement

Wortman and Silver (1989) challenged other common assumptions about bereavement loss:

- *Is distress or depression inevitable?* Studies of bereaved people show that depression affects 10 to 15 per cent of those who are bereaved (Bonanno 2004). Bonanno challenged Bowlby's assumptions that an absence of grief is pathological or that it indicates a superficial attachment to the deceased. Rather, he suggested it is relatively common for people to show great resilience in the face of trauma and loss, and to be able to continue functioning (this may relate to issues we discussed in the early part of this chapter). Bonanno calls for a re-evaluation of basic assumptions about responses to loss and more research into human fortitude.

- *Is it important to 'work through' feelings of loss?* It used to be assumed that resolution of grief requires cognitive-emotional processing (grief work), and this is the basis for offering bereavement counselling. However, Jordan and Neimeyer (2003) concluded that the scientific basis for accepting the efficacy of grief counselling appears weak and Currier *et al.* (2007) found no evidence to support grief counselling for children. Bonanno's (2004) review of the evidence went further to indicate that grief therapies can actually make matters worse when given for anything other than for those with chronic (prolonged) grief responses. This indicates that people should be allowed to decide for themselves if and when they need this type of support.

● *Do all people resolve their grief?* All models of loss assume that the final outcome of grieving will be a return to a normal psychological state. For some individuals, grieving may continue over many years, though this would not be considered abnormal unless it interferes with the individual's ability to function normally. However, a minority of people remain focused on the loss and engage in excessive rumination long after the event. This 'complicated grief' is amenable to psychological treatment, though there is no evidence that these complicated grief reactions can be prevented (Wittouck *et al.* 2011).

Ted was devastated when his wife Laura died. They had known each other since school, and had recently celebrated their golden wedding anniversary. She died of cancer after a relatively short illness and Ted was quite unprepared for this. He could not bear the thought of leaving the house or of anyone else touching Laura's things. He sought refuge in his greenhouse and in the evenings felt Laura's presence by having all of her things around him. The family were concerned, but he refused all offers of help.

Eventually, Ted developed bronchitis and moved in with Mark and Janice on a temporary basis. When he felt better, he visited his home and was able, with help, to start clearing a few things out. After a little longer he started making plans for the future and to look forward to the birth of his next great-grandchild. He still missed Laura very much, but being able to talk about her to the family helped.

It might be assumed that the stronger the marital relationship, the greater the sense of loss when the partner dies. However, Van Doorn *et al.* (1998) found that those who had experienced insecure attachment or dependent relationships were more likely to experience traumatic grief following the death of their spouse. Shear *et al.* (2007) suggested this is because they are caught in a seemingly endless state of acute grief, complicated by patterns of thoughts, feelings and behaviours that remain frozen at the time of the death.

Biographical interventions for loss

Bury (1982) introduced the concept of biographical disruption to explain the impact of loss. This means that many of the taken-for-granted aspects of daily life and future expectations are disrupted and the notion of 'self' has to alter to accommodate these changes. Borrowing the notion of schemas (see Chapter 3), some people are able to accommodate change within their existing schemas, while others cannot. Walter (1996) proposed that a person who has experienced an important change or loss needs to construct or reconstruct their identity in the light of the changes that have occurred.

Based on these notions, narrative psychologists (Crossley 2003) and gerontologists (Clark 2001) suggest that therapeutic work needs to involve the structuring of chaotic and disruptive memories into a meaningful story. Coming to terms with losses requires that loss events are integrated into continuing life, or mental health may suffer. Story-telling is the means by which people have traditionally achieved this (Walter 1999), which is why Kelly (1998) described the grief process as 're-storying one's life'. This means finding new goals and a sense of purpose to one's life and requires the individual to construct a new and different ongoing life story (see Neimeyer *et al.* 2010).

Research

Coming to terms with biographical change

Asbring (2001) interviewed women with fibromyalgia to find out how their illness had affected them. Fibromyalgia is a painful condition that affects the muscles and for which there is no known effective treatment. Losses included the ability to work and one participant described her life as similar to that of a pensioner. The main finding was that the illness led to a radical disruption in the women's biographies and had a profound effect on their sense of identity, particularly in relation to work and social life. However, not all of the changes were negative and many of the women also experienced gains as a result of their illness. For example, they felt they had learned to place more value on small joys and less on material goods.

Coping with other people's losses

If coping with our own losses is difficult, coping with other people's emotions following a loss can be extremely difficult. We have all heard of reports of people crossing the road to avoid facing someone who has recently had a bereavement or experienced a serious illness or disability. We mentioned earlier in this chapter how many nurses avoid opening up a conversation with someone who is upset for fear of opening the 'can of worms'.

Exercise

Can you think back to an encounter with someone who had just experienced a loss, or been diagnosed with a life-limiting illness?

- How did it make you feel?
- How did you respond?

Most of us have found ourselves in the position of not knowing what to say or do when faced with someone who has experienced a loss. On the one hand, we want to acknowledge their loss and let them know we care, but on the other we don't want to keep reminding them of their loss and risk upsetting them even more. Most people who have experienced a loss say that being ignored or avoided is the worst thing that can happen to them. Read the following extract from a letter written to a nursing journal by a nurse in 1970 and see if you think this could happen today.

Death in the first person (Anon., 1970)

I am a student nurse. I am dying.
I write this to you who are, and will become, nurses
in the hope that by my sharing my feeling with you,
you may someday be better able to help those who share my experience.
For me, fear is today and dying is now.
You slip in and out of my room,
give me medications and check my blood pressure.
Is it because I am a student nurse myself, or just a human being,
that I sense your fright?
And your fears enhance mine.
Why are you afraid? I am the one who is dying.
If only we could be honest, both admit our fear, touch one another.
If you really care,
would you lose so much of our valuable professionalism
if you even cried with me?…
Then it might not be so hard to die
– in a hospital – with friends close by.

Expressions of empathy (as opposed to sympathy) should be regarded as a right for all patients and clients who are facing up to a loss. Often, this can be achieved by looking the person in the eye, giving them a smile, and possibly a hug or a hand on the arm. You might wish to say 'You know I am here if you need me.'

Anticipatory grief

Some diseases involve a protracted period of illness and illness-related losses prior to death which affect caregivers as well as the patients. For example, in Alzheimer's disease, the spouse loses the person they married and loved, the friend, social companion, source of emotional support, lover, income-provider, car driver, person to argue with, and so on. These losses may occur gradually over many years, each loss to be mourned and requiring adjustment. This is termed 'anticipatory grief'. Very extended periods of anticipatory grief are not necessarily adaptive for the caregiver of someone with a chronic illness because withdrawal of emotional involvement during this period can induce a sense of guilt after the death has occurred. But there are examples of how it can help people to say and do things they might otherwise regret not doing. This can help adjustment when the death finally occurs.

Coming to terms with a death (Evans 1994: 160):

Some time after the death of her father, a young woman returned to the hospital ward on which he died to thank the nursing staff. She explained that, despite the distress and pain she experienced when informed of her father's terminal condition and his subsequent death, she was grateful for the time period between these two events. Among other things, it gave her time to resolve conflicts, express her love and say goodbye.

This extract suggests that care workers are able to help people face up to their imminent loss and start to mourn their loss before death actually occurs. But the support that people need prior to a death should not just focus on 'grief work'. Evans suggested that instead of focusing just on the death, we need to be aware of the multiple stresses that affect patients and their caregivers during a terminal illness and support them while they deal with these.

Maintaining hope

Perhaps one of the reasons why many health care professionals find it so hard to confront death is because of their desire to maintain hope. Hope is what most of us live for. But when pain, illness, disability or loss of someone we love occurs, our previously valued goals may be unattainable. This can engender hopelessness or it can bring acceptance or promote determination. It brings us back to where we started this chapter – the notion of resilience.

A feature of those who maintain high hope is the ability to modify or change some of their original goals (see also Chapters 9 and 10). It requires flexibility and a willingness to change one's personal biography. Snyder (1998) identified that resilient people with high hope have different goals within different life arenas. This means that they are able to switch to another goal when one appears unobtainable. He argued that grieving occurs when a previously attainable goal is no longer obtainable. But following a period of mourning, people with high hope turn their attentions to substitute goals that are achievable. Care professionals can help patients to face things one step at a time when faced with overwhelming challenges.

During her third year of training, Anna had a placement in a hospice for people approaching the end of life. She was very anxious because she did not really know how to talk to people who were dying or how to approach other patients following a death. However, once she had started on the ward her mentor carefully discussed with her the philosophy of hospice care, the holistic approach and the emphasis on openness and sharing with patient, family and staff. The mentor helped Anna to understand her own reactions to death and dying. This enabled Anna to communicate in a positive way with others who were exploring their own issues in relation to dying. Anna was surprised to discover that, rather than being a place of sadness, there was a real sense of hope which focused on maximizing quality of life for the patients and their families.

Example

Table 8.6 Dealing with negative emotions and loss: summary of key points

Concept(s)	Implications
Anxiety and depression	These are common human emotions which require assessment and management if symptoms cause an abnormal level of distress or interfere with the ability to lead a normal life
	Both may be explained from different psychological perspectives, each of which makes an important contribution to our understanding
Cognitive behaviour therapy (CBT)	An effective intervention for anxiety and depression that focuses on changing habitual ways of thinking and behaving
Mindfulness Based Stress Reduction (MBSR)	An effective intervention for anxiety which focuses the mind on what is happening in the immediate present. It reduces rumination on past and future problems
Post-traumatic stress disorder (PTSD)	A relatively common condition for which there are effective treatments. It causes considerable distress if not recognized
Grief	A normal, but not inevitable, response to loss
Empathetic listening	The most important contribution that those who do not have special training can offer to people who show emotional distress

Further reading

Segal, Z.V., Williams, J.M.G. and Teasdale, J.D. (2002) *Mindfulness-based Cognitive Therapy for Depression: A New Approach to Preventing Relapse.* New York: Guilford Press.

Wasserman, D. (2006) *Depression, The Facts: Expert Advice for Patients, Carers and Professionals.* Oxford: Oxford University Press.

Chapter 9

Psychology applied to health and illness

Key topics

- Health promotion
- Medical help-seeking
- Self-management in ill health

Introduction

This chapter combines theories and evidence from health psychology to address issues of importance to public health. The clients or patients we encounter on a daily basis in both health and social care include many people who are sick or disabled as a direct consequence of their lifestyle. This chapter addresses the following sorts of questions:

- Is lifestyle a choice?
- Is information and education likely to be sufficient to bring about change?

The chapter is divided into two distinct parts. The first part focuses on the promotion of health and the prevention of illness. The second part focuses on factors that influence medical help-seeking and addresses psychological approaches to the management of chronic ill health.

Lisa drives to work each day, skips lunch and buys crisps and chocolate bars from the nearby vending machine. She buys a ready meal to eat in the evening while slumped in front of the television. She is gaining weight and knows she needs to take exercise and eat a healthy diet that includes fresh fruit and vegetables. But somehow she never quite gets round to changing her lifestyle.

Vignette

Lisa's lifestyle is typical of many people who fail to act on sound health advice. How can we make sense of these lifestyle choices and help people like Lisa to change their behaviour? Is it just lack of willpower? Why does Lisa find it so difficult to make what would appear to be some simple changes? We invite you to reflect on these questions as you read this chapter.

Background

As professionals, we are good at telling other people what they ought to do, while not always particularly good at following the same advice ourselves. For example, during our careers we have met doctors and cardiovascular patients who smoked, nurses and physiotherapists who were overweight, and off-duty police officers who ignored parking restrictions. It would appear that following advice or sticking to rules is not entirely straightforward.

In order to understand both lay and professional understandings of health and illness, we start by considering what is actually meant by these terms.

Understanding health, illness and disease

Health and illness are concepts influenced by cultural and subjective beliefs which need to be understood from the perspective of each group or individual concerned. To a health professional, a mental or physical illness is usually diagnosed by an objective set of signs and symptoms. But Blaxter (1990) distinguished between illness and disease:

- *disease* is defined as a biological or clinically identified abnormality;
- *illness* is the subjective experience of symptoms.

Using these definitions, it is possible to have an illness without a disease, and a disease without feeling ill. People's subjective feelings of health and illness can sometimes seem to bear little relation to the medical assessment of their physical state. For example, when judging their state of health, people tend to compare themselves with others like themselves. This may help to explain why older people tended to describe themselves as healthy in spite of having a diagnosed disease or disorder (Grimby and Wiklund 1994).

A disease without illness

Mark's doctor diagnosed hypertension (high blood pressure). This disease places Mark at high risk of heart disease, stroke and kidney failure but there are few, if any, symptoms in the early stages. It is a disease without illness, which makes it difficult for Mark to see it as a serious problem.

Medical diagnoses are not static, but change as medical technologies improve and attitudes shift. For example, should infertility be regarded as a medical disorder? The diagnosis of mental illness is defined according to symptom classifications published in the latest edition of the

DSM (Diagnostic and Statistical Manual of Mental Disorders, published by the American Psychiatric Association; APA 2000) or ICD (International Classification of Diseases, published by the World Health Organization; WHO 2010). Both of these are subject to periodic modification in response to changes in cultural attitude as well as medical and psychological knowledge (WHO 2010). For example, homosexuality is no longer classified as a mental illness.

The classification of an addiction as a 'disease' can be problematic, as illustrated by Davison (2002: 229) in an interview with a woman who had experienced a serious drink problem:

> Just trying to stop drinking with willpower or doctor's pills wasn't working for me . . . I needed to get away from the idea of having an incurable disease before I could begin to control it.

Beyond western medicine, there are cultural variations in illness diagnosis. The Chinese Classification of Mental Disorders (CCMD) includes a condition called 'Koro', which refers to excessive fear of the genitals or breasts shrinking and may reflect cultural emphasis on fertility. People from different backgrounds have different concerns and, in an increasingly globalized world, it is important that health advice takes account of different cultural and individual understandings.

Promoting health and preventing ill health

In applying psychology to health, we distinguish between three distinct types of activity:

- *primary prevention*: measures to prevent disease in healthy people, such as eating a healthy diet;
- *secondary prevention*: the early detection of disease, usually through a screening programme, so that treatment will arrest the disease process at an early stage;
- *tertiary prevention*: rehabilitation and symptom management to restore function, maximize remaining capabilities and maintain quality of life.

The main aim of primary prevention is to motivate people to give up behaviours that pose a risk to their long-term health and take up behaviours likely to protect their health in the long term. Table 9.1 illustrates the systematic process required to evaluate the effectiveness of health promotion, using cardiovascular disease as an example.

The same principles can be applied to other diseases where there are known risk factors.

Do you have a health-related habit or behaviour you know you ought to change? It might be smoking or not taking enough exercise or eating too much chocolate. If so, do you know exactly how often this behaviour occurs? If you want to change, it is useful to take these 'baseline' measures so you can measure and monitor change. Why not start today?

Exercise

Table 9.1 Evaluating health promotion: example of cardiovascular disease

Priority health problem	Examples of modifiable risk factors	Risk behaviours	Behaviour change required	Example of self-report measure (daily diary)	Examples of objective measures
Cardiovascular disease	Inhalation of tobacco smoke	Smoking	Stop smoking	Number of cigarettes smoked each day	Salivary nicotine metabolites
	Lack of exercise	Sedentary lifestyle	Brisk 30 min walk 3 times a week	Minutes of brisk exercise	Treadmill tolerance
	High cholesterol	Saturated fat consumption	Cut down on fatty food intake	Intake of food containing saturated fat	Blood cholesterol

Social cognition

Social cognition is concerned with social influences on individual beliefs, attitudes and behaviour. Social cognition (or social cognitive) theories are based on the assumption that all health-related activities, including screening attendance, smoking, eating and taking exercise are voluntary behaviours. This implies that people are free to choose whether or not to engage in them or change them. Therefore changes in beliefs and attitudes are presumed to precede behaviour change, as illustrated in Figure 9.1.

The 'cues' identified in Figure 9.1 include health promotion messages, media images, health advice, illness symptoms and family and peer pressure. The social cognition theories or models most widely applied in health psychology are the health belief model (HBM) and the theory of planned behaviour (TPB).

Exercise

Before you read any further, we invite you to consider an aspect of your own behaviour that you have been meaning to change, but have not yet managed to achieve. It might concern a health-related behaviour, such as diet, exercise or smoking, or it might relate to other lifestyle habits, such as study or sleep routines.

Test how these psychological models relate to your own experience.

The health belief model (HBM)

The health belief model originated in the 1950s when Hochbaum, a social scientist, wanted to understand why people failed to attend for screening. The resulting components are shown in Figure 9.2.

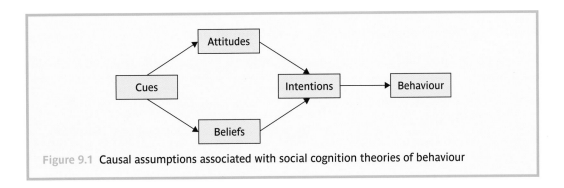

Figure 9.1 Causal assumptions associated with social cognition theories of behaviour

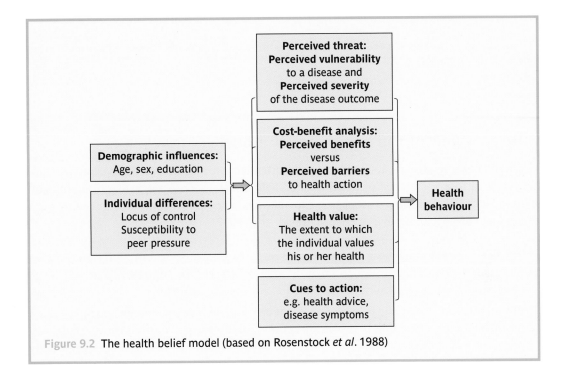

Figure 9.2 The health belief model (based on Rosenstock *et al.* 1988)

According to the health belief model, motivation to take action to protect health is subject to the following beliefs:

- *Perceived vulnerability and severity.* Individuals believe they may be at high risk of a serious disease.
- *Perceived benefits versus perceived barriers.* They believe that the benefits of taking action outweigh the barriers they need to overcome.
- *Health value.* They value their health enough to make the effort to change.
- *Cues to action.* Something prompts them to take appropriate action.

Predicting dietary change using the health belief model

Joe lives on takeaway foods and eats hardly any fresh fruit or vegetables. Applying the health belief model:

- Joe does not consider himself to be at risk. He reasons that there is no family history of premature death in his family.
- He sees little benefit to change, but identifies a range of barriers including lack of time to buy and prepare food and a strong preference for pizza and chips.
- Joe is young and takes his health for granted. He reasons that he does not want to live to a great age anyway.
- He is aware of health advice in the media, but does not feel that this applies to him.

The health belief model predicts that Joe is extremely unlikely to change to healthier eating habits at the present time.

Critical review of the health belief model

The health belief model was designed to predict attendance for medical screening, but has since been applied to a wide range of health-related habits such as smoking, eating, drinking and sexual activity. The following reasons may explain why the health belief model shows only weak ability to predict health behaviour change (Taylor *et al.* 2007).

1   The health belief model was designed specifically to predict a single action that requires minimal effort or disruption to an individual's lifestyle. In contrast, lifestyle change involves a complex set of actions that require considerable effort.

2   Attendance for screening is designed to detect and prevent a specific disease, which means there is a direct link between the action and disease prevention. However, disease prevention is not usually uppermost in most people's minds as they go about their daily activities.

3   Attendance at screening involves known barriers, such as leaving work early or making arrangements for child care. Making a lifestyle change often involves unforeseen and unpredictable barriers or distractions that lead the individual to deviate from a planned course of action.

4   Perceived threat, cost-benefit analysis and health value depend on the assumption that health-related behaviours and behaviour change involve conscious, deliberative cognitive processes. In contrast, most health-related activities such as smoking, eating and taking (or not taking) exercise are habits based on unconscious, automatic, low-effort cognitive processing (see Evans 2008: Chapter 1).

5   The health belief model focuses on individual beliefs and actions, whereas many involve social or group interactions where choice and control are reduced.

Nevertheless, the health belief model retains some practical use as part of individual assessment because it can highlight reasons why it is hard to make a change.

Reflect on your own experience. How useful is the health belief model for drawing attention to important reasons why you find it hard to change your own lifestyle behaviours or habits? Compare your experience with those of someone you know who is finding it difficult to make a change.

The advantages of disease prevention or reduction are often self-evident to a health professional, but may not be so obvious to those who see their behaviour as 'normal'. Many health risk behaviours are subject to social involvement, for example sharing meals, smoking outside work premises, or having sex. Social barriers can be particularly difficult to overcome.

Sexual risk in college students

Downing-Matibag and Geisinger (2009) observed that casual and unprotected sexual relationships are common among students. They conducted qualitative interviews which they analysed using a health belief model framework to understand students' reasons for taking sexual risks. They found:

- *Perceived invulnerability.* There was a high level of ignorance about the risks associated with unprotected oral sex, and belief that their partner was unlikely to have an STD because they were friends.
- *Benefits/barriers.* Condoms were more likely to be used during vaginal intercourse if the benefits of avoiding infection outweighed the barriers. Condoms were not used if students believed this might thwart the opportunity to have sex or compromise pleasure. Many were not confident in negotiating condom use during an unplanned sexual encounter. Some associated condom use with pornographic sex, not sex between friends. Alcohol frequently impaired judgement and some were just 'swept away' by sexual desire.

When giving advice about any type of lifestyle change, it is important to ensure that people correctly understand their individual risk. But it is also essential to explore with them all of the environmental, social and psychological barriers that might inhibit appropriate action, then help them to find the least onerous and most attractive ways of addressing or circumventing these.

Overcoming barriers to change

Ted's friend, Alan, was worried about a persistent cough and had been advised by his doctor to give up smoking. But his social life involved going to the pub with friends, who were all smokers. Alan couldn't resist the offer of a cigarette. At first, he felt he had to choose between keeping his friends or giving up smoking. Instead, he shared his dilemma with Ted and the others and they agreed to help him.

They set up a charity collection into which they put the savings from all the pub regulars for each cigarette they would have smoked, but didn't, while at the pub for the next three months. This proved very successful. Several regulars, including Alan, stopped smoking altogether and most of the others cut down considerably. They donated a large sum to the local children's hospice.

This example illustrates how it might be possible to overcome barriers using a combination of social support and incentive, rather than threat.

- Do you think you might be able to devise a plan of action that builds in sufficient incentives or treats to overcome the barriers you have identified?
- Based on your own analysis using the health belief model, how likely is it that you will change your behaviour in the near future?

Now read about the theory of planned behaviour and see if it offers a different perspective on the same issues.

The theory of planned behaviour (TPB)

The theory of planned behaviour (TPB) (Ajzen 1991) was designed by social psychologists to explain any behaviour, including buying a car, choosing a shirt or smoking a particular brand of cigarette. The key elements of the theory are illustrated in Figure 9.3 and explained below.

According to the theory, the intention to behave in a certain way, or make a change, is determined by the following key factors:

- *Attitude towards the behaviour* reflects a value judgement made by the individual about whether or not the action or change is 'a good thing'. It is based on an evaluation of the desirability of the outcome of the proposed action.
- *The subjective norm* refers to beliefs about what important or significant others think they should do, together with motivation to comply with these wishes.

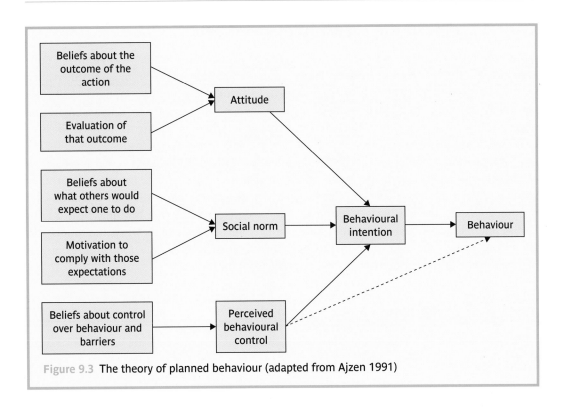

Figure 9.3 **The theory of planned behaviour (adapted from Ajzen 1991)**

● *Perceived behavioural control* refers to an assessment of the degree of self-efficacy or control the individual perceives him or herself to have over the particular course of action. It is based on an appraisal about whether or not they have the necessary skills, abilities, resources and/or support to achieve the behaviour and overcome barriers to action.

Apply each aspect of the theory of planned behaviour (below) to see how well it predicts your intention to change.

● Do you think it would be a good thing to change?
● Do those close to you think you should change? If so, how much do you value their opinion?
● How easily could you change if you really wanted to?

Based on your own analysis, using the theory of planned behaviour:

● How likely is it that you will change your behaviour during the next week? The next month? The next year? Sometime? Never?
● Has the theory of planned behaviour helped you to understand whether or not you will change?

Exercise

Critical review of the theory of planned behaviour

As indicated by its title, this model is also based on the assumption that behaviour is a consequence of rational decision-making. However, as we have already seen, most health-related behaviours need considerable effort or incentive to bring them under conscious, deliberate control. Even when individuals want to make a change, they frequently underestimate the degree of control they have over the behaviour change required, including the barriers likely to be encountered.

The model is reasonably good at predicting intentions (Ajzen 1991) but less good at predicting actual behaviour, particularly where the behaviour that needs changing is a habit that normally requires little forethought. In fact, the longer the gap between expressing an intention and making a change, the less likely the change is to take place. NICE (the National Institute for Health and Clinical Excellence) found little evidence of health benefits when the model was applied to individual behaviour in practice (Taylor *et al.* 2007). The following examples highlight some of the reasons for its modest predictive power.

Application of the TPB to individual behaviours

Janice has had an invitation to attend for a mammogram and must decide whether or not to attend.

- *Attitude*: Janice believes that attending for screening will have positive benefits. If it proves negative, it will reassure her. If it proves positive it will enable her to receive early treatment for breast cancer and this will improve the outcome for her.
- *Subjective or social norm*: Janice believes that her family would wish her to attend for screening. Her friends all attend and expect her to do the same.
- *Perceived behavioural control*: it is quite easy for Janice to attend for screening as the unit comes to her workplace. She knows about the procedure and is not frightened about what will happen.

Using this analysis, Janice is very likely to attend unless something unforeseen occurs to prevent this on the day.

Mark was advised by the cardiologist to walk for at least 20 minutes per day.

- *Attitude*: he believes that exercise would do him good.
- *Subjective norm*: his wife and sister both urged him to do this.
- *Perceived behavioural control*: he knows that he could easily do it if he wanted to because he has the ability and the resources (equipment, environment) to do it.
- *Behavioural intent*: he really intends to do it.

This analysis predicts strong intention to exercise. But the actual outcome is quite different. He keeps putting it off, giving the excuse that he will start when the weather is better, or he has more time. It appears that his level of behavioural control is much weaker than he likes to admit.

General critique of social cognition models

Social cognition models, by definition, treat health-related behaviours as if they are a consequence of conscious, rational cognitive processing (see Chapter 4). But most health behaviours are 'in a large part determined by combinations of circumstantial reality and individuals' habitual, emotional, unconscious and/or otherwise non-rational reactions to the external world' (Taylor *et al.* 2007: 5). It is easy to underestimate the conscious effort required to bring health habits under conscious control in order to implement change.

Second, social cognition models fail to distinguish between the different types of change required. For example:

- Smoking, drinking alcohol and substance misuse are behaviours that need to be reduced. Therefore, some other equally desirable activity needs to be introduced to compensate for the time that would have been spent engaged in these activities.
- Exercise involves the introduction of a new behaviour. Time must be found for this and it may mean displacing or discontinuing some other activity or routine. It is important to minimize disruption and introduce treats to ensure maintenance.
- Dietary change involves substitution, which is not so difficult provided it provides at least the same level of satisfaction.

When giving health advice, it is not good enough to focus only on disease prevention. Success in achieving health behaviour change is likely to depend on engaging with the individual and a careful analysis of their lifestyle, goals and desires, and on ways to overcome barriers to change. Making change as part of a social group increases normative pressures and can be more fun. Hence the popularity of slimming groups and leisure clubs.

Age-related differences in health behaviours

Høie *et al.* (2011) demonstrated that the theory of planned behaviour was better at predicting intention to stop smoking in those aged 35 to 55 (38 per cent), than in adolescents aged 16–19 (32 per cent). They found that the younger group were more likely to be responsive to subjective social norms, including peer group and media pressure. Older people seem more likely to change health behaviours for health reasons.

Research

Our third criticism of social cognition models is the lack of emphasis on the immediate social or environmental social cues or pressure, particularly in the younger age groups, as illustrated in the previous example of students' sexual activity.

A fourth criticism is that many health-related behaviours, including smoking, comfort eating, drinking alcohol and taking illegal drugs, are used as coping strategies for dealing with stress (Chapter 7). It is difficult to change these behaviours at a time when the individual is under stress. In fact, readiness to change is not accounted for in either the health belief model or the theory of planned behaviour.

Stages of change

Prochaska and DiClemente (1983) recognized that another important determinant of health-related behaviour change was the individual's motivational state – their readiness to make a change. They argued that interventions will be more successful if tailored to the individual's state of readiness to change. Prochaska and DiClemente produced their 'stages of change' model in order to classify people according to their level of readiness to make a change. It is also called the 'transtheoretical' model because it is designed for use in combination with theoretical models such as those we have previously described. The stages of change model is illustrated in Figure 9.4. The starting point is the stage of pre-contemplation.

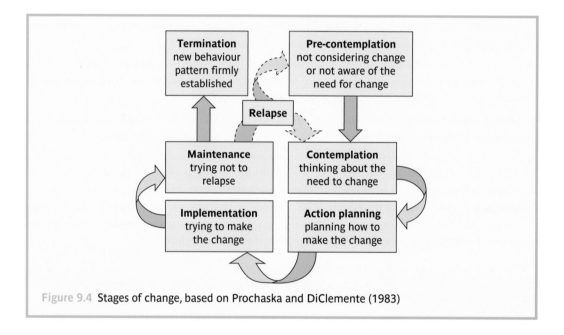

Figure 9.4 **Stages of change, based on Prochaska and DiClemente (1983)**

Reflect on the change you are contemplating. At which stage of change would you place yourself right now?

Have you previously attempted a change and then relapsed? If so, did you contemplate trying again or did you give up?

The stages of change model has been widely applied and tested in health promotion practice to address a variety of health habits. Logically, it makes sense to assess an individual's stage of change and adapt the intervention to suit the stage they are at. Table 9.2 Illustrates how the stages of change model might be useful in helping an individual to lose weight.

Table 9.2 Stages of change model applied to achieve weight loss

Stage of change	Key issues	Example of approach
Pre-contemplation	Overweight, but has not seen a reason to change	Focus on positive reasons and individual incentives to change
Contemplation	Wants to lose weight, but has failed before	Explore the easiest and more pleasurable dieting options, given personal food preferences
Planning	Not sure how to ensure it will succeed	Explore all possible barriers to success Involve family and friends Plan for gradual weight reduction, avoid crash dieting Incorporate plenty of treats
Implementation	Not sure how to get started	Avoid starting when celebrations or holidays are planned Plan menus, clear the larder Fix start date Recruit someone to monitor progress
Relapse prevention	Worried about failure Dealing with temptation	Plan how to deal with risky situations Incorporate regular treats Involve family and friends in removing temptations
Termination	How to decide when the programme is successful?	New diet enjoyed as part of lifestyle Weight stabilized at reasonable level

Table 9.2 illustrates how elements from the health belief model and theory of planned behaviour (such as overcoming barriers and translating good intentions into action) can be incorporated at a time that is appropriate to the individual's stage of change.

Critical review of the stages of change model

The stages of change model is intuitively attractive, extremely popular among clinicians and researchers, and widely used as a basis for planning health promotion interventions. However, Taylor *et al.* (2007: 19) found no overall evidence that assessing stage of change enhances the outcome of a health promotion programme. In fact, they found no empirical evidence that there are, in fact, observable discrete stages of change.

West (2005) offered the following critique of the stages of change model:

- On its own, the model is descriptive but not predictive. It is possible to classify people, but this gives little indication of their future progress.
- There is actually no evidence that people progress smoothly through a series of 'stages'. (This argument applies equally to other stage models of development and change; see Chapter 3).

- The model assumes that people make conscious and stable plans – many do not.
- People may not respond honestly to an assessment of their stage of change, particularly when engaging in a stigmatized behaviour such as substance misuse.
- To label someone as a 'pre-contemplator' when they have no intention to change is not helpful.
- The model allows health promoters, educators and researchers to claim success for an intervention just because people have moved from one stage to the next, even if no behavioural change has actually taken place.

As West noted, lifestyle behaviours often change in the absence of contemplation and planning.

Example

Unpremeditated change

Joe loved pizza and chips. Prior to meeting Sasha he had no intention at all of changing his unhealthy diet – he was at the stage of pre-contemplation. But after moving in with Sasha, he quickly came to like the fresh, healthy food she bought and cooked. Similarly, when Sasha found she was pregnant she immediately gave up smoking, even though she had not given it any serious consideration with respect to her own health.

No social cognition model can predict change in the context of unplanned life changes.

In spite of criticisms, West upheld the importance of assessing decision-making and motivation. Hodgins (2005) suggested that it might be helpful to outline the stages of change to patients or clients and invite them to make their own judgements about where they fit in. This fits with notion of partnership, whereby practitioners work with clients and patients to ensure that any course of action fits in with their personal goals and the resources they have to achieve these, as highlighted in the self-regulation model reviewed below.

Self-regulatory theory

Self-regulation implies that people have, or can develop, autonomy, self-control, self-direction and self-discipline (Purdie and McCrindle 2002). The assumption is that people's behaviours are motivated by their desire to achieve goals that are personally important.

The idea of self-regulation has its origins in systems theory, from which come the concepts of control and homeostasis. Self-regulation depends on feedback, through which individuals can appraise and adjust their performance. The amount of effort put into achieving a goal is likely to depend on its desirability and achievability. The emphasis within self-regulatory theory is on the relationship between an individual's action and his or her perception of its likely outcome.

Evaluating actions and outcomes: drinking alcohol

An evaluation of the consequences of drinking excess alcohol is quite different when viewed from different perspectives. Take the following scenario where Joe gets drunk at a party:

- Joe finds alcohol reduces his social inhibitions.
- Friends find his behaviour amusing.
- Strangers view Joe's behaviour as disturbing and offensive.
- Joe's family views his drinking as a normal part of growing up. They clean him up and put him to bed.
- Health professionals view his 'binge-drinking' as a threat to his health.

Joe is unlikely to gain control over his drinking unless or until he is able to find alternative sources of social ease with people who do not encourage him to drink or mitigate its consequences. The negative attitudes of strangers and professionals may actually increase his feelings of discomfort and his need to drink.

Example

A key proponent of the self-regulatory model is Bandura, whose concept of self-efficacy has proved influential within many aspects of health psychology (see Chapter 5). Bandura (2005) argued that if maintaining health is the goal, the best way to achieve this is through health promotion that is targeted at changing lifestyle habits. He reasoned that it is impossible to achieve success if the individual has a goal without a plan to achieve it; or has a plan without a clearly identified goal. According to Bandura, self-regulated change does not rely on willpower but on having a comprehensive plan that takes into account the following issues:

1 Many people enjoy their unhealthy lifestyle and do not share the same goals as health professionals.
2 When considering a lifestyle change, people often face competing or conflicting desires or demands. For example, many people who want to lose weight also love sweet or fatty foods. Or they want to give up drink or drugs, but find themselves in a social setting where these are the norm. Or they want to end a relationship, but can't face the repercussions or upheavals.
3 There is a tendency for people to be unrealistically optimistic in their beliefs about their ability to achieve their goals, and poor at anticipating the amount of effort required to overcome habits, social pressures and likely distractions (Taylor and Gollwitzer 1995).

Think back to the change you thought about making in your own life. How realistic were you in your assessment of the obstacles you might encounter on the road to change?

Exercise

The self-regulatory model predicts that behaviour change requires a goal implementation strategy and not just a goal-directed intention, as proposed in the theory of planned behaviour.

Example

Developing an implementation plan

When Mark developed angina, he needed a plan to avoid the temptation of buying crisps and chocolate. He enjoyed the daily chat with the newsagent from whom he bought chocolate bars and who had become a good friend. So he planned to share his problem with the newsagent and engage his help in buying chewing gum and nuts instead. Meanwhile, he and Janice worked out a lunchtime diet that would satisfy his hunger as well as his dietary needs. This new strategy worked very well. Mark lost weight and started to feel better.

Like Prochaska and DiClemente, Bandura pointed out the importance of identifying an individual's readiness to change. But he proposed alternative 'levels of readiness' (not stages), based on his concept of self-efficacy (see Chapter 5).

Bandura's levels of readiness (Bandura 2005)

Level 1: high sense of self-efficacy and positive expectations for achieving behaviour change. These people need minimal guidance.

Level 2: self-doubts about efficacy and the likely benefits of their efforts. These individuals make half-hearted attempts and are quick to give up when they run into difficulties. These people need individual support and guidance which may be provided by telephone or via the internet.

Level 3: believe that their health habits are beyond their personal control, effort is futile, and are highly sceptical of the need to change. These individuals need a great deal of personal guidance in a progressive structured programme.

Bandura (2000) recommended that the individuals at Levels 2 and 3 need to identify short-term attainable sub-goals to motivate and guide their efforts.

Applying Bandura's self-regulation model

Bandura's model is less prescriptive and more person-centred than other models. It requires the practitioner to work with individuals to recognize their readiness and ability to manage change, given the social situations and obstacles they are likely to encounter in everyday life. This enables the practitioner to assist the individual in the development of an implementation plan that will take full advantage of the resources available to them and overcome the barriers they are likely to encounter. We illustrate this application in Table 9.3.

Table 9.3 Application of self-regulatory theory to lifestyle change

Check list	Action
What is the individual's main goal?	Find out what the individual wants to achieve (e.g. weight loss, smoking cessation)
How ready is the individual to make a change?	Assess* using Bandura's state of readiness or Prochaska and DiClemente's stages of change for guidance
What resources are available to assist them to make the change?	Identify all relevant knowledge, skills, social and other tangible assets
What barriers or obstacles are likely to be encountered?	Identify all likely barriers to success. Help the individual think through all the situations he or she is likely to encounter
Is there a plan for dealing with barriers and obstacles?	Help the individual to find realistic and motivating ways of overcoming these
What can realistically be achieved in the short term?	Set an interim goal that is realistic and easily achievable
Is there an implementation plan?	Ensure that there is a written plan of action that takes account of how to deal with each obstacle identified
When will the plan start?	Make a contract to start straight away
How will you know the plan is working?	Take measurements and monitor change. Set a date to review progress. Has the interim goal been achieved? If not why not? If necessary, revise the contract to take account of unforeseen obstacles
What next?	Continue with new interim goals and revisions until the main goal is achieved or a new one negotiated

*Note that assessment is carried out in partnership *with* the individual.

Exercise

Applying Table 9.3 to your own need to change, how helpful do you think the checklist and action plan would be? Is there anything you might want to include in order to improve it?

In applying this self-regulatory process, it is really important that it is not only person-centred but is person-led, since it is individuals who must agree their own goals and develop their own strategy for achieving them. The practitioner may guide, but must not direct. One way of achieving this is by using the motivational interview.

The motivational interview

Didactic (instructional) approaches to health education (telling people what they ought to do) and those based on persuasion often fail because they imply criticism and produce resistance (see Chapter 6). Motivational interviewing was developed by Miller and Rollnick (2002) as a 'style of encounter' to overcome these effects in the field of addiction. It is now used increasingly to motivate change in other health settings (Britt *et al.* 2004). The motivational interview has certain key features:

- *Empathy*: express warmth towards clients and active interest in what they are saying.
- *Active listening*: listen carefully to the clients' point of view. Reflect back to clarify their interpretation, meaning and understanding.
- *Collaboration*: use negotiation; avoid persuasion or confrontation.
- *Evocation*: use a non-directive approach to steer clients into talking about their reasons for change; avoid giving advice or information unless it is requested.
- *Autonomy*: respect the wishes of clients, even if they choose not to change.
- *Rolling with resistance*: never challenge clients when they express resistance to change. Find a way to explore their reasons and regard these as legitimate – this approach is more likely to provide them with the opportunity to consider alternatives for themselves.

As part of the change process, many people know what they ought to do, but find themselves in a state of conflict between what they are actually doing and what they should do (see cognitive dissonance, Chapter 6). The motivational interview allows people to use problem-solving to change their behaviour, whereas directive approaches often elicit self-justification and reinforce resistance to change.

Using the motivational interview to increase exercise

Hillsdon *et al.* (2002) randomized a sample of 1658 inactive middle-aged men and women to receive a 30-minute session of either brief negotiation based on motivational interview, or direct health advice to take more exercise, or no intervention (controls). Brief negotiation consisted of inviting participants to think about the importance of physical exercise and the benefits and costs of increasing physical activity. Obstacles to change were acknowledged and the participant encouraged to think about ways of overcoming these. Of those who completed the study, the group who received brief negotiation increased their level of exercise significantly more than the controls, whereas the direct advice group did not. The average improvement amounted to 37 minutes of brisk walking per week.

A systematic review of motivational interviewing by Rubak *et al.* (2005) confirmed its potential to bring about a variety of lifestyle changes including diet and exercise. A more recent systematic review by Lai *et al.* (2010) showed that a single session of motivational interviewing delivered by a nurse or counsellor improved the likelihood of smoking cessation using bio-chemically validated measures. The outcome was likely to be better if the session lasted for longer than 20 minutes and if the motivational interview was used in conjunction with self-help materials. Telephone interview was almost as effective as face-to-face interview.

Using a motivational interview

Next time you encounter a friend or patient who appears resistant to what seems to be a sensible suggestion, try using the motivational interview approach.

- Be empathetic and express interest in their point of view.
- Acknowledge their right not to change and their reasons for not wanting to change.
- Listen to what they say and invite them to expand on their reasoning.
- Invite them to consider the rights and wrongs of alternative points of view.

BUT

- Only give information or express your point of view if it is requested.
- Don't attempt to offer advice or criticize their reasoning.

How long did this take? By the end, did you notice any shift in their attitude? Did they seem less resistant to change?

Medical help-seeking

The outcome of many illnesses depends on early detection. In order to seek medical help, it is first necessary for people to recognize that there is something wrong with them. Then it is essential that they seek medical help as soon as possible. Cancer and cardiovascular disease are common examples where delay in medical help-seeking leads to poor outcomes.

Why do people delay seeking help?

Grunfeld *et al.* (2003) surveyed well women about their beliefs and intentions to seek help for breast cancer symptoms, using the theory of planned behaviour. Older women were more likely to express the intention to seek help than younger women. The inability to recognize breast cancer symptoms predicted delay in all age groups. For women aged 35–54, lack of perceived behavioural control (not knowing what to expect or what to do) was found to be an important predictor of the intention not to seek help. In women aged over 65 years, beliefs about the disabling or disfiguring consequences of having breast cancer inhibited help-seeking.

Based on these findings, Grunfeld *et al.* suggest that providing information about cosmetic outcomes may be particularly important for older women whose friends or relatives might have received surgery at a time when aesthetic outcomes were poor.

In the case of myocardial infarction (MI, heart attack) or stroke, delay to the commencement of thrombolytic (clot-busting) intervention can have serious adverse consequences. Yet people often delay calling for help for several hours. Older people may be less likely to summon help because symptoms are less typical or pain less severe. Women may be more likely to delay than men if they view heart disease as a man's problem, but other than this there is little evidence that delay is due to lack of knowledge. An important reason for delay is likely to be found in the social process of help-seeking. Kentsch *et al.* (2002) found that key factors associated with delay included not wanting to bother anybody and waiting to ask others for advice.

Illustration of delay in help-seeking

When Mark first experienced chest pain, he did wonder if he might be having a heart attack and was very frightened. It was late afternoon and he was at work. He managed to convince himself that it was probably indigestion and made an excuse to leave early, knowing that Janice would be home to reassure or advise him. Janice quickly phoned for the ambulance. Fortunately, tests revealed it to be an angina attack and his symptoms responded to treatment. But had it been an MI, this delay could have been fatal.

People commonly seek help, advice and reassurance from others when they feel ill and it is often a family member or friend who prompts help-seeking. Those who are socially isolated are therefore at greater risk from delay.

People are particularly inclined to delay seeking medical help for mental health problems. Christiana *et al.* (2000) conducted an international survey of members of patient advocate groups suffering from anxiety disorders and found a median delay of eight years. Older people were more likely to seek help earlier. An important reason for delay may be the stigma associated with mental illness (Chapter 2).

One practical lesson for health professionals is that they should take every opportunity to educate the public about what to look for and what to do if someone they know develops a symptom or appears unwell. While this might not overcome reluctance to seek personal help, it is likely to encourage appropriate action on behalf of someone else.

Taking opportunities for health education

Anna's friend, Zara, worked as a health visitor, dealing mainly with the development of babies and young children. The local mother and toddler group had meetings at which they discussed important health and safety issues related to child care. Zara recognized that this provided an opportunity to introduce other general topics, such as resuscitation techniques for adults and children. Leading on from this, the mothers requested additional topics including the health of male partners and care of older relatives.

The final sections of this chapter focus on what happens after a disease has been diagnosed or symptoms of illness become persistent.

Following medical advice

Disease management was traditionally regarded as a process of taking prescribed medicines and other courses of treatment. For an acute illness, such as infection, this often involves a short course of medication (which many people fail to complete). In the case of a chronic illness, it can mean a lifetime taking a range of drugs in addition to following regimes that include dietary restrictions, exercise programmes and self-monitoring. There is strong evidence that people find it really difficult to stick to their treatment schedule in spite of the potential consequences.

Compliance was the term traditionally used to describe acting in accordance with the doctor's instructions. It implies that 'doctor knows best'. Non-compliance by patients was viewed as deviant behaviour. However, it is important to understand the reasons why people fail to continue with a course of treatment. For example, many drugs have unpleasant or harmful side-effects. Talk to any group of patients and you will find some who just don't like taking tablets. Most people want to know *why* they need treatment and what to expect from it, rather than blindly following the doctor's instructions.

Compliance was replaced by the term adherence. This implies that the doctor and patient reach agreement about an appropriate course of treatment. However, compliance and adherence have both been accused of involving some degree of coercion, which discourages patients from taking personal control over the management of their condition. These issues led Anderson and Funnell (2000) to claim that both compliance and adherence are dysfunctional concepts.

The term 'concordance' is now encouraged within health care to reflect the need for shared understanding between health care professional and patient about the nature of the illness, its treatment and its management. The intention is to involve patients as partners in order to ensure that their needs are understood and can be met within the context of their own lifestyle. This is particularly important at a time when people have access to a wide range of information on the internet (not all of which is accurate).

Concordance involving children

Sanz (2003) identified that when dealing with children who have chronic diseases, concordance is required between three partners: doctor, parent and child. Sanz pointed out that the medical consultation frequently involves a two-way conversation between the doctor and parent. The child often plays a passive role in the consultation even though children with asthma or diabetes are expected to play an active role in the management of their disease.

Igoe (1988, 1991) evaluated an education programme to improve children's involvement in their own health and health care. Children were asked to draw the medical consultation. Typically, these depicted a large doctor, medium-sized mother and, in the bottom corner, a small child. After training in what to expect and how to ask questions, their drawings indicated a much more equal relationship between the three partners, as illustrated by the size and position of the three players.

Partnership involves give and take. People need to understand the reasons for and advantages of adhering to a particular course of action. Professionals need to understand the context in which changes to lifestyle will occur and the barriers likely to make change difficult to achieve.

Find time to talk to a patient or client who, you know, has been advised to follow a particular course of action or lifestyle change. Invite them to talk about this change, and what it will mean for them. Listen carefully to what they say. Ask them to clarify or expand on issues they raise. Invite them to consider what action they think they are likely to take. Only give information or advice if they request it.

How easy or difficult did you find it to encourage discussion? Did the patient/client seek to defend a contrary position? Did you resist the temptation to weigh in with counter-arguments?

The motivational interview approach outlined earlier is ideally suited to helping people with a chronic illness to achieve lifestyle change. But it is not easy to avoid coercive statements or pleas, particularly for professionals who are convinced they know what the best course of action should be.

Understanding chronic illness

In this section, we focus attention on psychological issues in the management of chronic or life-limiting illnesses. These are illnesses that involve persistent, recurrent or deteriorating symptoms which are not amenable to cure. Psychologists in the 1980s identified five key questions that people normally want answered when they become ill (Leventhal and Nerenz 1982; Lau and Hartman 1983).

- *Identity*: what is the name of the disease I have?
- *Consequences*: what will happen to me?
- *Time line*: what is the duration of the illness?
- *Causes*: why has this happened to me?
- *Cure*: what can be done about it?

Anticipating and responding to these sorts of questions is generally reassuring and can highlight misconceptions. It seems a paradox that some patients express relief when given a potentially life-threatening diagnosis such as cancer or multiple sclerosis, but not knowing can be even more worrying. However, not everybody wants the same type of information and it is important first to clarify what the person wants to know (see Chapter 4 on breaking bad news).

People who have a chronic or life-limiting disease often need help to come to terms with their sense of loss. These include loss of abilities, roles, job and sense of identity, accompanied by changed or lost relationships, loss of anticipated future and even loss of hope (Walker *et al.*

2006). Cancer is now talked about more openly and has, to a great extent, lost the stigma it once held; indeed, cancer invites a lot of sympathy. In contrast, people with a progressive or chronic illness, particularly where there is no clearly defined medical diagnosis, are often exposed to stigmatizing encounters in the health care system and in daily life, leading to emotional pain and isolation (Holloway *et al.* 2007). Avoidant reactions to people who have a life-limiting or chronic illness are frequently reported, for example former colleagues cross the street. Care staff may move people into a side room or encourage unrealistic optimism. Reasons include uncertainty about how to respond to someone who may never again be well and a sense of helplessness when faced with failure to respond to treatment.

Find half an hour to sit with someone who has a chronic condition. Explain that you are interested to find out more about the effects of the condition they have. Tell them how long you have. Ask them to talk about the effects that the condition has had on their lives. If they dry up or skate over an issue, signal or invite them to tell you a bit more about it, but only if they wish to.

What have you learned about the experience of chronic illness?

Exercise

The challenges of chronic disease

A chronic disease is incurable, but not necessarily life-threatening. Therefore, the aim of chronic disease management is to ensure that people have access to the information and support that will enable them to maintain or improve their level of function and quality of life, and achieve attainable goals.

Health services are well equipped with the knowledge, skills and structures to treat acute disease episodes that involve a single body system. But they are less well structured to meet the needs of those whose symptoms vary and whose illness involves multiple body systems. People who have a chronic disease often receive a short course of rehabilitation and are then told that they must 'learn to live with it'. The options are to suffer and do nothing; just take the medicine; or take charge and be an active self-manager (DoH 2002: 1; Lorig *et al.* 2007). Only the last option will help to preserve quality of life.

The transition from patient to self-manager

Health professionals and patients find this transition very difficult. The health professional has to admit the investigations are complete and there is no cure. The patient needs to accept that this is true, so that he or she can move on. This is particularly difficult where there is no real medical explanation for the patient's symptoms. Examples of conditions that remain medically unexplained in terms of pathology include fibromyalgia and chronic fatigue syndrome or ME (myalgic encephalopathy).

The transition from medical management to self-management is often difficult for patients and health professionals. Barriers to successful adaptation include:

- the length of time spent waiting for confirmation of the diagnosis;
- the number of referrals required to achieve a definitive diagnosis;
- a desire on the part of the doctor or the patient to 'just try one more treatment';
- attribution of physical symptoms (by the doctor) to a psychological cause;
- failure of health professionals to offer alternative hope in the form of self-management strategies and support.

Principles of self-management

Drawing on the self-regulatory model and principles of motivational interviewing discussed earlier in this chapter, it is important to help the individual develop a goal-directed plan for how to achieve successful self-management. Some of the important issues faced by people with a chronic disease include (from Miller 1992):

- maintain sense of the 'normal' in terms of daily routines and lifestyle;
- gain knowledge and skills for symptom management;
- make decisions about treatment;
- use effective coping strategies;
- comply with essential medical regimes;
- deal with stigma associated with the disorder;
- adjust to altered social relationships;
- come to terms with losses associated with the illness;
- maintain or resume work, occupational and/or leisure activity;
- maintain hope.

Maintaining quality of life

Quality of life implies more than just happiness. The World Health Organization (WHO 1997) identified key domains of quality of life, based on interviews worldwide, and incorporated these into the WHO quality of life measure (WHOQOL). They recommend this as an assessment tool for clinical practice as well as research. It increases the professional's understanding of the patient's needs, provides valuable information about aspects of an individual's life that is most affected and informs appropriate responses. We have incorporated key elements from the WHOQOL into Table 9.4, in which we have included practical suggestions for people who have a chronic illness. These are based on our own evidence-based clinical practice and experience.

Most encounters in hospital or primary care settings are too short to deal effectively with these complex issues. But it is important for all staff to keep information about support services and groups that can help after discharge, and to use empathetic skills to encourage their use.

Table 9.4 Improving quality of life, based on WHOQOL indicators

Domain	Contributory factors	Suggestions to promote self-management
Physical	Energy and fatigue Pain and discomforting symptoms Sleep and rest	Improve overall bodily fitness Promote balance of exercise and rest Address full range of symptoms Promote good fluid and dietary intake Complementary therapies may help – placebo effects can be very strong
Psychological	Negative/positive feelings and self-esteem Concentration Bodily image and appearance	Address reasons for negativity If necessary, treat depression Review side effects of medication Highlight relevant self-help groups Make good use of internet resources (e.g. www.patient.co.uk)
Level of Independence	Mobility Activities of daily living Dependence on others Dependence on medicinal and other substances Availability and use of appropriate aids to independence Work capacity	Promote exercises that improve muscle strength Work with family to promote independence Review medication use Review access to and appropriate use of aids Encourage active engagement in work, household activities and hobbies
Social relationships	Quality of personal relationships Availability of emotional support and practical help Intimacy and sexual activity	Review personal relationships/offer counselling as necessary Encourage contact with relevant self-help group Discourage unnecessary practical help Be open to discussing topics related to intimacy and sex
Environmental	Financial resources Suitability of the home environment Opportunities for acquiring new information and skills Participation in and opportunities for recreation/ leisure Access to transport	Refer to appropriate agencies for advice and help as necessary Encourage contact with appropriate self-help groups and internet sources of information, as necessary Encourage self-referral to the Expert Patient Programme, as necessary: www.expertpatients.co.uk Highlight shopmobility and other local transport schemes
Spiritual	Engagement in activities that promote spiritual well-being	Be open to spiritual needs Support individual beliefs Help with access to religious support

Table 9.4 *Continued*	
Domain	**Suggestions to promote self-management**
Overall	When hospitalized, most people with an established chronic disease have become experts in their own symptom management and, provided it is safe, should be encouraged to remain in control
	You should be in a position to provide appropriate internet addresses or print-outs that give accurate and relevant self-help information about their condition and treatment
	Use non-directive strategies from the motivational interview to elicit the individual's beliefs, needs and goals, and to help them find effective solutions to their problems
	Don't forget the importance of whole-body fitness: exercise, diet and fluid intake are often neglected
	Don't forget to advise on dealing with common side-effects from medication, such as constipation, abdominal discomfort, loss of concentration and fatigue

Exercise

Find another half hour to talk to another patient who has had a chronic condition for a long time. Ask them how they have learned to manage the condition, who helped them, and what resources or supports they have found useful.

- What have you learned about self-management? Do you think that this patient is managing his or her condition effectively? Do you think that the help this person received was adequate?

- What advice are you able to give about the support available in your area following discharge?

Most hospitals in the UK have a patient advice and liaison service (PALS) where patients and their friends and relatives can find out information about support services. Local libraries are another source of information in the community.

Self-management programmes

Self-management programmes are group cognitive-behavioural programmes, based on self-regulatory principles, in which patients come together to learn ways of controlling their symptoms and regaining control over their lives. Programmes may be generic or disease-specific and may be led by professionals or lay people.

Self-management of asthma for children

An early example of a successful self-management programme was designed by Creer to treat childhood asthma (Creer *et al.* 1992). As part of the programme, children were taught to understand their condition and their symptoms, use their inhalers correctly, monitor their own symptoms and learn to recognize early signs of an attack. This enabled them to use their inhaler to prevent or reduce an attack. The children rehearsed these skills for implementation at home and at school. The evaluation of the programme identified that the child's locus of control shifted from external to internal, meaning that they felt more control over their lives. However, the researchers noted that parents felt some loss of their parental role, which would need to be addressed.

An evaluation by Muntner *et al.* (2001) of asthma self-management for adults identified that those who declined to participate in the programme had less knowledge about what to do in the event of an attack and less knowledge about the correct use of inhalers. It seems to confirm that those with the greatest need for knowledge and skills are among those least likely to attend a self-management programme. It is also worth noting that autonomy and control are not valued equally by all people, therefore self-management programmes may not appeal to people who passively see themselves as victims.

Many self-management programmes, such as multi-disciplinary pain management programmes, are run by health professionals. These programmes are likely to be disease- or symptom-specific and may be most appropriate for those requiring rehabilitation or symptom management for specific conditions, such as lung disease, stroke or myocardial infarction. Lay-led programmes, such as the Expert Patient Programme, give more emphasis to lifestyle impact and management.

The Expert Patient Programme, originally developed by Lorig and Holman (1989), is a structured generic chronic disease self-management programme consisting of six weekly sessions. Its aim is to improve self-efficacy and personal control, symptom management, activity and function. The reason for introducing this programme across the UK was to reduce demands on health services in terms of consultations and admissions. A full health economic evaluation (Richardson *et al.* 2008) showed it to be a cost-effective alternative to usual care for people with chronic conditions. Online self-management programmes may be an acceptable alternative for some (Lorig *et al.* 2010).

Look up www.expertpatients.co.uk and print off details of programmes and contacts near to where you work. You may find this information useful to give to patients who have a chronic condition and are finding it difficult to cope.

Self-help groups

Self-help groups offer continuing information and support for those with any type of chronic benign or malignant disease. Some involve attending local meetings, while others offer online support and chat rooms. People need some guidance to help them make best use of appropriate organizations. For example, it is important to avoid organizations whose main aim is to make money or to sell a product – people with a chronic disease are vulnerable to those offering magic cures. Groups need to concentrate on sharing positive aspects of coping, rather than dwelling predominantly on negative aspects of living with the disease. The advantages of a good support group are highlighted in the following account.

The benefit of a support group

In the following extract, Nadine Johnson describes the support she and her husband, Peter, received from the National Association of Laryngectomy Clubs following cancer treatment:

> A wealth of essential, practical tips that you don't learn about in hospital and, to my mind, help to complete the circle of care. Peter learned that in his condition coughing up blood was not necessarily a sign of lung cancer. To a seasoned laryngectomee [sic], this could be a sign of a comparatively innocuous chest infection or dryness of the chest. The differences are mammoth when you live constantly with the fear of a relapse.
>
> (Johnson 2004: 30)

In the final chapter, we provide further examples of how to help someone who has a painful condition.

Further reading

Bandura, A. (2005) The primacy of self-regulation in health promotion, *Applied Psychology: An International Review*, 54(2): 245–54.

Lorig, K., Holman, H., Sobel, D., Laurent, D., Gonzalez, V. and Minor, M. (2007) *Self-management of Long-Term Health Conditions: A Handbook for People with Chronic Disease*, 2nd edition. Boulder, CO: Bull Publishing.

Naidoo, J. and Wills, J. (2009) *Foundations for Health Promotion*, 3rd edition. London: Bailliere Tindall Elsevier.

Chapter 10

Pain: reducing suffering

Key topics

- Understanding and interpreting pain
- Gate control theory of pain
- Psychological principles in pain assessment
- Pain management

Introduction

This chapter addresses the following issues:

- Why do some people experience pain that is well above or below the level that is normally expected?
- Why is the management of pain so often reported to be inadequate?
- How can care professionals help people who are in a lot of pain?

We start with a quote that was written by Professor Patrick Wall who, with Ronald Melzack, originated the 'gate control theory' of pain, which we focus on in this chapter. It was written at a time when Patrick himself was in a lot of pain. It gives some indication why psychology is so important in explaining the experience of pain and in its management.

> Fear generates anxiety and anxiety focuses the attention. The more attention is locked, the worse is the pain. A major aim of therapy should therefore be to identify, understand and treat the anxiety.
>
> (Wall 1999: 157)

We invite you to reflect on these words as you read the following vignettes.

Celia, aged 32, has come into hospital in an attempt to control pain from a chronic condition. Since her admission she has received increasingly high doses of strong analgesia, but cries most of the time because of the pain. Celia's close-knit family members are angry and upset that her pain has not been relieved. The medical staff feel frustrated and powerless.

Dick, aged 28, was born with congenital bone deformities and recently had hip replacement surgery. He found his rehabilitation unexpectedly slow and has been unable to return to work. He has become depressed and his relationship with his girlfriend is on the verge of breakdown. He attends the pain clinic complaining of pain 'all over'.

These vignettes, together with other examples we introduce in this chapter, represent some of the challenges involved in pain management. They typify situations in which physical pain fails to respond to analgesia, leaving patients and those close to them, and care professionals, feeling helpless.

In this chapter, we explore the reasons why people like Celia and Dick have unbearable pain. We illustrate how a psychological approach to pain and its management can help people like Celia and Dick to regain control over their pain. We present exercises related to the two vignettes during the course of the chapter and later reveal the outcomes for Celia and Dick.

Barriers to pain control

We start by listing known barriers to effective pain control found in the literature (Table 10.1).

Table 10.1 Barriers to effective pain control

Barriers	Patients and carers	Health professionals
Pain-related fears	Fear of addiction, tolerance and side-effects	Fear of drug addiction and tolerance
	Belief that pain signals damage, harm or disease progression	Belief that there is a direct relationship between tissue damage and pain
Lack of knowledge	Poor understanding of pain and limits to medicine	Inadequate knowledge about pain mechanisms and pain management
Poor assessment and explanation	Failure to understand the relationship between pain, stress and quality of life	Failure to conduct a holistic assessment of the person in pain
Social stigma	Belief that 'good patients' do not complain about pain	Belief that patients who complain about pain are attention-seeking
External control beliefs	Fatalism or unrealistic expectations of cure	Exclusive focus on treatment or cure

Look back at the two vignettes. Can you identify any barriers listed in Table 10.1 that might contribute to the problems faced by Celia and Dick?

Table 10.1 illustrates how the beliefs of health professionals reflect, or are reflected in, the concerns of the public. Nobody can feel someone else's pain. We are frequently reminded that 'pain is what the patient says it is', but do we continue to make judgements about pain based on how much we think people ought to have?

Pain is often referred to as a biopsychosocial phenomenon. This means that in order to understand an individual's pain, we need to take into account each of the following:

- *Biological factors*: the type and extent of tissue damage and complex physiological mechanisms involved in pain transmission.
- *Psychological factors*: individual beliefs about pain, the meaning attached to a particular pain, and patterns of pain response.
- *Social factors*: the social context in which the pain occurs and social and cultural influences on pain beliefs and pain expression.

Variations in pain experience and expression start at an early age. With the exception of a small minority who are unable to feel pain, we all experience pain. But the meaning each of us learns to attach to different types of pain and the ways we respond to it can be very different.

Learning to understand and interpret pain

Pain experience in babies

Painful sensations are felt from an early stage of development. This presents particular problems for the care of pre-term, low birth weight and sick babies who are exposed to considerable pain and stress during invasive monitoring and life-saving procedures. These include needle-stick, suctioning and surgery. The long-term effects of prenatal and neonatal pain are not yet well researched, but there is some evidence that these early experiences lead to hypersensitivity to pain (Grunau *et al.* 2006).

Research

Non-pharmacological interventions to reduce neonatal pain

Grunau *et al.* (2009) showed that cumulative exposure to pain in the neonatal period was associated with poorer cognitive and motor outcomes at eight and 18 months. The administration of intravenous morphine was associated with poorer motor development at eight months, highlighting the desirability of alternative methods of pain control.

A systematic review by Cignacco *et al.* (2004) indicated that soothing non-pharmaceutical interventions, such as 'non-nutritive sucking' (using a dummy), swaddling and 'facilitated tucking' (holding the baby in the foetal position), have pain-alleviating effects for neonates.

Pain experiences during childhood

The degree of unpleasantness associated with a painful stimulus depends largely on attitudes to pain that are learned during childhood, as illustrated in the next example.

Example

Learning to cope with pain

After he started walking, Lee fell over frequently but rarely injured himself, so Sasha became less concerned. When she heard a thud and a yell, she would call out 'you're all right'. Usually, the cry would stop immediately. If it didn't, she would run to find out what was wrong.

When Jack started walking, his mother was very afraid that he might hurt himself. She ran to check each time she heard a bump. She was upset and cuddled him whenever he cried.

Through these actions, Lee learned that pain did not automatically signal harm while Jack picked up on his mother's fear and became afraid of pain.

Children such as Jack are often very nervous on admission to hospital, as are their mothers. These experiences help to shape responses to pain in adolescence and adulthood.

Example

Contrasting adolescent responses to pain

When Anna and her friend Clare were aged 14, both experienced premenstrual pain. Each month, Anna's mother encouraged her to go to school as usual, while Clare's mother allowed her to stay at home. Anna learned to control the pain with exercise and distraction, whereas Clare relied on rest and painkillers. Clare also found that she could avoid demanding situations at school if she complained of pain. Thus Clare learned to use passive avoidant pain coping strategies, while Anna learned active approach strategies (see Chapter 7).

There is some evidence in the literature to suggest sex differences in pain, notably that women seem to experience more pain when undergoing experimental, surgical and medical procedures (Fillingim *et al.* 2009). These authors find no consistent evidence of biological sex differences in pain response, therefore we wonder if these findings are influenced by differences in pain experience. For example, musculoskeletal injuries are common in boys, but boys are less experienced than girls at dealing with abdominal pains. Therefore it seems reasonable to expect that boys and girls will grow up to respond differently to different types of pain.

Exercises

1 Think back to the different sorts of pain you experienced during your own childhood, such as injury, toothache, tummy ache. How did you learn to deal with these sorts of pain?

2 Compare your own experiences with those of male and female friends.

3 Can you think of reasons that might help to account for the responses of Celia or Dick (in our initial vignettes) to their present pain?

In order to understand why pain is so variable, both between individuals who have the same injury, and within the same individual at different points in time, it is necessary to understand how pain is transmitted and factors that modify it.

The gate control theory of pain

Prior to the 1960s, it was believed that there was a direct relationship between the extent of tissue damage or injury and the intensity of the pain felt. Melzack, a psychologist, and Wall, a neuroscientist, radically changed this biomedical view with the publication of their gate control theory of pain (Melzack and Wall 1965).

Gate control theory explains a number of mechanisms by which pain signals are modulated (altered) between leaving the site of tissue damage and reaching the cerebral cortex. Through these processes, sensory and cognitive mechanisms operate as a whole. These mechanisms are described in the following section.

Descending pain modulation

At the level of the dorsal horn of the spinal cord, the pain signal from the site of tissue damage is modulated by descending signals from the brain. These descending signals are strongly influenced by the emotional state of the individual at the time. The pain 'gate' is a metaphor for these processes of modulation. It actually consists of various neurotransmitters and inhibitors which are released in the dorsal horn. These either 'open the gate' to allow the full force of the pain to be transmitted to the brain, or 'close the gate' to prevent or limit pain transmission to the brain.

Research since the 1960s has identified a range of neurotransmitters that contribute to the pain gate mechanism, including endorphins (Basbaum and Fields 1984). Endorphins are the body's own (endogenous) opioid pain-relieving substances, similar to morphine. Table 10.2 identifies the main factors associated with the opening and closing of the pain gate.

Table 10.2 Factors associated with the opening and closing of the pain gate		
	Factors that open the gate and increase pain sensation	**Factors that close the gate and decrease pain sensation**
Physical	Extent of injury	Analgesic medication
		Counterstimulation (rubbing, electrical stimulation)
Emotional	Fear/anxiety	Confidence/relaxation
	Depression	Optimism
Beliefs and behaviours	Focusing on the pain	Focused distraction/active involvement
	Having nothing to do	Perceived control
	Sense of helplessness/hopelessness	Perceived emotional support

Exercise

From Table 10.2, can you identify factors that might be leaving the pain gate open for Celia and Dick in the introductory vignettes?

Next, we apply the gate control theory to provide meaningful explanations for certain curious features of pain and pain responses.

Fast and slow pain

Example

When Lee started walking, he fell over and banged his knee. He felt the initial sharp blow, but didn't start to cry until a few moments later when a dull intense throb set in.

Pain signals travel along fast and slow ascending pain transmission fibres from the site of tissue damage to the dorsal horn of the spinal cord. The timing of Lee's pain illustrates the effects of pain transmission along fast and slow pain fibres from the site of tissue damage. But when the pain signals reach the dorsal horn of the spinal cord, they may be modulated by competing ascending signals from touch fibres.

Counterstimulation

This refers to stimulating alternative nerves that effectively block pain transmission. For example, massaging the painful area is effective in reducing pain because it stimulates the touch fibres to override the pain signal before it reaches the spinal cord.

Rubbing it better

When Lee bumped his knee, Sasha rubbed the area until he stopped crying. (Of course, the act of rubbing also provides the child with emotional comfort.)

The effect of 'counterstimulation' led to the development of transcutaneous electrical nerve stimulation (TENS) for the management of pain (more on this later).

Attention and distraction

Distraction diverts the attention away from the pain.

Diverting attention

As Sasha was rubbing Lee's knee, she also drew his attention to a butterfly that had settled on a nearby flower. She had learned that by the time his interest in the butterfly had worn off, the pain had normally subsided.

Diversion can take any form that holds individual attention. Examples include socializing, meditation, or engaging in work or an absorbing hobby.

Post-traumatic absence of pain

Pain-free injury?

Mark read an account in the newspaper of a farmer whose arm was severed in farm machinery but felt no pain until he got to hospital. Anna had recently been on placement in accident and emergency and made a similar observation, but was not sure how to explain it.

It is not uncommon for someone to experience a total absence of pain immediately after a major trauma. Beecher (1959) observed this in soldiers injured on the battlefield during World War II and explained it in terms of relief at escaping from danger. In the light of recent research, it is more likely that the intense focus of attention on escape or task completion releases a flood of endorphins which close the pain gate (Wall 1999).

Factors that open the pain gate and increase pain sensation

In this section, we consider important factors that leave the pain gate wide open to pain and ways in which we, as health care professionals, can apply psychology to help our patients to close the gate on pain.

Pain, anxiety and suffering

The following account illustrates how a small niggle is capable of causing far more suffering than an excruciating pain.

Example

Anna visited Arthur, aged 82, who was awaiting leg amputation because of severe vascular disease. His leg pain was 'excruciating', but he was not interested in talking about that. His overwhelming concern was with a 'niggling' pain in his lower abdomen. It transpired that six years ago he had surgery for bladder cancer and he was very afraid this niggle might signal a recurrence.

Negative emotions such as fear, anxiety and depression are largely responsible for the operation of the pain gate. Causes of pain-related fear, anxiety and depression are often summed up by preoccupations that patients may be afraid to share, including:

- Have I picked up an infection?
- Is it cancer?
- Will the pain get worse; how long it will last?
- Will I end up in a wheelchair?
- Nothing seems to help this pain

These sorts of questions maintain the individual's focus of attention on the pain, as Wall explained in the quote at the start of this chapter.

Exercise

Look again at the vignettes of Celia and Dick. Can you think of reasons why their pain is uncontrollable right now?

Negative thoughts and emotions are often associated with loss and grief (Walker *et al.* 2006), which leave the pain gate open and can make pain unbearable. This helps to explain why responses to pain can vary so much, not just between individuals, but for the same person as circumstances change.

From bearable to unbearable pain

Margaret's friend Ellen had had trigeminal neuralgia (continuous intense facial pain) for 50 years, during which time she ran a dancing school, raised a family and spent a happy retirement with her husband. But in the last few months, she complained that painkillers were useless. She told Margaret that she could no longer bear the pain and wanted to die.

   The pain had not changed, but her circumstances had. During the last year, both her husband and her daughter had died, leaving her alone with her emotional and physical pain.

It is evident in Ellen's account that physical pain alone is not sufficient to cause suffering (see Bendelow 2006). This is also illustrated by the numerous examples of people who push themselves to the limits of human pain and endurance in order to achieve an important goal.

   The distinction between pain and suffering is a very important one, particularly where the total relief of pain is an unrealistic goal. For this reason, a group of nurses who attended a pain workshop proposed that a suitable aim for pain management would be:

No individual should ever have more pain than they are willing or able to bear.

   This goal is achievable if we focus on what makes pain more bearable and what renders it unbearable for a particular individual. Later in this chapter, we look at the implications of this for pain assessment.

Placebo and nocebo responses

Explaining placebo responses

Anna could not understand why some patients claimed their painkillers did not work as well in hospital as the same sort they took at home. In another situation, a patient reported that an infusion of saline had relieved her pain. Her colleagues claimed this demonstrated the pain was not real.

- *Placebo response* refers to a beneficial treatment effect that occurs in response to a treatment or intervention that has no intrinsic active ingredient.
- *Nocebo response* refers to a harmful treatment effect that occurs in response to a treatment or intervention that has no intrinsic active ingredient.

It is believed by most lay people, and many health professionals, that placebo effects are 'all in the mind'. In contrast, continuing scientific evidence confirms that the placebo response is a neurobiological event that involves actual effects on both body and brain (Price *et al.* 2008).

   Put simply, beliefs and expectations, and classical conditioning (Chapter 5), stimulate the body to produce its own version of the anticipated substance. The placebo response to pain is

Example

Example

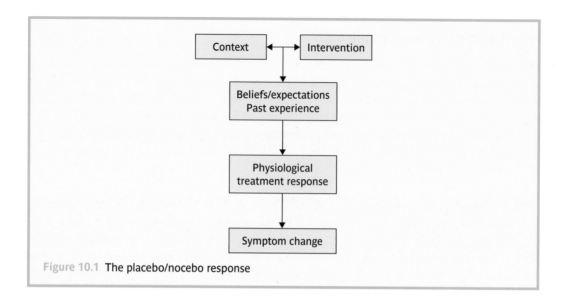

Figure 10.1 The placebo/nocebo response

mediated mainly by the release of endorphins that 'close the gate'. We know this because the administration of naloxone (the antidote to morphine) wipes out the placebo response (Benedetti *et al.* 2005). As with a real drug, the size of the effect is 'dose responsive' – it depends on the level and type of expectation. Classical conditioning occurs if the body has previously been primed with the real drug.

The context in which treatment is administered can have a strong influence on the strength of placebo response. Contextual influences include convincing instructions, treatment rituals and supportive behaviours, each of which helps to build up patient expectations of benefit or harm. The influences on placebo are illustrated in Figure 10.1.

The nature of the intervention imbues it with meaning. For example, injections generally have a stronger effect than tablets. Brand and colour of tablet both influence the strength of placebo effect. For instance, DeCraen *et al.* (1996) demonstrated that red, yellow and orange are associated with a stimulant effect, and blue and green with a tranquillizing effect.

A significant proportion of the effect of all medical and other therapeutic interventions is due to placebo. This is why Gracely (2000) observed that health professionals should seek to use their gifts of empathy to promote natural healing responses in their patients. These qualities of caring may help to explain the success of many complementary therapies. Below are some other interesting facts about placebo:

- Placebo analgesia can produce the same side-effects as the real drug. For example, respiratory depression may be caused by a placebo substitute for morphine (Benedetti 2006).
- It is possible that a placebo treatment will affect only the site at which the individual expects to gain pain relief (Benedetti *et al.* 1999).
- The placebo response is capable of producing a large effect. Benedetti *et al.* (2005) demonstrated that the application of a placebo cream reduced pain by between 46 and 57 per cent, compared to 'no treatment'.

- Placebo responses are not confined to pain. Placebo intervention in patients with Parkinson's disease triggers the release of dopamine; serotonin release is implicated in the placebo response for patients with depression (Benedetti *et al.* 2005). Placebo effects have also been found to influence blood pressure, asthma, social phobia, hot flushes and many other problems.

- The placebo effect may be diminished in people with Alzheimer's disease because expectations are not so strong (Benedetti *et al.* 2005).

Psychological principles of pain assessment

Pain assessment is a way of establishing a therapeutic relationship of trust as well as finding out important information, both of which are equally important for achieving pain control. As we have illustrated, it is important to focus on the holistic needs of the patient and not merely on pain intensity. It should never be seen merely as a 'tick-box' exercise.

Lasch (2000: 19) identified a series of questions that help to understand the needs of an individual who presents with pain. Clearly, these need to be adapted to suit the context in which the pain is being assessed:

- How would you describe your pain?
- Why do you think you have this pain?
- What has prompted you to seek help for your pain at this time?
- Do you have any fears about your pain? If so, what do you fear?
- What are the chief problems that your pain causes for you?
- What kind of treatment do you think you should receive? What do you hope this will achieve?
- What remedies have you tried that help you with pain?

These sorts of questions can save time and reduce unnecessary investigations, as illustrated in the next case study.

Pain-related fear

Brenda complained about persistent unilateral (one-sided) pain across her back, which she rated as 'mild'. Anna noticed that she seemed agitated and anxious. It transpired that her friend had died of breast cancer and she was convinced that she, too, might have the disease.

Anna passed this information on to the doctor who then gave Brenda a detailed examination to reassure her she did not have cancer. Instead, she diagnosed post-herpetic neuralgia – Brenda lived alone and had not seen the rash on her back caused by shingles (herpes zoster).

Brenda later told Anna that her life had been transformed by that clinic visit. The pain was still there, just the same, but now she hardly noticed it.

Example

Brenda's example illustrates how a little more time spent on listening and assessment can be both therapeutic and cost-effective.

Measuring and recording pain

In this section, we address some important points about pain measurement from a psychological perspective.

The location of the pain

Many people have difficulty locating the site of the pain. Adults often confuse right and left. Children often use the term 'headache' to refer to all sorts of pain, including tummy ache and sore throat. So it is always worth asking people to point to where it hurts.

Severity or intensity of the pain

There are numerous ways of measuring pain, based on visual, numerical and verbal descriptors.

Where visual devices such as visual analogue scales or touch screens are used, it is important to check that the patient can see well enough to differentiate the points on the scale.

Numerical rating and verbal descriptor scales are common in clinical practice. The 0 to 10 numerical scale has been widely tested for validity and reliability with adults, with children from the age of 8 (von Baeyer *et al.* 2009), and with people who have all but the severest levels of cognitive deficit (Closs *et al.* 2004). It has the advantage of verbal or visual presentation and is useful for those whose first language is not English.

Pain thermometers are popular because they combine a choice of visual, verbal and numerical options to suit individual needs or preferences (Figure 10.2). The background colour range is often based on red.

A 0 to 3 scale (0 no pain; 1 mild; 2 moderate; 3 severe) is now used on many clinical units. Limited options at the upper end of the scale can lead to the underestimation of very severe, excruciating or unbearable pain. It may be quick and convenient, but it is a simplistic approach that can easily become a meaningless and depersonalizing recording exercise.

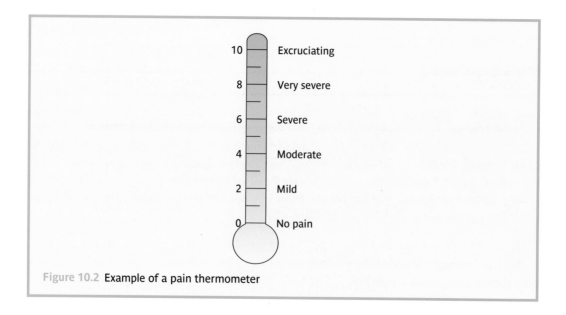

Figure 10.2 **Example of a pain thermometer**

A cautionary tale

One of Anna's friends described how, as a post-surgical patient, she had compared notes with other patients who wanted to work out the relationship between pain score and pain medication. This enabled them all to manipulate the 0–3 score to obtain the medication they wanted.

Pain assessment in those unable to communicate verbally

Pictorial scales using happy/sad faces are available for use with children up to the age of about 8 and those with communication difficulties, but these do not distinguish between pain and distress.

For babies, infants and people with severe cognitive deficits who are unable to communicate pain in this way, pain must be deduced from physical signs and behavioural expressions, such as the following:

- Signs of current or former physical trauma or disease normally associated with pain.
- Physiological responses indicative of stress (Chapter 7).
- Vocalizations such as grunting, whimpering, crying.
- Facial expressions including grimacing, signs of tension, fear.
- Body language such as rocking, agitation, guarding, flinching.
- Behaviour changes that can include loss of appetite, bouts of confusion or aggression.

A number of observational tools have been developed, based on these types of observation, but all require 'knowing the person'. Table 10.3 may be helpful, depending on the target group:

Table 10.3 Pain assessment schemes for special groups

Target group	Assessment tools	Additional sources of information
Premature babies and neonates	ABC pain scale (Bellieni *et al.* 2007)	AAP (American Academy of Pediatrics) (2006) – policy statement
	Bernese Pain Scale for Neonates (Cignacco *et al.* 2004)	
Pre- and non-verbal children	COMFORT behavioural scale (Johansson and Kokinsky 2009)	Royal College of Nursing: The recognition and assessment of acute pain in children (Quick reference guide and poster)
Children with severe neurological impairment	Paediatric Pain Profile (Hunt *et al.* 2007)	
Older people with dementia	Pain Assessment Checklist for Seniors with Limited Ability to Communicate (PACSLAC) (Fuchs-Lacelle *et al.* 2008)	www.geriatricpain.org (Zwakhalen *et al.* 2006)
People with profound learning disabilities	Look for changes in behaviour indicative of pain	Davies and Evans (2001)
	Disability Distress Assessment Tool (DisDAT) (Regnard *et al.* 2007)	

Example

The following responses could indicate the site of pain in cognitively impaired but otherwise healthy individuals:

- head-banging could indicate toothache
- head-holding and rocking could indicate headache
- doubling up with arms round the abdomen, accompanied by rocking, could indicate constipation (a common side-effect of opioid medication)
- guarding and flinching is likely to indicate a source of tissue damage
- regular difficulty in straightening or moving when encouraged to do so, accompanied by grunting and defensive reactions, is probably indicative of arthritic joint pain.

In many cases it is just not possible to identify signs and symptoms that are specific to pain. For example, some people with severe cognitive deficit grimace or grind their teeth in pleasure. Therefore, Regnard *et al.* (2007) recommend that, for each individual, responses indicative of contentment and distress should be routinely documented. Background knowledge of these makes it possible for carers to monitor the presence of pain and the therapeutic value of pain treatments.

Managing pain

Understanding, sympathy, comfort, security, reassurance, confidence and someone to listen are all rated highly by patients for promoting coping with pain. Lack of time is really no excuse for abruptness. As one patient observed: 'She [the community nurse] gave me the assurance that she had the time, even though she did not really' (Walker 1994: 225). Attending to a patient's pain with kindness and compassion usually reduces their demands and saves time.

Research

Empathy helps pain

Martin was partially sighted, had poor health and had attended hospital many times. He expressed much dissatisfaction with several episodes of care, but was very positive about his last emergency attendance with acute urinary retention. The doctor greeted him by observing, 'You poor thing, you must be in agony.' The pain immediately started to subside as he observed, 'I felt I could trust her' (Walker *et al.* 1998: 198).

The same approach applies from the moment of birth. For example Halimaa (2003) recommends that parental talking, singing, gentle stroking and cuddling should be encouraged as soon as is feasible for premature babies undergoing medical procedures.

Managing different types of pain

Different types of pain pose different demands and require different approaches to coping and management. In this chapter, we distinguish between the following types of pain:

- Acute pain caused by acute trauma, surgery or acute disease. This type of pain normally resolves spontaneously as healing takes place.
- Pain in the end stage of illness or disease that is progressive and time-limited.
- Chronic (persistent or intermittent) pain which may be caused by a chronic disease process or may be of unknown origin. It can last a lifetime.

All types of pain benefit from holistic assessment by caring staff. In the following sections, we focus on issues specific to these different types of pain.

Psychological issues in acute pain

Acute pain is caused by tissue damage due to injury, surgical intervention or acute inflammatory disease and analgesics are generally the mainstay of pain control. But professionals often feel helpless and even suspicious when analgesia fails to have the expected effect. In these cases, it is essential to consider psychological and emotional factors that leave the pain gate open and make the pain less bearable (see Table 10.4).

Table 10.4 Factors that affect pain control	
Factors that open the pain gate	**Actions that promote pain control**
Fear and anxiety	Prepare patients for what to expect when having painful procedures
	Listen to, assess, acknowledge and address concerns and information needs
Tension	Deal with causes of fear and anxiety
	Encourage focus on breathing, imagery and shoulder relaxation
Feeling alone or unsupported	Eye contact, smile, touch
Lack of pain self-efficacy	Facilitate individual coping strategies
	Promote patient control over analgesia
Lack of control over the pain-related situation	Attend to basic comfort measures
	Initiate regular pain assessment and medication
Focus of attention on the pain	Deal with causes of fear and anxiety
	Encourage distraction

Reflect on the experiences of Celia and Dick in the introductory vignettes. What do you imagine might be leaving the gate wide open to their pain? What are the implications for the management of their pain?

Exercise

Aside from pain assessment and drug treatment, very much can be achieved to improve pain control by providing adequate information and preparation, relieving stress, providing emotional support and facilitating individual coping strategies. When preparing adults or children for pain procedures, information needs to focus on what sensations to expect and how to deal with these; and when and how to ask for help (McCann and Kain 2001).

Research

Type of information matters

Langer *et al.* (1975) compared two groups of surgical patients. One was given standard procedural information about what would happen during surgery; the other group was taught how to use imagery to control their anxiety following surgery. Langer observed that procedural information raised anxiety in the immediate term and had no effect on post-operative anxiety or pain. In contrast, information about how to use imagery lowered levels of post-operative anxiety and need for pain relief.

Patient-controlled analgesia (PCA)

Numerous psychological experiments demonstrated that belief in the ability to terminate a painful stimulus enables people to tolerate more pain. These were instrumental in piloting PCA and introducing it into clinical practice. Hudcova *et al.* (2005) concluded that, in general, PCA leads to better pain control and patient satisfaction. PCA administered within predetermined limits is effective for children and adolescents (Berde *et al.* 1991), provided they are able to understand the concept (see Chapter 3 on cognitive development).

Not all patients have the capacity or want to control their own analgesia. In order to make effective use of PCA, patients require good preparation and continuing support from staff. Therefore PCA should not be seen as a time-saving option. The duration of PCA should be linked to assessment of the pain and analgesia consumption. Its removal should be a matter of negotiation between staff and patient, though we are aware that this does not always happen.

Acute pain that persists

If a patient remains in severe or increasing pain, it is unethical to reduce or withdraw analgesia without a full medical examination since this may indicate a complication, such as infection or nerve damage. Pain caused by a neurological complication (nerve damage) is more likely to be reversible if it is identified and treated appropriately at an early stage.

Avoidable pain

Diane was mother to two children who had severe learning difficulties and required a lot of physical care. She developed carpal tunnel syndrome (trapped nerves) in both wrists and opted for surgery to her right (dominant) hand. Post-operatively, her complaints about increasing pain in her arm and shoulder were met with the comment 'Your operation was on your hand, not your shoulder.'

Following discharge, the pain became unbearable. After several months, she attended the pain clinic where she was diagnosed as having intractable neuropathic pain caused by surgical nerve damage. If recognized and treated immediately, this outcome could have been avoided.

Pain management towards the end of life

Symptom management, particularly pain control, is one of the most common reasons for referral to specialist palliative care and the main reason why Dame Cicely Saunders started the modern hospice movement. However, many people nearing the end of life are cared for in general or specialist hospital wards or at home, particularly older patients (Grande *et al.* 2006). Therefore all nurses need to understand the principles of end-of-life pain management. According to the World Health Organization (Sepúlveda *et al.* 2002), palliative care for adults and children should start at an early stage of the illness. The following recommendations are additional to medical treatments to relieve pain and other distressing symptoms such as breathlessness and nausea:

- integrate psychological and spiritual aspects of patient care (adults); evaluate and alleviate physical, psychological and social distress (children);
- support patients to live as actively as possible until death;
- enhance quality of life according to the individual's needs and wishes;
- maintain support for the family.

One of the main barriers to effective end-of-life care (Payne *et al.* 2007) is determining when this phase actually starts. Payne *et al.* observed that, in community hospitals, the majority of older patients are already moribund when palliative care is initiated, particularly if they have a diagnosis other than cancer, or co-morbidities. This means that it is too late to help prepare individuals and their loved ones for a peaceful death.

Twycross *et al.* (1996) found that most cancer patients have pain from more than one source. The same applies to older patients who have co-morbidities. Each source of pain needs to be assessed separately and there needs to be negotiation between professionals and the patient to decide which needs most urgent attention.

Intervention at an early stage should aim to facilitate self-management (see Chapters 8 and 9). Numerous support networks and self-help information are available on the internet. Patients should be encouraged to maintain their desired lifestyle or substitute other enjoyable activities for as long as they can in order to stimulate the release of endorphins and provide distraction from pain. Those who are dying, and their caregivers, face considerable psychological threat and loss but often try to put on a brave face for each other and for professional carers. The following extracts illustrate some of the conflicts patients face in a social context.

Research

Interview extracts (McCreaddie *et al*. 2010: 5–6)

Janet: I wasn't a person that moaned or groaned. I was a good patient . . . well I think a good patient is if you don't moan, what's the sense in moaning . . . try and help yourself.

Sarah: People close to you, they feel it, but they feel helpless because there is nothing they can do. So you have to try and be positive and show a bright side . . . I think medical people like you to be positive because it makes their job easier doesn't it?

Irene: I am really positive about it most of the time but I don't think anybody is positive all the time . . . and the very few times when I don't feel positive, I do want to have a wee cry. I want to have a cuddle.

In the context of end-of-life care, much has been written about the need for good emotional care, but Rigby *et al.* (2010) identified that little attention had been given to the role of the physical environment. Their review of the literature showed that patients and relatives found contact with the natural world, in the form of sunshine, garden or green open space, therapeutic. A 'homely' environment was preferred, but preference for a single or shared room was variable. Some preferred the opportunity for mutual support afforded by a shared room. Problems of loneliness and boredom were often overlooked by care staff (see Chapter 8 on emotional resilience).

There is good evidence that many patients are reluctant to complain of pain or take adequate analgesia to control the pain, no matter how advanced their disease (Coward and Wilkie 2000). Some resist strong analgesia because they see it as a sign of weakness or that the end is drawing near.

Example

Pain and conflict

Wendy was in the late stages of cancer and nursed at home by her husband and daughters. Her family did not want her to have morphine because they believed that signalled 'the end', so Wendy refused it. Her pain became so bad that she screamed when the nurses tried to move her. They found this very distressing and blamed the family. At her funeral, the family and the nurses were no longer able to communicate with each other.

An important problem in this scenario is that the focus of the nurses' attention was on the pain, rather than on the spiritual and emotional needs of Wendy and her family. It has been shown that didactic or authoritarian approaches to pain management are less likely to achieve effective pain control (Schumacher 2002). A shared problem-solving approach involving dialogue between nursing staff, the family and Wendy was more likely to achieve mutual agreement about the cause of the problem and possible solutions. As it was, Wendy's death involved immense suffering which left the family and the nurses with distressing memories to resolve. This experience may be contrasted with a positive scenario.

A good death

Janice's neighbour, Cynthia, was diagnosed with untreatable cervical cancer at the age of 36. Her main concern was for her four children, aged between 6 and 16 years. Cynthia, her husband, the social worker and community nurse collaborated to find the best way to tell the children. As her symptoms became less controllable, she requested admission to the local hospice. Social work support ensured that the needs of the husband and children were adequately addressed, which gave Cynthia peace of mind. After admission, she enjoyed the support of other patients and elected to take up painting. The combination of relief from anxiety, increased support and distraction made her pain bearable without the need for increased analgesia. She died peacefully two weeks later having prepared a small painting as a special keepsake for each family member.

Chronic benign pain

Chronic pain is often defined as pain that has lasted for at least three months. Others define it as pain that has persisted beyond the healing time needed for recovery from injury or tissue damage (Chapman *et al.* 1999). Chronic benign pain is pain that is not life-threatening but may last for years and is an important cause of disability and distress. Causes include musculoskeletal pain (pain that involves muscles, ligaments and joints), including arthritis and back pain, pain caused by a variety of chronic diseases and pain such as fibromyalgia whose origin is medically unexplained.

Chronic benign pain has no known medical cure and complete relief is not possible. Therefore, the approach to pain management is very different from that for acute pain and pain near the end of life, where analgesia is the mainstay of treatment. Chronic pain, notably musculoskeletal pain, is very common in the general population. Health care professionals are very likely to encounter patients who have acute exacerbations of chronic pain, or a source of chronic pain in addition to the acute condition they are being treated for. Therefore, it is essential to have up-to-date knowledge about its management.

Opioid analgesia in chronic benign pain

The use of opioid analgesia in the treatment of chronic benign pain is controversial. The relatively modest benefits that many people gain from this type of analgesia in the long term need to be weighed against common adverse effects (including loss of concentration and constipation) and the problem of tolerance. Drug tolerance is not the same as drug addiction.

- Addiction refers to a psychological or physiological overdependence on the drug. It often involves tolerance.
- Tolerance means that the body requires increasing levels of the drug to achieve the same effect. This does not necessarily imply addiction.

Analgesia offers limited respite from chronic pain. In contrast, the key aim of chronic pain management is to reduce suffering and to improve or sustain quality of life in spite of the pain. This can be achieved through the use of effective self-management (coping) strategies.

Research

Living with chronic or persistent pain (Wall 1999: 190–1)

"People have to learn to live with their pain in a realistic context. Coping is the beginning of a series of steps that give a sense of understanding and a type of control. Coping is a skill that may be learned with help. There is no chance of coping if attention is monopolized by fear, anxiety and depression. There is no chance of coping while passively awaiting the invention of a cure. Coping is an active process directed at everything other than the pain itself. It needs inspiration and inspired help to live with pain."

Patients with chronic pain are often told, 'There is nothing we can do for you. You will have to learn to live with it', but are rarely told how. As Wall pointed out, people need help to learn to cope with pain.

Coming to terms with chronic pain

Chronic pain often starts out as an acute episode of pain. When pain persists, it leads people to a search for a diagnosis and cure (Chapter 9). Some people spend years searching for a 'magic bullet' cure as doctors, focused on diagnosis and cure, refer them for consultations, investigations and ineffective medical treatments only for them to be told that nothing more can be done. Other care professionals, reluctant to destroy hope, collude in this process, which serves to maintain false hope and prevent effective coping. To make matters worse, patients who lack a confirmed diagnosis, or whose condition fails to respond to treatment, are often stigmatized by health care staff and members of the public (Higgins 2005). Stigmatization (see Chapter 2) appears to be associated with the belief that in the absence of obvious disease or injury the pain is not 'real'.

The stigma of back pain (Holloway *et al.* 2007: 1458)

Judith, aged 58, described her experience of seeking help for persistent back pain: 'You don't actually see the consultant. You wait for ages and ages and ages and you come out feeling totally baffled really. He [the doctor] doesn't really seem to understand your problem and you feel like bursting into tears, you have wasted such a lot of time and energy . . . You don't feel that you're being treated as a person at all.'

Managing the transition from acute to chronic pain is a challenge for all health care professionals, particularly those who view the inability to cure or eliminate pain as defeat. Patients need help to find positive ways of coping with their own pain from an early stage. Below we address beliefs and behaviours that have been identified as important barriers to effective coping.

- *Catastrophizing* refers to the belief that things are awful and can only get worse. Casey *et al.* (2008) found that people with neck and back pain who initially believed their pain to be both uncontrollable and permanent were most likely to report longer term pain and disability.

- *Avoidance* of activities that increase pain, rather than the pain itself, has been identified as the main cause of disability in people with conditions such as back pain (Vlaeyen and Linton 2000).
- *Dependence* on an attentive spouse or partner, the sort who takes over roles or activities from the person in pain, has been shown to be associated with greater levels of pain behaviours and depression (Thieme *et al.* 2005). Help is often inadvertent – it is hard not to help a loved one who is struggling. But it leaves the person in pain with nothing to do but focus on the pain. Financial compensation and benefits are also barriers to effective coping if support is reduced or withdrawn once the individual is judged fit to resume work or normal activities.
- *Blame and anger* may be directed at the individual or organization that the person holds responsible for their injury, or the system that failed to prevent it, or health care professionals who failed to treat it successfully, or even God (Fernandez 2005). Blame and anger are associated with helpless and depression. Self-blame is less common and in cases of benign (non-cancer) pain is generally associated with better coping outcomes.

Managing chronic pain

The main aim for the management of chronic pain is for the individual to control the pain, rather than the pain controlling that person's life. In Table 10.5 we summarize objectives for managing chronic pain, with some ways to achieve them.

Table 10.5 Managing chronic pain

Objectives	Implications
Reduce pain-related distress	Listen and identify the causes of distress
	May need referral to deal with unresolved loss, anger, blame or PTSD
Reduce avoidance due to pain-related fear	Explain that activity-related pain does not imply further tissue damage
	Avoid explanations that introduce the idea of 'wear and tear'
	Encourage activity and gentle exercise
Replace unrealistic hopes and expectations with realistic ones	Offer mind–body explanations that relate to manageable outcomes (e.g. stress, anxiety and tension)
Increase pain self-efficacy	Promote a wide range of pain-coping strategies including exercise
	Give information about pain management or expert patient programmes, as appropriate
	Consider complementary therapies (see below)
Ensure adequate support	Provide information about credible support groups/internet support
Maximize independence	Ensure that the individual is encouraged to do as much for themselves as they possibly can
	Be aware that welfare benefits may be reduced as activity and independence increases
Deal with loss, anger, blame	Counselling may be helpful
Enhance quality of life	Encourage hobbies and interests and, if possible, return to work
	Review and address all sources of stress that are not related to pain

Managing chronic pain during hospital admissions

Chronic pain often gets worse on admission to hospital because patients are under stress because of their illness and lose access to their usual pain coping strategies. Increased analgesia might be necessary while in hospital, but it is important to prepare patients for discharge by addressing their concerns, encouraging increased activity and referring for continuing support where necessary.

Case study: Celia (see vignette at the start of this chapter)

Celia had an incurable painful condition and had a long history of contact with health and social services as a result of her demands and those of her family for pain relief. She had no pain coping strategies or distractions because all attention was narrowly focused on medical treatment. As a result, Celia had developed a high level of tolerance to analgesia.

Celia and her family needed help to understand that there was no cure for this type of pain, but there are alternative and more effective ways of helping Celia to improve her quality of life. This could not happen in hospital. Following a joint meeting at which their hopes, fears and expectations were addressed, they all agreed the priority was for Celia to return home as quickly as possible.

Prior to discharge, a case conference was convened at which the GP and representatives of the community support services all agreed their shared task was to help Celia and her family find new ways to help Celia achieve important goals in ways that would keep her occupied, make her feel useful and divert her attention away from the pain.

In the following sections, we examine ways of promoting effective pain control for people who live with chronic pain.

Pain management resources

The management of chronic pain involves making use of available positive social supports and regaining a sense of personal control. Sources of information, advice and support are available through individual consultation, in groups and online. They include the following:

- Multidisciplinary pain management programmes, based on cognitive behavioural principles, combine individual and group work delivered by local or regional pain services. Some programmes are residential; most are non-residential.
- The Expert Patient Programme (see Chapter 9) is a lay-led national programme offered in groups or online. It is based on cognitive behavioural principles to improve quality of life for people with chronic conditions, including chronic pain. An online version is available for those who do not like to join groups.
- Local pain self-help and support groups.
- Internet-based self-help and support.

Self-help groups and internet chat rooms need careful monitoring to ensure that they maintain their focus on positive coping and do not degenerate into shared catastrophizing sessions.

Pain management programmes

Some key elements of a pain management programme are illustrated in the following example:

Example of pain management programme

Dysvik *et al.* (2010) developed a nurse-led cognitive-behavioural programme to address the following needs:

1 Accept the chronic pain diagnosis
2 Understand the body–mind connection, based on gate control theory
3 Orientate towards self-management
4 Address influences that maintain pain problems
5 Find a good match between the patient's needs and treatment options

Their programme was typical in containing the following types of session:

Session	Topics
1	Establish goals
2	Relationship between physical activity and pain
3	Pain as a complex mind–body phenomenon
4	Muscle tension, relaxation and pain
5	Coping strategies and pain
6	Self-esteem, social network and pain
7	Thoughts, feelings and behaviour
8	Communication with others, self-help

Most multidisciplinary pain management programmes include input from a physiotherapist to reduce postural strain and teach and supervise paced or graded exercise (start very gently and increase very gradually), which improves fitness, increases range of activity and releases endorphins. Occupational therapists give ergonomic advice to promote good posture and reduce pain while engaging in activities such as food preparation, reading and computer use.

Research

Research

Evidence from systematic reviews

Scascighini *et al.* (2008) found that multidisciplinary pain management programmes offered better outcomes than standard treatment, or programmes run by a single professional, for patients with fibromyalgia and chronic back pain.

Morley *et al.* (2008) identified that between 1 in 3 and 1 in 7 (depending on the outcome measure used) programme participants achieved clinically significant gains. Most notable were the improvements between pre-treatment and follow-up in pain self-efficacy, catastrophizing and five-minute walk.

People who experience persistent pain need to be introduced to the principles of effective pain management at an early stage and advised about the resources available to help, should it prove resistant to medical treatment. Exercise and activity are important aspects to consider.

Example

Case study: Dick (see vignette at the start of this chapter)

In our initial vignette, Dick felt depressed and complained of pain all over. But within six months, Dick's pain was limited to a single site. He had set up his own business; his girlfriend had moved in and was expecting his baby.

Dick explained that his upbringing had taught him to be very self-reliant in spite of his disability. He had felt demoralized when elderly women recovered from their hip operations more quickly than he did. He said the turning point for him came when we turned our attention away from the pain and asked: 'How physically fit are you these days?' This prompted him to go straight to the gym. As a result of exercise and fitness training, he was now feeling fit and well and his pain was quite manageable.

Our case examples highlight the need to attend to the physical, psychological and social needs of the whole person and not to focus attention solely on the pain. Next we review complementary approaches that support effective coping for all types of pain.

Complementary pain therapies

These are therapies used in conjunction with the pain management strategies mentioned above. Most work on psychological principles by increasing sense of personal control over the pain (pain self-efficacy) or diverting attention away from the pain.

Transcutaneous electrical nerve stimulation (TENS)

TENS is based on the principle of counter-stimulation (see gate control theory). It consists of a battery-operated device that delivers a small variable electrical current to the region of the pain via adhesive pads. Because it is operated by the patient, it serves the additional purpose of promoting personal control (Chapter 7). TENS has been shown to be effective in improving pain control in labour (van der Spank *et al.* 2000) and in chronic pain due to known pathologies such as knee pain (Osiri *et al.* 2000). Reviews of its effect on other chronic pains, including back pain, have proved inconclusive (Khadilkar *et al.* 2005; Carroll *et al.* 2006). But TENS is non-invasive and worth a trial for those who are interested in using it.

Acupuncture

A recent review of all systematic reviews (Ernst *et al.* 2011) concluded that most of the reported benefit is due to placebo influences, such as therapist and patient enthusiasm.

Placebo effects of non-acupuncture

A qualitative study by Scott *et al.* (2011), conducted alongside a clinical trial of acupuncture, confirmed that the therapeutic ritual was often sufficient to convince patients of its therapeutic value. In a control condition, sticky pads were attached to the skin (similar to TENS) and leads attached to an inert box with impressive but non-functional dials. One man noticed an immediate effect: 'When [practitioner] switched and then put the [inert] electrodes on me, the tingling went all the way down my leg. Now, how can that be ineffective? I don't think it was, because after three or four of those treatments, I stopped taking painkillers.'

Anecdotal information from patients receiving acupuncture at pain clinics suggests that even if acupuncture does not relieve pain it can promote relaxation and sleep for a limited period. Some clinics now offer group acupuncture where patients additionally provide each other with mutual support.

Relaxation and imagery

Relaxation is intended to counter anxiety (Chapter 5) and reduce muscle tension, which contributes to muscle spasm and pain. The most common approach, as taught in antenatal classes, is progressive muscle relaxation in which each muscle group is tensed and then relaxed in turn until a complete state of relaxation is achieved. Imagery helps to maintain relaxation by diverting the mind from other concerns and promoting calmness.

Systematic review of relaxation

Kwekkeboom and Gretarsdottir (2006) found that of 13 studies in which patients used relaxation repeatedly over a period of time, eight demonstrated significant results for pain relief. One-off use (for acute pain) showed no effect. The authors suggested that frequent practice of relaxation over several weeks or months is required to achieve positive outcomes.

When faced with a patient in acute pain, instruction to 'relax' is potentially unhelpful since it can trigger a stress response in individuals who have no prior training and find relaxing difficult to achieve.

Mindfulness meditation

Unlike other forms of mental imagery where the individual is encouraged to focus attention away from the body, mindfulness encourages the individual to focus on the reality of the present moment, without allowing the intrusion of thoughts about or emotional reactions to the situation (Kabat-Zinn *et al.* 1983; we review this concept in some detail in Chapter 8). It has regained popularity as 'mindfulness-based stress reduction' (MBSR), which has been shown to be effective in assisting in the self-management of chronic pain, cancer pain and a variety of other medical conditions.

Effectiveness of mindfulness meditation for pain

Evidence suggests that mindfulness meditation achieves better results than other forms of relaxation (Rosenzweig *et al.* 2010). Studies report significant improvements in anxiety, depression, stress, sexual difficulties, physiological arousal and immune function, combined with subjective benefits and no adverse consequences. Improvements in pain acceptance, engagement in activities and physical function have been recorded in older adults with chronic back pain (Morone *et al.* 2008).

The following in-depth case study is based on an encounter that took place in an outpatient clinic and involves multiple problems of the kind that makes care professionals feel helpless. We use it to illustrate how a person-centred approach, rather than a pain-centred approach, can help all concerned. We use cross-referencing to demonstrate how the interventions used were informed by aspects of psychology introduced in this book.

Case study: Pam

Introduction

The nurse met Pam and Rob in the corridor after they had attended for a consultation with the pain consultant. Pam was in tears and her husband looked angry.

Non-verbal signs of anger and distress suggested that neither Pam nor Rob felt their needs had been addressed as a result of their consultation (Chapter 6). The nurse took them to a private room and asked them to tell their story.

The pain problem

Rob spoke while Pam sat with her head in her hands and cried. He explained that Pam had extremely poor circulation. Pam held out her blue hands as he explained that the fingers on her left hand had already been part amputated and those on her right hand caused excruciating pain most of the time. They had come to the clinic to seek relief from the pain, but the doctor told them he was unable to provide treatment until Pam gave up smoking. Rob expressed the view that everyone in health care was anti-smoking, but that it was unreasonable to expect Pam to succeed in view of her problems.

The treatment considered was sympathectomy. This involves cutting the sympathetic nerve supply to the arms to increase the circulation to the hands. But smoking would negate this because nicotine constricts the peripheral blood vessels. The doctor had probably explained this, but neither Pam nor Rob had either heard or understood it (Chapter 4). They had interpreted the advice to stop smoking as an instruction, but the doctor had not offered an action plan to help them (Chapter 9).

Gaining trust

The nurse explained why it was necessary to stop smoking. She sympathized and commented that since the doctor was himself a heavy smoker he would appreciate these difficulties.

The psychology of persuasion suggests that health advice is better received if it appears unbiased (Chapter 6). Rob felt Pam was being stigmatized for lack of will-power (Chapter 2). But it was becoming clear that Pam was under a lot of stress due to her illness and possibly other issues (Chapter 7), leading to a sense of helplessness and hopelessness, which in turn increased the pain. The nurse decided to adopt a motivational interview style (Chapter 9), starting by inviting Pam and Rob to tell their story.

Personal background: Rob's account

Rob explained that he and Pam, aged 42, had been married for over 20 years. About 10 years ago, Pam had developed a drink problem which became so bad that he left her.

Alcohol is often used as self-medication to reduce pain and help people to forget traumatic experiences. It is a form of emotion-focused coping (Chapter 7). A little later, it might be helpful to find out the reasons for her drinking, as it could contribute to her current emotional state.

Medical background: Rob's account

Pam's circulation had gradually worsened. Then, two years ago, Pam had a stroke that left her with a slight right-sided weakness (she was left-handed) and slow in formulating speech. This, Rob explained, was why Pam did not like talking to people. Rob returned home to look after her on the promise that she would give up drinking, which she did.

Rob paused at this point while both he and the nurse shared their admiration for Pam. Alcoholism in women is stigmatized (Chapter 2), and there is a tendency to focus on the addiction, rather than the success of stopping.

Current circumstances: Rob's account

Rob explained how he cared for Pam. He took her breakfast in bed, helped her dress and undress, did all the housework and cooking. He was self-employed and went home at lunchtime to get her a midday meal.

The literature on chronic pain suggests that too much instrumental support (practical help) can reduce personal control and lead to dependence (Chapter 7 and this chapter). By this time, Pam had gained confidence to join in the conversation and it was obvious that speech therapy was no longer needed. The nurse asked Pam to describe her typical day.

Current circumstances: Pam's account

Pam described how she watched television all day. But she could identify only one programme that she enjoyed and this was something she and Rob watched together in the evening.

Pam appeared to have little positive reinforcement in her life (Chapter 5), other than Rob's company and smoking. The nurse asked about her life prior to the pain.

Personal history: Pam's account

Pam described how she had spent her early life in a children's home. She had then married Rob and had one child who was born with a severe mental and physical handicap and died at the age of 6. They had no other children. After the death of their son, Pam became withdrawn and started drinking. It became clear that she had not come to terms with this and had a very low opinion of herself.

It was important that Pam chose to present this aspect of her biography. She appears to have had little opportunity to develop a secure attachment relationship during her childhood (Chapter 3), which might have left her vulnerable to low self-esteem, depression and substance abuse. Since marrying Rob, she had experienced a series of serious losses, uncontrollable life events and hassles associated with the death of their son and her subsequent illness (Chapter 7). Although Rob appears to be a good source of emotional support, she may fear that Rob will leave again. This highlights the importance of keeping him involved in her pain management.

It was necessary to clarify Pam's main goal (Chapter 9), which was to obtain relief from pain. So the nurse focused next on assessing the pain. What was it like? When was it worst? Could she find any ways of gaining relief? Was she ever pain-free?

Pam's pain

Pam likened the pain to a constant toothache in her hands. She took a high dose of sustained release oral morphine and was on an antidepressant, which also helped her pain and sleep. Her main goal at this point was just to reduce the pain.

The nurse then focused on the pattern of Pam's pain. Were there any things that made it better or worse? Was she ever pain-free?

Pain triggers and alleviating factors

These questions prompted Rob to observe that Pam usually awoke free of pain and the pain commenced after she had her first cigarette. Pam nodded agreement.

The identification of pain as an immediate negative consequence of smoking (Chapter 5) validated the doctor's advice and provided an important incentive to quit. As a check, the nurse asked Pam to keep a pain diary for a week, in which she would record her levels of pain intensity at regular intervals, together with how she felt, what was happening and what she was doing, immediately before and after the pain started.

This simple form of behaviour analysis (Chapter 5) would provide important feedback on factors that influenced pain, including smoking. As a start, the nurse suggested a simple technique to reduce the desire to smoke, based on a self-help smoke-stop programme (Marks 1993). Pam's personal message to be read out before smoking each cigarette read:

> This cigarette will cause me a lot of pain.
> This cigarette is making me ill.
> I don't want to smoke this cigarette.

Smoking serves a number of important functions (Chapter 5) and it was necessary to compensate for these if Pam were to cut down. In Pam's case it appeared to calm her feelings of anxiety, gave her something to do, and she enjoyed it. Pam and Rob were encouraged to think about alternative enjoyable ways of filling her time, focusing on things that Pam could do, rather than what she could not do. It was emphasized that active involvement leads to the release of endorphins that help to alleviate pain. It was important to find activities that kept Rob involved.

Increasing independence

Pam agreed that she could prepare sandwiches for their lunch, instead of Rob getting them. Rob would continue to come home at lunchtime to provide company and help to break up the day.

Stress management is an important part of smoking cessation, pain and depression management programmes, so the nurse asked if Pam would consider attending a CBT programme (Chapter 8). Pam rejected this. Rob explained that she was embarrassed because people stared at her hands and she found it difficult to speak to strangers. So the nurse enquired about relaxation techniques to help her control her anxiety.

Stress management

Pam had learned yoga years ago and found it beneficial. She was willing to try relaxation exercises at home and Rob agreed to support this.

It was important to find means of distraction from the pain, and the nurse asked about any enjoyable activities she thought she might be able to do.

Distraction

Pam had been good at crochet and thought she might try this again if the pain was not so severe. Rob agreed to buy some thread for her to try. The nurse then mentioned the possibility of getting a dog trained to help people with physical disabilities.

In addition to the practical support a helping dog might afford, it would provide company and occupation, as well as unconditional love (humanistic psychology, see Chapter 1). It might also provide an incentive for Pam to walk outside and meet people. Conversations with strangers are easier when focused on the dog.

The interview had covered a lot of ground and much of it might be forgotten by the time Pam and Rob arrived home, therefore a written summary was given. (This also gave the opportunity to check agreement.)

Making a plan

The nurse wrote out a list of key points for Pam and Rob to take home, their action plan, and contact details including web addresses for further support. This might encourage Pam to learn computer skills.

Continued support is important. The nurse would have considered referral to a clinical psychologist specializing in chronic pain and depression if Pam had shown severe symptoms of depression (see Chapter 8). If at further appointments she was unable to demonstrate progress, this would be considered.

During the one-hour interview, the nurse had begun to establish a therapeutic relationship; identified reasons for Pam's current state of hopelessness and low self-esteem; assessed her goals, coping strategies, coping resources and barriers; negotiated an action plan and provided information for continuing support.

Satisfaction with the consultation

Rob and Pam thanked the nurse for her time and interest and left smiling. They made an appointment to share their progress and review the likelihood of having minor surgery to help control the pain.

This case study illustrates how a seemingly bleak situation can turn out to have many positive aspects and generate optimism. As often happens in health care, the nurse did not meet Pam or her husband again and this highlighted the problem of lack of continuity. As a result, the nurse practitioner now writes a letter detailing the key issues agreed, along with the agreed goals and action plan, including the support and resources needed to achieve it. The letter is sent to the referring pain consultant, with a copy to the patient and one to the family doctor. Colleagues report that patient motivation to engage in self-management is considerably increased as a result of this approach.

Further reading

Chronic pain

Caudill, M. (2002) *Managing Pain Before It Manages You*, 2nd edition. New York: Guilford Press.
Shone N. (2002) *Coping Successfully With Pain*, revised edition. London: Sheldon.
Wall, P. (1999) *Pain: The Science of Suffering*. London: Weidenfeld & Nicholson.

Pain in babies and children

AAP (2006) *Prevention and management of pain in the neonate: an update*, American Academy of Pediatrics, Committee on Fetus and Newborn and Section on Surgery, Canadian Pediatric Society and Fetus and Newborn Committee, 118(5): 2231–41.

Royal College of Nursing (2009) *The Recognition and Assessment of Acute Pain in Children: Update of Full Guideline.* London: Royal College of Nursing.

A

A priori: refers to an assumption, hypothesis or prediction produced before an experiment or intervention takes place.

Active versus passive coping: doing something versus doing nothing when faced with a problem.

Adaptation: a process of change that achieves a desired outcome or has survival value.

Adherence: following an agreed plan of action developed with a doctor or health care professional.

Amnesia: memory loss.

Anxiety: a state of emotional and physiological arousal associated with perceptions of threat or lack of control.

Appraisal: thought processes used to evaluate a potential stressor (from Lazarus 1966).

Approach/avoidance: ways of coping with problems, either by confronting them (approach) or avoiding them.

Attachment: a strong emotional bond between two people that elicits caring behaviours.

Attribution theory: from social psychology, a theory of how people make inferences about the causes of behaviour.

Avoidance: behaviours associated with ignoring the existence of problems and any negative consequences.

B

Behaviourism: an approach to psychology that proposes that all behaviour is determined by its antecedents (cues) and its consequences.

Behaviourist, behavioural: based on the principles of behaviourism.

Bereavement: a perception of loss caused by death.

Biopsychosocial: an approach that views biological, psychological and social systems in combination, rather than separately.

Bond, bonding: the formation of a strong attachment relationship.

Burnout: a response to stress in the caring professions that leads to feelings of emotional exhaustion and depersonalizing behaviours towards patients.

C

Catharsis: a term from psychoanalysis used to describe the therapeutic release of negative emotions.

CBT: Cognitive behaviour therapy.

Classical conditioning: from behaviourism, a simple form of associative learning in which reflex behaviours come under the unconscious control of an external stimulus.

Cognition: thought processes, including perception, memory and information processing.

Cognitive behaviour therapy: a structured therapy based on principles from behavioural and cognitive psychology.

Cognitive dissonance: a state of emotional tension created by two inconsistent beliefs, or incompatibility between the individual's beliefs and their behaviour (from Festinger 1957).

Compliance: actions undertaken in accordance with the instructions of others.

Conditioning: a process by which simple associative learning takes place.

Conformity: the tendency for perceptions, attitudes and behaviours to conform to those of powerful others, or the majority, in social situations.

Coping: ways of dealing with problems.

Coping strategies: conscious methods of dealing with problems.

D

Daily hassles: minor events that disrupt or interrupt daily routines.

Decentre: in developmental psychology, the ability to see or feel things from the point of view of another person.

Decentred: in mindfulness practice, the ability to see thoughts and emotions as phenomena to be observed, rather than indicators of well-being.

Defence mechanisms: from psychoanalysis, the term used to describe unconscious processes that are assumed to defend the ego from unmanageable threats and anxiety.

Denial: from psychoanalysis, a defence mechanism by which the individual fails to accept the reality of a situation.

Depersonalization: the treatment of an individual as an object, rather than a person.

Depression: a state of hopelessness and helplessness.

Determinism: a doctrine that assumes that every event has a cause. Therefore all human behaviour is a response to some external stimulus or occurrence.

Dualism: philosophical position that separates mind from body.

E

Eclectic: in psychotherapy, a mix of psychological approaches drawn from different schools of thought.

Ego: in psychoanalysis, the part of the mind concerned with conscious self-regulation.

Egocentrism: the inability to see or feel things from the point of view of another individual.

Emotional support: helping people to feel loved, cared for and valued.

Emotion-focused coping: a form of coping that is intended to relieve unpleasant emotions such as anxiety or fear.

Empiricism: a philosophical belief that all knowledge is gained from experience (the opposite of nativism).

Evolutionary psychology: the aspect of psychology that seeks to understand psychological processes in terms of their survival value.

Explanatory style: the way that an individual habitually understands past events.

F

Fight or flight response: state of immediate readiness for action, stimulated by a perception of threat (from Cannon 1932).

Focus groups: a group of people who share an experience, brought together to identify common problems and solutions.

Functional analysis: from behaviourism, a systematic analysis of immediate cues and consequences that influence behaviour.

Fundamental attribution error: tendency to blame people for their own problems or mistakes, rather than looking for situational causes.

G

Generalized/generalizable: implies that findings from a sample, or situation, are applicable to the whole population, or to all situations.

Grief: the emotional response to feelings of loss.

Groupthink: group interaction that can lead to erroneous beliefs in the correctness of group decisions (from Janis 1972).

H

Habit, habitual: a routine pattern of behaviour, not subject to deliberation or conscious awareness.

HBM: health belief model.

Health behaviour: a behaviour directed towards achieving a health goal.

Health-related behaviour: a behaviour that has an impact on health, but is not necessarily directed towards achieving a health goal.

Homeostasis: process by which physiological systems are maintained in a state of balance.

Hypothesis: a prediction that a particular action will lead to a particular outcome.

I

Iatrogenesis: medically induced illness.

Illness behaviour: behavioural responses to illness that include signalling the need for help.

Inductive: a process of generating theory from observational data.

Informational support: giving advice or information to enhance well-being.

Instrumental support: practical or tangible help.

Intervention: used in research to refer to any action or change likely to have an effect on an individual or group.

Introspection: examination of one's own mental experiences.

L

Learned helplessness: a state of depression caused by perceived uncontrollability and associated with cognitive, motivational and behavioural deficits (from Seligman 1975).

Life events: events involving loss or change that require major adjustment or adaptation.

LOC: Locus of control.

Locus of control: a set of beliefs about internal (personal) or external (other or chance) responsibility for achieving a desired outcome (from Rotter 1966).

Loss: an unpleasant experience caused by separation from a loved person or object.

M

Maladaptive: responding to change in a way that leads to adverse outcomes or unintended consequences.

Meta-analysis: analysis of combined data from all good quality randomized controlled trials of a specific intervention.

Mindfulness: the non-judgemental awareness of events, thoughts and emotions as they happen.

Mnemonic: a technique of visual or verbal association used to improve memory for facts.

Modelling: the learning of new skills by observing and copying others (from Bandura 1977a).

Mourning: the behavioural expression of grief, shaped by cultural expectations.

N

Narrative psychology: psychology based on the belief that our biographical stories constitute our sense of self.

Narrative therapy: therapy that uses therapeutic writing or verbal storytelling, with or without the presence of a therapist.

Nativism: a philosophical belief that humans are born with unique abilities to organize knowledge and respond to their environment.

Non-verbal communication: communication by facial expression and body movement.

Normative: in social psychology, social influences to conform.

O

Operant conditioning: learning by which voluntary behaviours and activities are brought under the control of external stimuli.

P

PCA: Patient-controlled analgesia.

Peer teaching: refers to education delivered by lay people who have gained knowledge from similar types of experience.

Phenomenology: a philosophical doctrine that advocates the study of subjective or 'lived' experience.

Phobia: persistent and intense irrational fear that produces a strong desire to escape from or avoid the feared object or situation.

Placebo: an inert substance that elicits an expectation of an effect and leads to physiological change.

Placebo response: physiological change brought about by expectation.

Positive psychology: a movement within psychology that places emphasis on positive emotions, strengths and successes.

Positivism: philosophical stance which holds that legitimate knowledge can only be obtained using scientific methods of inquiry.

Post hoc: refers to an explanation given after the event (opposite of a priori).

Primacy effect: information given first is remembered best.

Primary appraisal: cognitive process by which the individual determines whether there is a threat (from Lazarus 1966).

Primary prevention: preventive actions to maintain health in the absence of any signs or symptoms of disease.

Problem-focused coping: a response to stress that focuses on resolving the cause of the problem.

Pseudoscience: a body of theory that is not testable using scientific methods.

Psychoanalysis: a method of investigation, theory of mind, and form of treatment invented by Sigmund Freud.

Psychodynamic: refers to psychological systems that emphasize processes of development and change across the lifespan.

Psychogenic: a disease that has a psychological origin.

Psychoneuroimmunology: study of psychological factors that affect the immune system.

Psychosocial: an approach that views psychological and social systems in combination, rather than separately.

Psychosomatic: a disease that involves both mind and body.

Punishment: in behaviourism, an intervention that decreases the likelihood that the target behaviour will occur.

Q

Qualitative research: focuses on subjective experience.

Quantitative research: based on objective and measurable data.

R

Random, randomly: occurs by chance.

Randomized controlled trial: a research method used to test a new intervention; attempts to control for effects not attributable to the intervention by random allocation of participants to receive either a new (test) intervention or a comparable alternative (control) treatment.

Recency effect: information given last is remembered best.

Reductionism: the belief that complex phenomena can be understood by breaking them down into more simple fundamental elements.

Reference group: a group of people who share desired attributes and goals.

Reinforcement: in behaviourism, an intervention that increases the likelihood that the target behaviour will occur.

Reliability: when applied to a psychological measurement tool, consistency in producing the same result on separate occasions in similar circumstances.

Repertory grid: a method used to measure the self-concept (from Kelly 1955).

Repression: from psychoanalysis, a defence mechanism that suppresses memories that cause anxiety.

Resilience: the capacity to respond well to, or to recover rapidly from, adverse events.

Rogerian counselling: based on the work of Carl Rogers, non-directive client-centred therapy provided in an atmosphere of 'unconditional positive regard'.

S

Schedule of reinforcement: from behaviourism, the frequency or regularity by which reinforcement is received.

Schema: mental representation that informs understanding.

Secondary appraisal: cognitive process by which the individual determines what to do about a perceived threat (from Lazarus 1966).

Secondary prevention: preventive actions designed to detect and treat illness or disease at an early stage, as in attending for screening tests.

Self: personal identity.

Self-actualization: from humanistic psychology, a process of personal growth, or the pinnacle of achievement.

Self-efficacy: belief in one's ability to achieve a desired outcome (from Bandura 1977b).

Self-esteem: feeling good about oneself.

Self-management: learning to deal with an illness and its consequences through one's own actions.

Self-regulation: conscious efforts to achieve a desired goal in a changing environment.

Sense of coherence: the feeling that one's life is meaningful (from Antonovsky 1985).

Social cognition: study of thought processes in the context of the social environment in which they arise.

Social norm: expected standards of belief or behaviour determined by one's social or cultural reference group.

Social support: actions that impact on the well-being of others.

Socialization: process of learning about socially and culturally acceptable norms of behaviour.

Stigma: distinguishing features that have a negative impact on the attitudes of others (from Goffman 1963).

Stimulus: from behavioural psychology, an internal or external event or change that alerts attention and precipitates arousal.

Stimulus control: from behavioural psychology, the automatic triggering of a response by an external event or situational cue.

Stressor: an internal or external event that is perceived as a potential cause of threat or harm.

Systematic review: review of all research data on a particular topic, including unpublished data.

T

Tangible support: see instrumental support.

Tertiary prevention: actions to promote or preserve well-being and quality of life after the onset of illness or disease.

Threat: any event that potentially threatens physical or psychological well-being.

TPB: Theory of planned behaviour.

U

Unconditional positive regard: from humanistic psychology, esteem that is freely given, regardless of the behaviour or demeanour of the other.

V

Validity: when applied to a psychological measure, the extent to which it measures what it is intended to measure, and not something else.

Variable: in statistics, a measurable factor that is subject to variation or change.

W

Whitehall studies: a series of studies over several decades to identify causes of morbidity and mortality in UK civil servants.

AAP (American Academy of Pediatrics) (2006) Prevention and management of pain in the neonate: an update, *Pediatrics*, 118(5): 2231–41.

Abrams, D. and Hogg, M.A. (2004) Collective identity: group membership and self-conception, in M.B. Brewer and M. Hewstone (eds) *Self and Social Identity*, pp. 147–81. Oxford: Blackwell.

Ader, R., Cohen, N. and Felton, D. (1995) Psychoneuroimmunology: interactions between the nervous system and the immune system, *The Lancet*, 345: 99–103.

Adler, P.S. and Kwon, S-W. (2002) Social capital: prospects for a new concept, *The Academy of Management Review*, 27(1): 17.

Ainsworth, M.D.S., Blehar, M.C., Waters, E. and Wall, S. (1978) *Patterns of Attachment*. Hillsdale, NJ: Lawrence Erlbaum Associates.

Ajzen, I. (1991) The theory of planned behavior, *Organizational Behavior and Human Decision Processes*, 50: 179–211.

Aked, J. and Thompson, S. (2011) *Five Ways to Wellbeing: New Applications, New Ways of Thinking.* London: New Economics Foundation.

Al-Ghazal, S.K., Fallowfeld, L. and Blamey, R.W. (2000) Comparison of psychological aspects and patient satisfaction following breast conserving surgery, simple mastectomy and breast reconstruction, *European Journal of Cancer*, 36: 1938–43.

Andersen, B.L., Farrar, W.B., Golden-Kreutz *et al.* (2004) Psychological, behavioral, and immune changes after a psychological intervention: a clinical trial, *Journal of Clinical Oncology*, 22(17): 3671–9.

Anderson, R.M. and Funnell, M.M. (2000) Compliance and adherence are dysfunctional concepts in diabetes care, *Diabetes Educator*, 26(4): 597–604.

Ando, M., Morita, T. and Okamoto, T. (2008) One-week short-term life review interview can improve spiritual well-being of terminally ill cancer patients, *Psycho-Oncology*, 17(9): 885–90.

Ando, M., Morita, T., Akechi, T. and Okamoto, T. (2010) Efficacy of short-term life-review interviews on the spiritual well-being of terminally ill cancer patients, *Journal of Pain and Symptom Management*, 39(6): 993–1002.

Ångström-Brännström, C., Norberg, L. and Jansson, L. (2008) Narratives of children with chronic illness about being comforted, *Journal of Pediatric Nursing*, 23(4): 310–16.

Anon. (1970) Death in the first person, *American Journal of Nursing*, 70(2): 336–8.

Antonovsky, A. (1985) *Health, Stress and Coping*. San Francisco, CA: Jossey-Bass.

APA (American Psychiatric Association) (2000) *Diagnostic and Statistical Manual of Mental Disorders: DSM-IVfi-TR*, 4th edition. Washington, DC: APA.

Asarnow, J.R., Jaycox, L.H. and Tompson, M.C. (2001) Depression in youth: psychosocial interventions, *Journal of Clinical Child Psychology*, 30(1): 33–47.

Asbring, P. (2001) Chronic illness – a disruption in life: identity-transformation among women with chronic fatigue syndrome and fibromyalgia, *Journal of Advanced Nursing*, 34(3): 312–19.

Asch, S.E. (1956). Studies of independence and conformity: A minority of one against a unanimous majority. *Psychological Monographs*, 70, 416 (whole issue).

Baer, R. (2003) Mindfulness training as a clinical intervention: a conceptual and empirical review, *Clinical Psychology: Science and Practice*, 10(2): 125–43.

Bajor, J.K. and Baltes, B.B. (2003) The relationship between selection optimization with compensation, conscientiousness, motivation, and performance, *Journal of Vocational Behavior*, 63: 347–67.

Ballard, C.G., Gauthier, S., Cummings, J.L., Brodaty, H., Grossberg, G.T., Robert, P. *et al.* (2009) Management of agitation and aggression associated with Alzheimer disease, *Nature Reviews, Neurolology*, 5: 245–55.

Bandura A. (1971) Vicarious and self-reinforcement processes, in R. Glaser (ed.) *The Nature of Reinforcement*, A symposium of the Learning Research and Development Center, University of Pittsburgh, pp. 228–78. New York: Academic Press.

Bandura, A. (1977a) *Social Learning Theory*. Englewood Cliffs, NJ: Prentice Hall.

Bandura, A. (1977b) Self-efficacy: towards a unifying theory of behavioural change, *Psychological Review*, 84(2): 191–215.

Bandura, A. (1997) *Self-efficacy: The Exercise of Control*. New York: W.H. Freeman.

Bandura, A. (2000) Health promotion from the perspective of social cognitive theory, in P. Norman, C. Abraham and M. Conner (eds) *Understanding and Changing Health Behaviour: From Health Beliefs to Self-regulation*, pp. 299–342. Amsterdam: Harwood.

Bandura, A. (2005) The primacy of self-regulation in health promotion, *Applied Psychology: An International Review*, 54(2): 245–54.

Bandura, A., Ross, D. and Ross, S.A. (1961) Transmission of aggression through imitation of aggressive models, *Journal of Abnormal and Social Psychology*, 63: 575–82.

Barnes, D.E., Cauley, J.A., Lui, L.Y., Fink, H.A., McCulloch, C., Stone, K.L. *et al.* (2007) Women who maintain optimal cognitive function into old age, *Journal of the American Geriatric Society*, 55(2), 259–64.

Barnett, K., Harrison, C., Newman, F., Bentley, C. and Cummins, C. (2005) A randomised study of the impact of different styles of patient information leaflets for randomised controlled trials on children's understanding, *Archives of Disability in Children*, 90: 364–66.

Baron, R.M. and Kenny, D.A. (1986) The moderator–mediator variable distinction in social psychological research: conceptual, strategic, and statistical considerations, *Journal of Personality and Social Psychology*, 51(6): 1173–82.

Barrett, R. and Randle, J. (2008) Hand hygiene practices: nursing students' perceptions, *Journal of Clinical Nursing*, 17(14): 1851–7.

Bartlett, G. (1932) *Remembering*. Cambridge: Cambridge University Press.

Basbaum, A.I. and Fields, H.L. (1984) Endogenous pain control systems: brainstem spinal pathways and endorphin circuitry, *Annual Review of Neuroscience*, 7: 309–38.

Baumrind, D. (1967) Child care practices anteceding three patterns of preschool behaviour, *Genetic Psychology Monographs*, 75: 43–8.

Baumrind, D. (1971) Current patterns of parental authority, *Developmental Psychology Monographs*, Part 2, 4(1): 1–103.

Beecher, H.K. (1959) *Measurement of Subjective Responses*. New York: Oxford University Press.

Bellieni, C.V., Maffei, M., Ancora, G., Cordelli, D., Mastrocola, M., Faldella, G. *et al.* (2007) Is the ABC pain scale reliable for premature babies?, *Acta Pædiatrica*, 96: 1008–101.

Bendelow, G.A. (2006) Pain, suffering and risk, *Health, Risk & Society*, 8(1): 59–70.

Benedetti, F. (2006) Placebo analgesia, *Neurological Science*, 27: S100–2.

Benedetti, F., Arduino, C. and Amanzio, M. (1999) Somatotopic activation of opioid systems by target-directed expectations of analgesia, *The Journal of Neuroscience*, 19(9): 3639–48.

Benedetti, F., Mayberg, H.S., Wager, T.D., Stohler, C.S. and Jon-Kar Zubieta, J-K. (2005) Neurobiological mechanisms of the placebo effect, *The Journal of Neuroscience*, 25(45): 10390–402.

Benner, P. (1984) *From Novice to Expert: Excellence and Power in Clinical Nursing Practice*. Menlo Park, CA: Addison-Wesley.

Berde, C.B., Lehn, B.M., Yee, J.D., Sethna, N.F. and Russo, D. (1991) Patient-controlled analgesia in children and adolescents: a randomized prospective comparison with intramuscular administration of morphine for postoperative analgesia, *Journal of Pediatrics*, 118(3): 460–6.

Bhawuk, D.P.S. and Brislin, R.W. (2000) Cross-cultural training: a review, *Applied Psychology: An International Review*, 49(1): 162–91.

Birtwistle, J., Payne, S., Smith, P. and Kendrick, T. (2002) The role of the district nurse in bereavement support, *Journal of Advanced Nursing*, 38(5): 467–78.

Bisson, J. and Andrew, M. (2007) Psychological treatment of post-traumatic stress disorder (PTSD) (Review), *Cochrane Database of Systematic Reviews*, Issue 3. Art No. CD003388. www.thecochranelibrary.com/userfiles/ccoch/files/CD003388.pdf (accessed 31 December 2011).

Blaxter, M. (1990) *Health and Lifestyles*. London: Tavistock/Routledge.

Boccardi, M. and Frisoni, G.B. (2006) Cognitive rehabilitation for severe dementia: critical observations for better use of existing knowledge, *Mechanisms of Ageing and Development*, 127: 166–172.

Boersma, K., Linton, S., Overmeer, T., Jansson, M., Vlaeyen, J. and de Jong, J. (2004) Lowering fear-avoidance and enhancing function through exposure *in vivo*: a multiple baseline study across six patients with back pain, *Pain*, 108: 8–16.

Bohlmeijer, E., Smit, F. and Cuijpers, P. (2003) Effects of reminiscence and life review on late-life depression: a meta-analysis, *International Journal of Geriatric Psychiatry*, 18(12): 1088–94.

Bonanno, G.A. (2004) Loss, trauma, and human resilience: have we underestimated the human capacity to thrive after extremely aversive events?, *American Psychologist*, January: 1–28.

Borkenau, P., Riemann, R., Angleitner, A. and Spinath, F.M. (2001) Genetic and environmental influences on observed personality: evidence from the German observational study of adult twins, *Journal of Personality and Social Psychology*, 80(4): 655–68.

Boulos, M.N. (2005) British internet-derived patient information on diabetes mellitus: is it readable?, *Diabetes Technology and Therapy*, 7(3): 528–35.

Bowlby, J. (1969) *Attachment and Loss: Vol. 1. Attachment*. London: Hogarth Press.

Brissette, I., Scheier, M.F. and Carver, C.S. (2002) The role of optimism in social network development, coping, and psychological adjustment during a life transition, *Journal of Personality and Social Psychology*, 82(1): 102–11.

Britt, E., Hudson, S.M. and Blampied, N.M. (2004) Motivational interviewing in health settings: a review, *Patient Education and Counseling*, 53: 147–55.

Bury, M. (1982) Chronic illness as biographical disruption, *Sociology of Health and Illness*, 4: 167–82.

Butler, A.C., Chapman, J.E., Forman, E.M. and Beck, A.T. (2006) The empirical status of cognitive-behavioural therapy: a review of meta-analyses, *Clinical Psychology Review*, 26(1): 17–31.

Cacioppo, J.T., Reis, H.T. and Zautra, A.J. (2011) Social resilience: the value of social fitness with an application to the military, *American Psychologist*, 66(1): 43–51.

Cannon, W.B. (1932) *The Wisdom of the Body*. New York: W.W. Norton.

Carroll, D., Moore, R.A., McQuay, H.J., Fairman, F., Gramer, M. and Leijon, G. (2006) Transcutaneous electrical nerve stimulation (TENS) for chronic pain, *The Cochrane Database of Systematic Reviews*, Issue 4. Chichester: Wiley.

Carver, C.S., Scheier, M.F. and Segerstrom, S.C. (2010) Optimism, *Clinical Psychology Review*, 30: 879–89.

Casey, C.Y., Greenberg, M.A., Nicassio, P.M., Harpin, R.E. and Hubbard, D. (2008) Transition from acute to chronic pain and disability: a model including cognitive, affective, and trauma factors, *Pain*, 134: 69–79.

Cassidy, J. and Shaver, P.R. (1999) *Handbook of Attachment: Theory, Research and Applications*. New York: Guilford Press.

Chaiken, S. (1980) Heuristic versus systematic information processing and the use of source versus message cues in persuasion, *Journal of Personality and Social Psychology*, 39(5): 752–66.

Chaiken, S. (1987) The heuristic model of persuasion, in M.P. Zanna, J.M. Olson and C.P. Herman (eds) *Social Influence*. Hillsdale, NJ: Laurence Erlbaum Associates.

Chapman, C.R., Nakamura, Y. and Flores, L.Y. (1999) Chronic pain and consciousness: a constructivist perspective, in R.J. Gatchel and D.C. Turk (eds) *Psychosocial Factors in Pain*. New York: The Guilford Press.

Chapman, R., Styles, I., Perry, L. and Combs, S. (2010) Examining the characteristics of workplace violence in one non-tertiary hospital, *Journal of Clinical Nursing*, 19(3–4): 479–88.

Charles, K., McKee, L. and McCann, S. (2011) A quest for patient-safe culture: contextual influences on patient safety performance, *Journal of Health Services Research & Policy*, 16 (Suppl. 1): 57–64.

Chesney, M.A., Neilands, T.B., Chambers, D.B., Taylor, J.M. and Folkman, S. (2006) A validity and reliability study of the coping self-efficacy scale, *British Journal of Health Psychology*, 11: 421–37.

Chida, Y. and Steptoe, A. (2009) The association of anger and hostility with future coronary heart disease: a meta-analytic review of prospective evidence, *Journal of the American College of Cardiology*, 53(11): 936–46.

Christiana, J.M., Gilman, S.E., Guardino, M., Mickelson, K., Morselli, P.L., Olfson, M. *et al.* (2000) Duration between onset and time of obtaining initial treatment among people with anxiety and mood disorders: an international survey of members of mental health patient advocate groups, *Psychological Medicine*, 30(3): 693–703.

Christie, D. and Wilson, C. (2005) CBT in paediatric and adolescent health settings: a review of practice-based evidence, *Pediatric Rehabilitation*, 8(4): 241–7.

Cialdini, R.B. and Goldstein, N.J. (2004) Social influence: compliance and conformity, *Annual Review of Psycholology*, 55: 591–621.

Cignacco, E., Hamers, J.P.H., Stoffel, L. and Lingen, R.A. (2007) The efficacy of non-pharmacological interventions in the management of procedural pain in preterm and term neonates: a systematic literature review, *European Journal of Pain*, 11: 139–52.

Cignacco, E., Mueller, R., Hamers, J.P. and Gessler, P. (2004) Pain assessment in the neonate using the Bernese Pain Scale for Neonates, *Early Human Development*, 78(2): 125–31.

Clark, P. (2001) Narrative gerontology in clinical practice: current applications and future prospects, in G. Kenyon, P. Clark and B. de Vries (eds) *Narrative Gerontology: Theory, Research, and Practice*. New York: Springer.

Closs, S.J., Barr, B., Briggs, M., Cash, K. and Seers, K. (2004) A comparison of five pain assessment scales for nursing home residents with varying degrees of cognitive impairment, *Journal of Pain and Symptom Management*, 27(3): 196–205.

Coleman, P.G. (1999) Creating a life story: the task of reconciliation, *The Gerontologist*, 39(2): 133–9.

Coleman, P.G. and O'Hanlon, A. (2004) *Ageing and Development*. London: Arnold.

Connolly, D. (2004) Post-traumatic stress disorder in children after cardiac surgery, *Journal of Pediatrics*, 144(4): 480–4.

Cooley, C.H. (1902) *Human Nature and the Social Order*. New York: Scribners.

Costa, P.T. and McCrae, R.R. (1992) The five-factor model of personality and its relevance to personality disorders, *Journal of Personality Disorders*, 6(4): 343–59.

Coulon, M., Guellai, B. and Streri, A. (2011) Recognition of unfamiliar talking faces at birth, *International Journal of Behavioral Development*, 35(3): 282–7.

Coward, D.D. and Wilkie, D.J. (2000) Metastatic bone pain: meanings associated witih self-report and self-management decision making, *Cancer Nursing*, 23(2): 101–8.

Cowin, L., Davies, R., Estall, G., Fitzerald, M. and Hoot, S. (2003) De-escallating aggression and violence in the mental health setting, *International Journal of Mental Health Nursing*, 12(1): 64.

Craig, K.D. (2004) Social communication of pain enhances protective functions: a comment on Deyo, Prkachin and Mercer (2004), *Pain*, 107: 5–6.

Creer, T.L., Stein, R.E., Rappaport, L. and Lewis, C. (1992) Behavioural consequences of illness: childhood asthma as a model, *Pediatrics*, 90(5): 808–15.

Cross, M.J., March, L.M., Lapsley, H.M., Byrne, E. and Brooks, P.M. (2006) Patient self-efficacy and health locus of control: relationships with health status and arthritis-related expenditure, *Rheumatology*, 45: 92–6.

Crossley, M. (2003) 'Let me explain': narrative emplotment and one patient's experience of oral cancer, *Social Science and Medicine*, 56: 439–48.

Crowne, D.P. and Marlowe, D. (1960) A new scale of social desirability independent of psychopathology, *Journal of Consulting Psychology*, 24: 349–54.

Cuijpers, P., van Straten, A. and Andersson, G. (2008) Internet-administered cognitive behavior therapy for health problems: a systematic review, *Journal of Behavioral Medicine*, 31: 169–77.

Currier, J.M., Holland, J.M. and Neimeyer, R.A. (2007) The effectiveness of bereavement interventions with children: a meta-analytic review of controlled outcome research, *Journal of Clinical Child and Adolescent Psychology*, 36(2): 253–9.

Davies, D. and Evans, L. (2001) Assessing pain in people with profound learning disabilities, *British Journal of Nursing*, 10(8): 513–16.

Davis , C., Patte, K., Curtis, C. and Reid, C. (2010) Immediate pleasures and future consequences: a neuropsychological study of binge eating and obesity, *Appetite*, 54(1): 208–13.

Davison, J. (2002) Women with drinking problems. Unpublished PhD thesis, University of Southampton.

De Craen, A.J., Roos, P.J., de Vries, L.A. and Kliejnen, J. (1996) Effect of colour of drugs: systematic review of perceived effect of drugs and of their effectiveness, *British Medical Journal*, 313(7072): 1624–6.

Depp, C., Vahia, I.V. and Jeste, D. (2010) Successful aging: focus on cognitive and emotional health, *Annual Review of Clinical Psychology*, 6: 527–50.

DiClemente, C.C. (1993) Changing addictive behaviours: a process perspective, *Current Directions in Psychological Science*, 2: 101–6.

Dixon, M., Benedict, H. and Larson, T. (2001) Functional analysis and treatment of inappropriate verbal behaviour, *Journal of Applied Behavior Analysis*, 34: 361–3.

DoH (Department of Health) (2002) *Self-management of Long-term Health Conditions: A Handbook for People With Chronic Disease.* Boulder, CO: Bull Publishing.

Donaldson, M. (1978) *Children's Minds.* London: Fontana.

Donaldson, M. (1990) *Children's Minds,* 2nd edition. Glasgow: Fontana.

Downing-Matibag, T.M. and Geisinger, B. (2009) Hooking up and sexual risk taking among college students: a health belief model perspective, *Qualitative Health Research*, 19: 1196.

Dünser, M.W. and Hasibeder, W.R. (2009) Sympathetic overstimulation during critical illness: adverse effects of adrenergic stress, *Journal of Intensive Care Medicine*, 24(5): 293–316.

Dysvik, E., Kvaløy, J.T., Stokkeland, R. and Natvig, G.K. (2010) The effectiveness of a multidisciplinary pain management programme managing chronic pain on pain perceptions, health-related quality of life and stages of change: a non-randomized controlled study, *International Journal of Nursing Studies*, 47(2010): 826–35.

Erikson, E.H. (1980) *Identity and the Life Cycle.* New York: Norton.

Eriksson, M. and Lindstrom, B. (2006) Antonovsky's sense of coherence scale and the relation with health: a systematic review, *Journal of Epidemiology and Community Health*, 60: 376–81.

Ernst, E., Lee, M.S. and Choi, T-Y. (2011) Acupuncture: does it alleviate pain and are there serious risks? A review of reviews, *Pain*, 152: 755–64.

Evans, A. (1994) Anticipatory grief: a theoretical challenge, *Palliative Medicine*, 8: 159–65.

Evans, J.T.B. (2008) Dual-processing accounts of reasoning, judgment and social cognition, *Annual Review of Psychology*, 59: 255–78.

Falkner, T.M. and de Luce, J. (1992) A view from antiquity: Greece, Rome and elders, in T.R. Cole, D. van Tussel and R. Kastenbaum (eds) *Handbook of the Humanities and Aging*, pp. 3–39. New York: Springer.

Fallowfield, L. and Jenkins, V. (1999) Effective communication skills are the key to good cancer care, *European Journal of Cancer*, 35(11): 1592–7.

Fallowfield, L.J., Jenkins, V.A. and Beveridge, H.A. (2002) Truth may hurt but deceit hurts more: communication in palliative care, *Palliative Medicine*, 16(4): 297–303.

Feinstein, L. and Hammond, C. (2004) The contribution of adult leanring to health and social capital, *Oxford Review of Education*, 30(2): 199–221.

Fernandez, E. (2005) The relationship between anger and pain, *Current Pain and Headache Reports*, 9(2): 101–5.

Ferrie, C.P., Prince, M., Bravne, C. *et al.* for Alzheimer's Disease International (2005) Global prevalence of dementia: a Delphi consensus study, *The Lancet*, 366: 2112–17.

Ferri, J.E. (ed.) (2004) *Work, Stress and Health: The Whitehall II Study.* London: ccsu/Cabinet office.

Festinger, L. (1954) A theory of social comparison, *Human Relations*, 7: 117–40.

Festinger, L. (1957) *A Theory of Cognitive Dissonance.* Stanford, CA: Stanford University Press.

Field, D., Payne, S., Relf, M. and Reid, D. (2007) An overview of adult bereauement support in the United Kingdom: issues for policy and practice, *Social Science and Medicine*, 64(2): 428–38.

Fillingim, R.B., King, C.D., Ribeiro-Dasilva, M.C., Rahim-Williams, B. and Riley, J.L. (2009) Sex, gender, and pain: a review of recent clinical and experimental findings, *The Journal of Pain*, 10(5): 447–85.

Finlayson, T., Lee, S. and Oyserman, D. (2005) Social identity and the perceived efficacy of and engagement in health behaviors among a low-income, minority community sample, *Abstracts of the Academy of Health Meeting*, 22: 3289.

Folkman, S. (2009) Questions, answers, issues and next steps in stress and coping research, *European Psychologist*, 14(1): 72–7.

Folkman, S. and Lazarus, R.S. (1985) If it changes it must be a process: study of emotion and coping during three stages of a college examination, *Journal of Personal and Social Psychology*, 48(1): 150–70.

Folkman, S. and Moskowitz, J.T. (2004) Coping: pitfalls and promise, *Annual Review of Psychology*, 55: 745–74.

Folstein, M.F., Folstein, S.E. and McHugh, P.R. (1975) Mini mental state, *Journal of Psychosomatic Research*, 12: 196–8.

Fox, N.A. and Card, J.A. (1999) Psychophysiological measures in the study of attachment, in J. Cassidy and P.R. Shaver (eds) *Handbook of Attachment: Theory, Research and Clinical Applications*. New York: Guilford Press.

Frank, A.W. (1995) *The Wounded Storyteller: Body, Illness and Ethics*. Chicago, IL: University of Chicago Press.

Frederickson, B.L. (2001) The role of positive emotions in psychology: the broaden-and-build theory of positive emotions, *American Psychologist*, 56(3): 218–26.

Friedman, M.S. (2000) Long-term relations of personality and health: dynamisms, mechanisms, tropisms, *Journal of Personality*, 68(6): 1089–1107.

Fry, J.P. and Neff, R.A. (2009) Periodic prompts and reminders in health promotion and health behavior interventions: systematic review, *Journal of Medical Internet Research*, 11(2): e16. www.jmir.org/2009/2/e/16/ (accessed 31 December 2011).

Fuchs-Lacelle, S., Hadjistavropoulos, T. and Lix, L. (2008) Pain assessment as intervention: a study of older adults with severe dementia, *Clinical Journal of Pain*: 24(8): 697–707. www.ncbi.nlm.nih.gov/pubmed/18806535 (accessed 31 December 2011).

Garand, L., Buckwalter, K.C., Lubaroff, D., Tripp-Reimer, T., Frantz, R.A. and Ansley, T.N. (2002) A pilot study of immune and mood outcomes of a community-based intervention for dementia caregivers: the PLST intervention, *Archives of Psychiatric Nursing*, XVI (4): 156–67.

Garossa, E., Rainho, C., Moreno-Jiménez, B. and Monteiro, M.J. (2010) The relationship between job stressors, hardy personality, coping resources and burnout in a sample of nurses: a correlational study at two time points, *International Journal of Nursing Studies*, 47: 205–15.

Gaston, C.M. and Mitchell, G. (2005) Information giving and decision-making in patients with advanced cancer: a systematic review, *Social Science & Medicine*, 61: 2252–64.

Glazener, C.M. and Evans, J.H. (2002) Simple behavioural and physical interventions for nocturnal enuresis in children, *Cochrane Database of Systematic Reviews*, 2: CD003637.

Goffman, E. (1959) *The Presentation of Self in Everyday Life*. London: Penguin.

Goffman, E. (1963) *Stigma: Notes on the Management of Spoiled Identity*. Harmondsworth: Penguin.

Gottlieb, B.H. (1985) Social support and the study of personal relationships, *Journal of Social and Personal Relationships*, 2: 351–75.

Gouin, J-P., Hantsoo, L. and Kiecolt-Glaser, J.K. (2008) Immune dysregulation and chronic stress among older adults: a review, *NeuroImmunoModulation*, 155: 251–9.

Gracely, R.H. (2000) Charisma and the art of healing, in M. Devor, M.C. Rowbotham and Z. Wiesenfed-Hallin (eds) *Proceedings of the 9th World Congress on Pain*. Seattle, WA: IASP Press.

Graham, H. (1993) *Hardship and Health in Women's Lives*. New York: Harvester Wheatsheaf.

Grande, G.E., Farquhar, M.C., Barclay, S.I.G. and Todd, C.J. (2006) The influence of patient and carer age in access to palliative care services, *Age and Ageing*, 35: 267–73.

Greenberg, M.T., O'Brien, M.U., Zins, J.F., Fredericks, L., Rosnik, J. and Elias, M.J. (2003) Enhancing school-based prevention and youth development through coordinated social, emotional, and academic learning, *American Psychologist*, 58(6–7): 466–74.

Grimby, A. and Wiklund, I. (1994) Health-related quality of life in old age: a study among 76-year-old Swedish urban citizens, *Scandivanian Journal of Social Medicine*, 22(1): 7–14.

Gross, R. (2010) *Psychology: The Science of Mind and Behaviour*, 6th revised edition. London: Hodder Education.

Grossman, P., Niemann, L., Schmidtc, S. and Walach, H. (2004) Mindfulness-based stress reduction and health benefits: a meta-analysis, *Journal of Psychosomatic Research*, 57: 35–43.

Grunau, R.E., Holsti, L. and Peters, J.W.B. (2006) Long-term consequences of pain in human neonates, *Seminars in Fetal and Neonatal Medicine*, 11: 268–75.

Grunau, R.E., Whitfield, M.F., Petrie-Thomas, J., Synnes, A.R., Cepeda, I.L., Keidar, A. *et al.* (2009) Neonatal pain, parenting stress and interaction, in relation to cognitive and motor development at 8 and 18 months in preterm infants, *Pain*, 143: 138–46.

Grunfeld, E.A., Hunter, M.S., Ramirez, A.J. and Richards, M.A. (2003) Perceptions of breast cancer across the lifespan, *Journal of Psychosomatic Research*, 54(2): 141–6.

Halimaa, S-L. (2003) Pain management in nursing procedures on premature babies, *Journal of Advanced Nursing*, 42(6): 587–97.

Hall, S., Abramsky, L. and Marteau, T.M. (2003) Health professionals' reports of information given to parents following the prenatal diagnosis of sex chromosome anomalies and outcomes of pregnancies: a pilot study, *Prenatal Diagnosis*, 23(7): 535–8.

Harlow, H.F. (1959) Love in infant monkeys, *Scientific American*, 200: 68–74.

Harris, B. (1979) Whatever happened to little Albert?, *American Psychologist*, 34(2): 151–60.

Hartley, L.C. (2005) The consequences of conflicting stereotypes: Bostonian perceptions of US dialects, *American Speech*, 80(4): 388–405.

Hedden, T. and Gabrieli, J.D.E. (2004) Insights into the ageing mind: a view from cognitive neuroscience, *Nature Reviews, Neuroscience*, 5(2): 87–96.

Helson, R., Jones, C. and Kwan, V.S.Y. (2002) Personality change over 40 years of adulthood: hierarchical linear modeling analyses of two longitudinal samples, *Journal of Personality and Social Psychology*, 83(3): 752–66.

Hendriks, G.J., Voshaar, O., Keijsers, G.P.J., Hoogduin, C.A.L. and van Baldom A.J.L.M. (2008) Cognitive-behavioural therapy for late-life anxiety disorders: a systematic review and meta-analysis, *Acta Psychiatrica Scandinavia*, 117: 403–11.

Hewison, D. (1997) Coping with loss of ability: 'good grief' or episodic stress responses?, *Social Science and Medicine*, 44(8): 1129–39.

Hewstone, M. (1989) *Causal Attribution: From Cognitive Processes to Collective Beliefs*. Oxford: Blackwell.

Higgins, I. (2005) The experience of chronic pain in elderly nursing home residents, *Journal of Research in Nursing*, 10(4): 369–82.

Hillsdon, M., Thorogood, M., White, I. and Foster, C. (2002) Advising people to take more exercise is ineffective: a randomized controlled trial of physical activity promotion in primary care, *International Journal of Epidemiology*, 31: 808–15.

Hobfoll, S.E. (1988) *The Ecology of Stress*. New York: Hemisphere.

Hodgins, D. (2005) Weighing the pros and cons of changing change models: a comment on West (2005), *Addiction*, 100: 1042–3.

Hoel, H., Glas, L., Hetland, J., Cooper, C.L. and Einarsen, S. (2010) Leadership styles as predictors of self-reported and observed workplace bullying, *British Journal of Management*, 21: 453–68.

Hoeve, M., Dubas, J.S., Eichelsheim, V.I., van der Laan, P.H., Smeenk, W. and Gerris, J.R.M. (2009) The relationship between parenting and delinquency: a meta-analysis, *Journal of Abnormal Child Psychology*, 3(7): 749–75.

Hoffman, G.A., Harrington, A. and Fields, H.L. (2005) Pain and the placebo: what we have learned, *Perspectives in Biology and Medicine*, 48(2): 248–65.

Hofling, C.K., Brotzman, E., Dalrymple, S., Graves, N. and Pierce, C.M. (1966) An experimental study in nurse–physician relationships, *Journal of Nervous and Mental Disease*, 143(2): 171–80.

Hofmann, S.G., Sawyer, A.T., Witt, A.A. and Oh, D. (2010) The effect of mindfulness-based therapy on anxiety and depression: a meta-analytic review, *Journal of Consulting and Clinical Psychology*, 78(2): 169–83.

Hofmann, W., Friese, M. and Strack, F. (2009) Impulse and self-control from a dual-systems perspective, *Perspectives on Psychological Science*, 4: 162–76.

Hogbin, B. and Fallowfield, L. (1989) Getting it taped: the 'bad news' consultation with cancer patients, *British Journal of Hospital Medicine*, 41(4): 330–3.

Høie, M., Moan, I.S., Rise, J. and Larsen, E. (2011) Using an extended version of the theory of planned behaviour to predict smoking cessation in two age groups, *Addiction Research and Theory*, http://informahealthcare.com/doi/abs/10.3109/16066359.2011.557165 (accessed 31 December 2011).

Holloway, I., Sofaer, B. and Walker, J. (2007) The stigmatisation of people with chronic back pain, *Disability and Rehabilitation*, 29(18): 1456–64.

Holmes, T.H. and Rahe, R.H. (1967) The Social Readjustment Rating Scale, *Journal of Psychsomatic Research*, 11: 213–18.

Holt, C.L., Clark, E.M., Krueter, M.W. and Scharff, D.P. (2000) Does locus of control moderate the effects of tailored health education materials?, *Health Education Research*, 15(4): 393–403.

Homer, S.D., Surratt, D. and Juliusson, S. (2000) Improving readability of patient education materials, *Journal of Community Health Nursing*, 17: 15–23.

Houts, P.S., Witmer, J.T., Egeth, H.E., Loscalzo, M.J. and Zabora, J.R. (2001) Using pictographs to enhance recall of spoken medical instructions II, *Patient Education and Counseling*, 43(3): 231–42.

Hudcova, J. *et al.* (2005) Patient controlled opioid analgesia versus conventional opioid analgesia for postoperative pain, *Cochrane Database of Systematic Reviews*, 18(4): CD003348.

Hung, L-W., Kempen, G.I.J.M. and de Vries, N.K. (2010) Cross-cultural comparison between academic and lay views of health ageing: a literature review, *Ageing and Society*, 30: 1373–91.

Hunt, A., Wisbeach, A., Seers, K., Goldman, A., Crichton, N., Perry, L. *et al.* (2007) Development of the Paediatric Pain Profile: role of video analysis and saliva cortisol in validating a tool to assess pain in children with severe neurological disability, *Journal of Pain and Symptom Management*, 33(3): 276–89.

Igoe, J.B. (1988) Healthy long-term attitudes on personal health can be developed in school-age children, *Pediatrician*, 15(3): 127–36.

Igoe, J.B. (1991) Empowerment of children and youth for consumer self-care, *American Journal of Health Promotion*, 6(1): 55–64.

Jackson, D., Firtko, A. and Edenborough, M. (2007) Personal resilience as a strategy for surviving and thriving in the face of workplace adversity: a literature review, *Journal of Advanced Nursing*, 60(1): 1–9.

Janis, I.L. (1972) *Victims of Groupthink: A Psychological Study of Foreign-policy Decisions and Fiascos*. Oxford: Houghton Mifflin.

Janssen, C.G., Schuengel, C. and Stolk, J. (2002) Understanding challenging behaviour in people with severe and profound intellectual disability: a stress attachment model, *Journal of Intellectual Disability Research*, 46(6): 445–53.

Johansson, M. and Eva Kokinsky, E. (2009) The COMFORT behavioural scale and the modified FLACC scale in paediatric intensive care, *Nursing in Critical Care*, 14(3): 122–30.

Johnson, A. and Sandford, J. (2004) Written and verbal information versus verbal information only for patients being discharged from acute hospital settings to home: systematic review, *Health Education Research*, 20(4): 423–9.

Johnson, M. and Webb, C. (1995) Rediscovering unpopular patients: the concept of social judgement, *Journal of Advanced Nursing*, 21(3): 466–74.

Johnson, N. (2004) *Cancer – My Partner*. Southampton: Paul Cave Publications.

Jonassaint, C.R., Siegler, I.C., Barefoot, J.C., Edwards, C.L. and Williams, R.B. (2011) Low life course socioeconomic status (SES) is associated with negative NEO PI-R personality patterns, *International Journal of Behavioral Medicine*, 18: 13–21.

Jordan, J.R. and Neimeyer, R.A. (2003) Does grief counseling work?, *Death Studies*, 27(9): 765–86.

Jost, J.T., Banaji, M.R. and Nosek, B.A. (2004) A decade of system justification theory: accumulated evidence of conscious and unconscious bolstering of the status quo, *Political Psychology*, 25(6): 881–919.

Kabat-Zinn, J., Lipworth, L. and Burney, R. (1983) The clinical use of mindfulness meditation for the self-regulation of chronic pain, *Journal of Behavioural Medicine*, 8(2): 163–90.

Kaltenthaler, E., Brazier, J., De Nigris, E., Tumur, I., Ferriter, M., Beverley, C. *et al.* (2006) Computerised cognitive behaviour therapy for depression and anxiety update: a systematic review and economic evaluation, *Health Technology Assessment*, 10(33): 1–6.

Kaltenthaler, E., Sutcliffe, P., Parry, G., Beverley, C., Rees, A. and Ferriter, M. (2008) The acceptability to patients of computerized cognitive behaviour therapy for depression: a systematic review, *Psychological Medicine*, 38: 1521–30.

Kaviani, H., Javaheri, F. and Hatami, N. (2011) Mindfulness-based Cognitive Therapy (MBCT) reduces depression and anxiety induced by real stressful setting in non-clinical population, *International Journal of Psychology and Psychological therapy*, 11(2): 285–96.

Kelly, G.A. (1955) *A Theory of Personality: The Psychology of Personal Constructs*. New York: W.W. Norton.

Kelly, P. (1998) Loss experienced in chronic pain and illness, in J.H. Harvey (ed.) *Perspectives on Loss: A Sourcebook*. Philadelphia, PA: Brunner Mazel.

Kentsch, M., Rodemerk, U., Müller-Esch, G., Schnoor, U., Münzel, T., Ittel, T-H. *et al.* (2002) Emotional attitudes toward symptoms and inadequate coping strategies are major determinants of patient delay in acute myocardial infarction, *Zeitschrift für Kardiologie*, 91(2): 147–55.

Khadilkar, A., Milne, S., Brosseau, L., Wells, G., Tugwell, P., Robinson, V. *et al.* (2005) Transcutaneous Electrical Nerve Stimulation for the treatment of chronic low back pain: a systematic review, *Spine*, 30(23): 2657–66.

Kiecolt-Glaser, J., Preacher, K.J., MacCallum, R.C., Atkinson, C., Malarkey, W.B. and Glaser, R. (2003) Chronic stress and age-related increases in the proinflammatory cytokine IL-6, *Proceedings of the National Academy of Science*, USA, 100(15): 9090–5.

Kiecolt-Glaser, J.K., McGuire, L., Robles, T.F. and Glaser, R. (2002) Psychoneuroimmunology: psychological influences on immune function and health, *Journal of Consulting and Clinical Psychology*, 70(3): 537–47.

Klaus, H.M. and Kennell, J.H. (1976) *Maternal–Infant Bonding.* St Louis, MO: Mosby.

Kleinhesselink, R.R. and Edwards, R.E. (1975) Seeking and avoiding belief-discrepant information as a function of its perceived refutability, *Journal of Personality and Social Psychology*, 31: 787–90.

Kobasa, S.C. (1979) Stressful life events, personality and health: an inquiry into hardiness, *Journal of Personality and Social Psychology*, 37: 1–11.

Kobau, R., Seligman, M.E.P., Peterson, C., Zack, M.M., Chapman, D. and Thompson, W. (2011) Health promotion in public health: perspectives and strategies from positive psychology, *American Journal of Public Health*, 101(8): e1–9.

Koenig, H.G. and Cohen, H.J. (eds) (2002) *The Link Between Religion and Health: Psychoneuroimmunology.* Oxford: Oxford University Press.

Kohlberg, L. (1969) Stage and sequence: the cognitive-developmental approach to socialization, in D.A. Goslin (ed.) *Handbook of Socialization Theory and Research.* Skokie, IL: Rand McNally.

Korpershoek, C., Van der Bijl, J. and Hafsteinsdóttir, T.B. (2011) Self-efficacy and its influence on recovery of patients with stroke: a systematic review, *Journal of Advanced Nursing*, 67(9): 1876–94.

Krueger, P.M. and Chang, V.W. (2008) Being poor and coping with stress: health behaviors and the risk of death, *American Journal of Public Health*, 98(5): 880–96.

Kübler-Ross, E. (1969) *On Death and Dying.* London: Tavistock/Routledge.

Kwekkeboom, K.L. and Gretarsdottir, E. (2006) Systematic review of relaxation interventions for pain, *Journal of Nursing Scholarship*, 38(3): 269–77.

Lai, D.T.C., Cahill, K., Qin, Y. and Tang, J.L. (2010) Motivational interviewing for smoking cessation (Review), *The Cochrane Library*, 3: 1–37.

Lam, D. and Gale, J. (2000) Cognitive behaviour therapy: teaching a client the ABC model – the first step towards the process of change, *Journal of Advanced Nursing*, 31(2): 444–51.

Lamontagne, A.D., Keegel, T., Louie, A.M., Ostry, A. and Landsbergis, P.A. (2007) A systematic review of the job-stress intervention evaluation literature, 1990–2005. *Job-Stress Evaluation*, 13(3): 268–80.

Langer, E.J., Janis, I.L. and Wolfer, J.A. (1975) Reduction of psychological stress in surgical patients, *Journal of Experimental Social Psychology*, 11: 155–65.

Langille, M., Bernard, A., Rodgers, C., Hughes, S., Leddin, D. and van Zanten, S.V. (2010) Systematic review of the quality of patient information on the internet regarding inflammatory bowel disease treatments, *Clinical Gastroenterology and Hepatology*, 8(4):322–8.

Lasch, K.E. (2000) Culture, pain, and culturally sensitive pain care, *Pain Management Nursing*, 1(3), Suppl. 1: 16–22.

Latané, B. and Darley, J.M. (1968) Group inhibition of bystander intervention in emergencies, *Journal of Personality and Social Psychology*, 10: 215–21.

Lau, R.R. and Hartman, K.A. (1983) Common sense representations of common illness, *Health Psychology*, 2: 319–32.

Lazarus, R.S. (1966) *Psychological Stress and the Coping Process*. New York: McGraw-Hill.

Lazarus, R.S. and Averill, J.R. (1972) Emotion and cognition: with special reference to anxiety, in C.D. Spielberger (ed.) *Anxiety: Current Trends in Therapy and Research, Volume II*. New York: Academic Press.

Lazarus, R.S. and Folkman, S. (1984) *Stress, Appraisal and Coping*. New York: Springer-Verlag.

LeBlanc, M. and Ritchie, M. (2001) A meta-analysis of play therapy outcomes, *Psychology Quarterly*, 14(2): 149–63.

Levenson, H. (1974) Activism and powerful others: distinctions within the concept of internal–external control, *Journal of Personality Assessment*, 38: 377–83.

Leventhal, H. and Nerenz, D. (1982) Representations of threat and the control of stress, in D. Meichenbaum and J. Jaremki (eds) *Stress Management and Presention: A Cognitive-Behavioural Approach*. New York: Plenum Press.

Levett-Jones, T. and Lathlean, J. (2009) 'Don't rock the boat': nursing students' experiences of conformity and compliance, *Nurse Education Today*, 29(3): 342–9.

Levin, J. (2003) Spiritual determinants of health and healing: an epidemiologic perspective on salutogenic mechanisms, *Alternative Therapies in Health and Medicine*, 9(6): 48–57.

Levinson, D.J., Darrow, D.N., Klein, E.B., Levinson, M.H. and McKee, B. (1978) *The Seasons of a Man's Life*. New York: A.A. Knopf.

Lewin, K., Lippit, R. and White, R.K. (1939). Patterns of aggressive behavior in experimentally created social climates. *Journal of Social Psychology*, 10, 271–301.

Lewinsohn, P.M. (1974) A behavioural approach to depression, in R.J. Freidman and M.M. Katz (eds) *The Psychology of Depression: Contemporary Theory and Reseach*, pp. 157–86. Washington, DC: V.H. Winston.

Ley, P. (1997) *Communicating with Patients: Improving Satisfaction and Compliance*. Cheltenham: Stanley Thornes.

Leydon, G.M., Boulton, M., Moynihan, C., Jones, A., Mossman, J., Boudioni, M. *et al.* (2000) Faith, hope, and charity: an in-depth interview study of cancer patients' information needs and information-seeking behavior, *Western Journal of Medicine*, 173(1): 26–31.

Lin, C-H., Chiu, Y-C. and Huang, J-T. (2009) Gain–loss frequency and final outcome in the Soochow Gambling Task: a reassessment, *Behavioral and Brain Functions*, 5: 45. www.behavior. and brainfunctions.com/content/5/1/45 (accessed 31 December 2011).

Link, B.G. and Phedan, J.C. (2006) Stigma and its public health implications, *The Lancet*, 367: 528–9.

Linville, P.W. (1987) Self-complexity as a cognitive buffer against stress-related illness and depression, *Journal of Personality and Social Psychology*, 52(4): 663–76.

Lissek, S., Biggs, A.L., Ratin, J., Cornwell, B.R., Alvarez, R.P., Pine, D.S. *et al.* (2008) Generalization of conditioned fear-potentiated startle in humans: experimental validation and clinical relevance, *Behaviour Research and Therapy*, 46: 678–87.

Litz, B.T., Gray, M.J., Bryant, R.A. and Adler, A.B. (2002) Early intervention for trauma: current status and future directions, *Clinical Psychology: Science and Practice*, 9(2): 112.

Lloyd, J. (2010) Peering through the SMOG: adult literacy in the UK and its potential impact upon political marketing communication strategy and content. Paper given at 60th Political Studies Association Annual Conference, Edinburgh, 29 March–1 April.

Loftus, E. (2005) Planting misinformation in the human mind: a 30-year investigation of the malleability of memory, *Learning and Memory*, 12: 361–6.

Lorig, K. and Holman, H. (1989) Arthritis self-management studies: a twelve year review, *Health Education Quarterly*, 20: 17–28.

Lorig, K. Holman, H., Sobel, D., Laurent, D., Gonzalez, V. and Minor, M. (2007) *Self-management of Long-term Health Conditions: A Handbook for People with Chronic Disease*, 3rd edition. Boulder, CO: Bull Publishing.

Lorig, K., Ritter, P.L., Laurent, D.D., Plant, K., Green, M., Jernigan, V.B.B. *et al.* (2010) Online diabetes self-management program: a randomized study, *Diabetes Care*, 33(6): 1275–81. http://care.diabetesjournals.org/content/early/2010/03/10/dc09–2153 (accessed 31 December 2011).

Lyubomirsky, S., Sheldon, K.M. and Schkade, D. (2005) Pursuing happiness: the architecture of sustainable change, *Review of General Psychology*, 9: 111–31.

McAllister, M. and McKinnon, J. (2009) The importance of teaching and learning resilience in the health disciplines: a critical review of the literature, *Nurse Education Today*, 29: 371–9.

McCann, M.E. and Kain, Z. (2001). The management of preoperative anxiety in children: an update, *Anesthesia and Analgesia*, 93: 98–105.

Maccoby, E.E. (1980) *Social Development: Psychological Growth and the Parent–Child Relationship*. New York: Harcourt Brace Jovanovich.

McCreaddie, M., Payne, S. and Froggatt, K. (2010) Ensnared by positivity: a constructivist perspective on 'being positive' in cancer care, *European Journal of Oncology Nursing*, 14(4): 283–90.

McDermut, W., Miller, I.W. and Brown, R.A. (2001) The efficacy of group psychotherapy for depression: a meta-analysis and review of the empirical research, *Clinical Psychology: Science and Practice*, 8(1): 98–116.

McGrath, J.E. (1970) A conceptual formulation for research on stress, in J.E. McGrath (ed.) *Social and Psychological Factors in Stress*. New York: Holt, Rinehart & Winston.

Maddux, J.E. (1993) Social cognitive models of health and exercise behavior: an introduction and review of conceptual issues, *Journal of Applied Sport Psychology*, 5(2): 116–40.

Malle, B.F. (2006) The actor–observer asymmetry inattribution: a (surprising) meta-analysis, *Psychological Bulletin*, 132(6): 895–919.

Marks, D.F. (1993) *The Quit for Life Programme: An Easier Way to Stop Smoking and Not Start Again*. Leicester: The British Psychological Society.

Marks, D.F., Murray, M., Evans, B. and Estacio, E.V. (2011) *Health Psychology: Theory, Research and Practice*, 3rd edition. London: Sage Publications.

Marmot, M., Siegrist, J., Theorell, T. and Feeney, A. (1999) Health and the psychosocial environment at work, in M. Marmot and R.G. Wilkinson (eds) *Social Determinants of Health*, pp. 105–31. Oxford: Oxford University Press.

Marsland, A.L., Bachen, E.A., Cohen, S., Rabin, B. and Manuck, S.B. (2002) Stress, immune reactivity and susceptibility to infectious disease, *Physiology and Behaviour*, 77: 711–16.

Martin, C.J.H. and Bull, P. (2006) What features of the maternity unit promote obedient behaviour from midwives?, *Clinical Effectiveness in Nursing*, 952: e221–e231.

Maslach, C., Schaufeli, W.B. and Leiter, M.P. (2001) Job burnout, *Annual Review of Psychology*, 52: 397–422.

Matthews, S., Stansfeld, S. and Power, C. (1999) Social support at age 33: the influence of gender, employment status and social class, *Social Science and Medicine*, 49(1): 133–42.

Maunder, R.G. and Hunter, J.J. (2008) Attachment relationships as determinants of physical health, *Journal of the American Psychoanalytic and Dynamic Psychiatry*, 36(1): 11–32.

Meadows, S. (1993) *The Child as Thinker*. London: Routledge.

Meins, E., Fernyhough, C., Wainwright, R., Gupta, M.D., Fradley, E. and Tuckey, M. (2002) Maternal mind-mindedness and attachment security as predictors of theory of mind understanding, *Child Development*, 73(6): 1715–26.

Melzack, R. and Wall, P.D. (1965) Pain mechanisms: a new theory, *Science*, 150: 971–9.

Merritt, M.M., Bennett, G.G., Williams, R.B., Sollers, J.J. and Thayer, J.F. (2004) Low educational attainment, John Henryism, and cardiovascular reactivity to and recovery from personally relevant stress, *Psychosomatic Medicine*, 66: 49–55.

Miller, G.A. (1956) The magical number seven, plus or minus two: some limits to our capacity for processing information, *Psychological Review*, 63: 81–97.

Miller, J.F. (1992) Analysis of coping with illness, in J.F. Miller (ed.) *Coping with Chronic Illness: Overcoming Powerlessness*, 2nd edition. Philadelphia, PA: F.A. Davis.

Miller, W.R. and Rollnick, S. (2002) *Motivational Interviewing: Preparing People to Change Addictive Behaviour*, 2nd edition. New York: The Guilford Press.

Mills, M. and Walker, J.M. (1994) Memory, mood and dementia, *Journal of Aging Studies*, 8(1): 17–27.

Mirowsky, J. and Ross, C.E. (2003) *Social Causes of Psychological Distress*, 2nd edition. New York: Aldine de Gruyter.

Mischel, W., Ebbesen, E.B. and Zeiss, R.A. (1972) Cognitive and attentional mechanisms in delay of gratification, *Journal of Personality and Social Psychology*, 21(2): 204–18.

Mischel, W., Ayduk, O., Berman, M.G., Casey, B.J., Gotlib, I.H., Jonides, J. *et al.* (2011) 'Willpower' over the life span: decomposing self-regulation, *Social Cognitive and Affective Neuroscience*, 6(2): 252–6.

Mols, F. and Denollet, J. (2010) Type D personality in the general population: a systematic review of health status, mechanisms of disease, and work-related problems. *Health and Quality of Life Outcomes* 8: 9. http://www.hqlo.com/content/8/1/9 (accessed 31 December 2011).

Montgomery, C., Fisk, J.E. and Craig, L. (2008) The effects of perceived parenting style on the propensity for illicit drug use; the importance of parental warmth and control, *Drug and Alcohol Review*, 27: 640–9.

Morley, S., Williams, A. and Hussain, S. (2008) Estimating the clinical effectiveness of cognitive behavioural therapy in the clinic: evaluation of a CBT informed pain management programme, *Pain*, 137 (2008): 670–80.

Morone, N.E., Lynch, C.S. Greco, C.M., Tindle, H.A. and Weiner, D.K. (2008) 'I felt like a new person': the effects of mindfulness meditation on older adults with chronic pain: qualitative narrative analysis of diary entries, *The Journal of Pain*, 9(9): 841–8.

Morris, J. and Ingham, R. (1988) Choice of surgery for early breast cancer: psychosocial considerations, *Social Science and Medicine*, 27(11): 1257–62.

Muntner, P., Sudre, P., Uldry, C., Rochat, T., Courteheuse, C., Naef, A.F. *et al.* (2001) Predictors of participation and attendance in a new asthma patient self-management education program, *Chest*, 120(3): 778–84.

Murray, M. (2003) Narrative psychology, in J.A. Smith (ed.) *Qualitative Psychology: A Practical Guide to Research Methods*, pp. 111–31. Thousand Oaks, CA: Sage Publications.

Nabi, H., Singh-Manoux, A., Ferrie, J.E., Marmot, M., Melchior, M. and Kivimäki, M. (2010) Hostility and depressive mood: results from the Whitehall II prospective cohort study, *Psychological Medicine*, 40: 405–13.

Neimeyer, R.A., Burke, L.A., Mackay, M.M. and Stringer J.G. van D. (2010) Grief therapy and the reconstruction of meaning: from principles to practice, *Journal of Contemporary Psychotherapy*, 40: 73–83.

Newell, R. (2002a) Living with disfigurement, *Nursing Times*, 98(15): 34–5.

Newell, R. (2002b) The fear-avoidance model: helping patients to cope with disfigurement, *Nursing Times*, 98(16): 39–9.

NHS Wales (2010) *Standards for Spiritual Care Services in the NHS in Wales*. Cardiff: Welsh Assembly Government. http://www.wales.nhs.uk/news/16376, accessed 16 August 2011.

NICE (**National Institute for Health and Clinical Excellence**) (2005) *Post-traumatic Stress Disorder (PTSD): The Management of PTSD in Adults and Children in Primary and Secondary Care, Clinical Guideline No. 26*. London: National Institute for Health and Clinical Excellence.

NICE (2009) *Depression: Treatment and Management of Depression in Adults, Including Adults With a Chronic Physical Health Problem*. London: NHS National Institute for Health and Clinical Excellence.

NICE (2011) *Generalised Anxiety Disorder and Panic Disorder (With or Without Agoraphobia) in Adults: Management in Primary, Secondary and Community Care*. London: NHS National Institute for Health and Clinical Excellence.

NMC (**Nursing and Midwifery Council**) (2010) *Raising and Escalating Concerns: Guidance for Nurses and Midwives*. London: Nursing and Midwifery Council.

Omoto, A.M. and Snyder, M. (1995) Sustained helping without obligation: motivation, longevity of service, and perceived attitude change among AIDS volunteers, *Journal of Personality and Social Psychology*, 68(4): 671–86.

Osiri, M., Welch, V., Brosseau, L., Shea, B., McGowan, J., Tugwell, P. *et al.* (2000) Transcutaneous electrical nerve stimulation for knee osteoarthritis, *The Cochrane Database of Systematic Reviews*, Issue 4. Chichester: Wiley.

Palmer, S., Cooper, C.L. and Thomas, K. (2003) *Creating a Balance: Managing Stress*. London: British Library Publishing.

Park, C.L., Folkman, S. and Bostrom, A. (2001) Appraisals of controllability and coping in caregivers and HIV men: testing the goodness-of-fit hypothesis, *Journal of Consulting and Clinical Psychology*, 69(3): 481–8.

Park, D.C., Hertzog, C., Leventhal, H., Morrell, R.W., Leventhal, E., Birchmore, D. *et al.* (1999) Medication adherence in rheumatoid arthritis patients: older is wiser (comments), *Journal of the American Geriatrics Society*, 48(4): 457–9.

Parkes, C.M. (1972) *Bereavement: Studies of Grief in Adult Life*. Harmondsworth: Penguin.

Parliamentary and Health Services Ombudsman (2010) Listening and learning: the Ombudsman's review of complaint handling by the NHS in England 2009–10. London: TSO. www.official-documents.gov.uk (accessed 14 December 2011).

Parsons, S., Neale, H.R., Reynard, G. *et al.* (2000) Development of social skills amongst adults with Asperger's Syndrome using virtual environments: the 'AS Interactive' project, *Proceedings of the 3rd International Conference in Disability, Virtual Reality and Associated Technologies*, pp. 163–70. Alghero, Italy: International Society for Virtual Rehabilitation.

Payne, S., Hawker, S., Kerr, C., Seamark, D., Jarrett, N., Roberts H. and Smith, H. (2007) Healthcare workers' skills: perceived competence and experiences of end-of-life care in community hospitals, *Progress in Palliative Care*, 15(3): 118–25.

Payne, S.A., Dean, S.J. and Kalus, C. (1998) A comparative study of death anxiety in hospice and emergency nurses, *Journal of Advanced Nursing*, 28(4): 700–6.

Pence, L.B., Thorn, B.E., Jensen, M.P. and Romano, J.M. (2008) Examination of perceived spouse responses to patient well and pain behavior in patients with headache, *Clinical Journal of Pain*, 24(8): 654–61.

Penley, J.A., Tomaka, J. and Wiebe, J.S. (2002) The association of coping to physical and psychological health outcomes: a meta-analytic review, *Journal of Behavioral Medicine*, 25(6): 551–603.

Petty, R.E. and Cacioppo, J.T. (1986) *Communication and Persuasion: Central and Peripheral Routes to Attitude Change*. New York: Springer-Verlag.

Piaget, J. (1952) *The Origins of Intelligence in Children*. New York: Norton.

Piaget, J. and Inhelder, B. (1956) *The Child's Conception of Space*. London: Routledge & Kegan Paul.

Powell, H. and Gibson, P.G. (2003) Options for self-management education for adults with asthma, *Cochrane Database Systematic Review*, 3(1): CD004107.

Powers, B.J., Trinh, J.V. and Bosworth, H.B. (2010) Can this patient read and understand written health information?, *JAMA*, 304(1): 76–84.

Price, D.D., Finniss, D.G. and Benedetti, F. (2008) A comprehensive review of the placebo effect: recent advances and current thought, *Annual Review of Psychology*, 59: 565–90.

Prochaska, J.O. and DiClemente, C.C. (1983) Stages and processes of self change in smoking: towards an integrative model of change, *Journal of Consulting and Clinical Psychology*, 51: 390–5.

Puhl, R.M. and Latner, J.D. (2007) Stigma, obesity, and the health of the nation's children, *Psychological Bulletin*, 133(4): 557–80.

Purdie, N. and McCrindle, A. (2002) Self-regulation, self-efficacy and health behavior change in older adults, *Educational Gerontology*, 28(5): 379–400.

Rank, S.G. and Jacobson, C.K. (1977) Hospital nurses' compliance with medication overdose orders: a failure to replicate, *Journal of Health and Social Behaviour*, 18(2): 188–93.

Raphael, H. (2008) A grounded theory study of men's perceptions, understanding and experiences of osteoporosis. Unpublished PhD thesis, Southampton University.

Rasmussen, H.N., Scheier, M.F. and Greenhouse, J.B. (2009) Optimism and physical health: a meta-analysis review. *Annals of Behavioral Medicine*, 37: 239–56.

RCN (Royal College of Nursing) (2005) *Bullying and Harassment at Work*, revised edition. London: RCN.

Regnard, C., Reynolds, J., Watson, B., Matthews, D., Gibson, L. and Clarke, C. (2007) Understanding distress in people with severe communication difficulties: developing and assessing the Disability Distress Assessment Tool (DisDAT), *Journal of Intellectual Disability Research*, 51(4): 277–92.

Richardson, G., Kennedy, A., Reeves, D., Bower, P., Lee, V., Middleton, E. *et al.* (2008) Cost effectiveness of the Expert Patients Programme (EPP) for patients with chronic conditions, *Journal of Epidemiology and Community Health*, 62: 361–7.

Rigby, J., Payne, S. and Froggatt, K. (2010) What evidence is there about the specific environmental needs of older people who are near the end of life and are cared for in hospices or similar institutions? A literature review, *Palliative Medicine*, 24(3): 268–85.

Roberts, N.P., Kitchiner, N.J., Kenardy, J. and Bisson, J.I. (2010) Early psychological interventions to treat acute traumatic stress symptoms, *Cochrane Database of Systematic Reviews*, Issue 3, CD007944. www.ncbi.nlm.nih.gov/pubmed/20238359 (accessed 31 December 2011).

Robertson, J. and Robertson, J. (1967–73) Young children in brief separation (videos), www.robertsonfilms.info/young_children_in_brief-separation.htm (accessed 21 December 2011).

Romer, D., Duckworth, A.L., Sznitman, S. and Park, S. (2010) Can adolescents learn self-control? Delay of gratification in the development of control over risk taking, *Prevention Science*, 11: 319–30.

Rose, S., Bisson, J. and Wessely, S. (2002) Psychological debriefing for preventing post traumatic stress disorder (PTSD) (Cochrane Review), *The Cochrane Library*, Issue 1. Chichester: Wiley.

Rosenhan, D.L. (1973) On being sane in insane places, *Science*, 179: 365–9.

Rosenstiel, A.K. and Keefe, F.J. (1983) The use of coping strategies in chronic low back pain patients: relationship to patient characteristics and current adjustment, *Pain*, 17: 33–44.

Rosenstock, I.M., Strecher, V.J. and Becker, M.H. (1988) Social learning theory and the health belief model, *Health Education Quarterly*, 15: 175–83.

Rosenthal, R. and Jacobson, L. (1968) *Pygmalion in the Classroom: Teacher Expectations and Pupils' Intellectual Development*. New York: Holt, Rinehart & Winston.

Rosenzweig, S., Greeson, J.M., Reibel, D.K., Green, J.S., Jasser, S.A. and Beasley, D. (2010) Mindfulness-based stress reduction for chronic pain conditions: variation in treatment outcomes and role of home meditation practice, *Journal of Psychosomatic Research*, 68: 29–36.

Ross, C.E. and Mirowsky, J. (1989) Explaining the social patterns of depression: control and problem solving – or support and talking?, *Journal of Health and Social Behavior*, 30(2): 206–19.

Ross, L. (1977) The intuitive psychologist and his shortcomings: distortions in attribution process, in L. Berkowitz (ed.) *Advances in Experimental Social Psychology*, Vol 10. New York: Academic Press.

Roth, S. and Cohen, L.J. (1986) Approach, avoidance and coping with stress, *American Psychologist*, 41(7): 813–19.

Rotter, J.B. (1966) Generalized expectancies for internal versus external control of reinforcement, *Psychological Monographs: General and Applied*, 80(1): 1–28.

Rubak, S., Sandbaek, A., Lauritzen, T. and Christensen, B. (2005) Motivational interviewing: a systematic review and meta-analysis, *British Journal of General Practice*, 55(513): 305–12.

Rumsey, N. (2004) Psychological aspects of face transplantation: read the small print carefully, *The American Journal of Bioethics*, 4(3): 22–5.

Rumsey, N. and Harcourt, D. (2004) Body image and disfigurement: issues and interventions, *Body Image*, 1: 83–97.

Rumsey, N., Bull, R. and Gahagan, D. (1982) The effect of facial disfigurement on the proxemic behaviour of the general public, *Journal of Applied Social Psychology*, 12: 137–50.

Rushforth, H. (1999) Practitioner review. Communicating with hospitalized children: review and application of research pertaining to children's understanding of health and illness, *Journal of Child Psychology and Psychiatry*, 40(5): 683–91.

Rutter, M. (1979) Maternal deprivation, 1972–1978: new findings, new concepts, new approaches, *Child Development*, 50: 282–305.

Salmon, C.T. and Atkin, C. (2003) Using media campaigns for health promotion, in D.L. Thompson, A. Dorsey, K.L. Miller and R. Parrott (eds) *Handbook of Health Communication*, pp. 449–72. Mahwah, NJ: Laurence Erlbaum Associates.

Sanders-Dewey, N.E.J., Mullins, L.L. and Chaney, J.M. (2001) Coping style, perceived uncertainty in illness, and distress in individuals with Parkinson's disease and their caregivers, *Rehabilitation Psychology*, 46(4): 363–81.

Sanz, E.J. (2003) Concordance and children's use of medicines, *British Medical Journal*, 327(7419): 858–60.

Scascighini, L., Toma, V., Dober-Spielmann, S. and Sprott, H. (2008) Multidisciplinary treatment for chronic pain: a systematic review of interventions and outcomes, *Rheumatology*, 47: 670–8.

Schumacher, K. (2002) Putting cancer pain management regimens into practice at home, *Journal of Pain and Symptom Management*, 2(5): 369–82.

Scott, C., Walker, J., White, P. and Lewith, G. (2011) Forging convictions: the effects of active participation in a clinical trial, *Social Science & Medicine*, 72(12): 2041–8.

Seligman, M.E.P. (1975) *Helplessness: On Development, Depression and Death.* New York: Freeman.

Seligman, M.E.P. (2003) *Authentic Happiness: Using the New Positive Psychology to Realise Your Potential for Lasting Fulfilment.* London: Nicholas Brealey.

Seligman, M.E.P. and Maier, S.F. (1967) Failure to escape traumatic shock, *Journal of Experimental Psychology*, 74: 1–9.

Seligman, M.E.P., Maier, S.F. and Geer, J.H. (1968) Alleviation of learned helplessness in the dog, *Journal of Abnormal Psychology*, 73(3): 256–62.

Selye, H. (1956) *The Stress of Life.* New York: McGraw-Hill.

Sephton, S.E., Koopman, C., Schaal, M., Thorsens, C. and Spiegel, D. (2001) Spiritual expression and immune status in women with metastatic breast cancer: an exploratory study, *The Breast Journal*, 7(5): 345–53.

Sepúlveda, C., Marlin, A., Yoshida, T. and Ullrich, A. (2002) Palliative care: the World Health Organization's global perspective, *Journal of Pain and Symptom Management*, 24(2): 91–6.

Shear, K., Monk, T., Houck, P., Melhem, N., Frank, E., Reynolds, C. *et al.* (2007) An attachment-based model of complicated grief including the role of avoidance, *European Archives of Psychiatry and Clinical Neuroscience*, 257: 453–61.

Shennan, C., Payne, S. and Fenlon, D. (2011) What is the evidence for the use of mindfulness-based interventions in cancer care?. A review, *Psycho-Oncology*, 20: 681–697.

Silverman, J. and Kinnersley, P. (2010) Doctors' non-verbal behaviour in consultations: look at the patient before you look at the computer, *British Journal of General Practice*, 60(571): 76–8.

Sinclair, H.A.H. and Hamill, C. (2007) Does vicarious traumatisation affect oncology nurses? A literature review, *European Journal of Oncology Nursing*, 11: 348–56.

Sitzer, D.L., Twamley, E.W. and Jeste, D.V. (2006) Cognitive training in Alzheimer's disease: a meta-analysis of the literature, *Acta Psychiatrica Scandinavica*, 114: 75–90.

Skinner, B.F. (1953) *Science and Human Behavior.* Oxford: Macmillan.

Smith, E.R. and Collins, E.C. (2009) Contextualizing person perception: distributed social cognition, *Psychological Review*, 116: 343–64.

Smith, P. (1992) *The Emotional Labour of Nursing: Its Impact on Interpersonal Relations, Management and Educational Environment.* London: Palgrave Macmillan.

Snyder, C.R. (1998) A case for hope in pain, loss and suffering, in J.H. Harvey (ed.) *Perspectives on Loss: A Sourcebook.* Philadelphia, PA: Brunner Mazel.

Sodian, B. (2011) Theory of mind in infancy, *Child Development Perspectives*, 5(1): 39–43.

Spector, P.E., Zapf, D., Chen, P.Y. and Frese, M. (2000) Why negative affectivity should not be controlled in job stress research: don't throw out the baby with the bath water, *Journal of Organizational Behavior*, 21: 79–95.

Srivastava, S., John, O.P., Gosling, S.D. and Potter, J. (2003) Development of personality in early and middle adulthood: set like plaster or persistent change?, *Journal of Personality and Social Psychology*, 84(5): 1041–53.

Stansfield, S.A. (1999) Social support and social cohesion, in M. Marmot and R.G. Wilkinson (eds) *Social Determinants of Health*, pp. 155–78. Oxford: Oxford University Press.

Stern, M. and Hildebrandt, K.A. (1986) Prematurity stereotyping: effects on mother–infant interaction, *Child Development*, 57(2): 308–15.

Stockwell, F. (1984) *The Unpopular Patient*. London: Croom Helm.

Strauss, R.P., Ramsey, B.L., Edwards, T.C., Topolski, T.D., Kapp-Simon, K.A., Thomas, C.R. *et al.* (2007) Stigma experiences in youth with facial differences: a multi-site study of adolescents and their mothers, *Orthodontic and Craniofacial Research*, 10: 96–103.

Stroebe, M.S. and Schut, H. (1998) Culture and grief, *Bereavement Care*, 17(1): 7–10.

Tajfel, H. (1982) *Social Identity and Intergroup Relations*. Cambridge: Cambridge University Press.

Talwar, V., Harris, P.L. and Schleifer, M. (2011) *Children's Understanding of Death: From Biological to Religious Conceptions*. New York: Cambridge University Press.

Taris, T.W. and Bok, I.A. (1996) Effects of parenting style upon psychological wellbeing of young adults: exploring the relations among parental care, locus of control and depression, *Early Child Development and Care*, 132: 93–104.

Taylor, D., Bury, M., Campling, N., Carter, S., Garfield, S., Newbould, J. *et al.* (2007) *A Review of the Use of the Health Belief Model (HBM), the Theory of Reasoned Action (TRA), the Theory of Planned Behaviour (TPB) and the Trans-Theoretical Model (TTM) to Study and Predict Health Related Behaviour Change*. London: Department of Health.

Taylor, S.E. (1979) Patient hospital behaviour: reactance, helplessness, or control?, *Journal of Social Issues*, 35: 156–84.

Taylor, S.E. and Gollwitzer, P.M. (1995) Effects of mindset on positive illusions, *Journal of Personality and Social Psychology*, 69: 213–26.

Taylor, S.E. and Stanton, A.L. (2007) Coping resources, coping processes, and mental health, *Annual Review of Clinical Psychology*, 3: 377–401.

Teresi, J.A., Holmes, D., Ramirez, M., Gurland, B.J. and Lantigua, R. (2001) Performance of cognitive tests among different racial/ethnic and education groups: findings of differential item functioning and possible item bias, *Journal of Mental Health and Aging*, 7(1): 79–89.

Thieme, K., Spies, C., Sinha, P., Turk, D.C. and Flor, H. (2005) Predictors of pain behaviours in fibromyalgia syndrome, *Arthritis & Rheumatism*, 53(3): 343–50.

Thorne, S.E., Hislop, G., Armstrong, E-A. and Oglov, V. (2008) Cancer care communication: the power to harm and the power to heal?, *Patient Education and Counseling*, 71: 34–40.

Todd, S. and Shearn, J. (1997) Family dilemmas and secrets: parents' disclosure of information to their adult offspring with learning disabilities, *Disability and Society*, 12(3): 341–66.

Twycross, R., Harcourt, J. and Bergl, S. (1996) A survey of pain in patients with advanced cancer, *Journal of Pain and Symptom Management*, 12(5): 273–82.

Uchino, B.N. (2006) Social support and health: a review of physiological processes potentially underlying links to disease outcomes, *Journal of Behavioral Medicine*, 29(4): 377–387.

Van der Spank, J.T., Cambier, D.C., De Paepe, H.M.C., Danneels, I.A.G., Witvrouw, E.E. and Beerens, L. (2000) Pain relief in labour by transcutaneous electrical nerve stimulation (TENS), *Archives of Gynecology and Obstetrics*, 264(3): 131–6.

Van Doorn, C., Kasl, S.V., Beery, L.C., Jacobe, H.G. and Prigerson, H.G. (1998) The influence of marital quality and attachment styles on traumatic grief and depressive symptoms, *Journal of Nervous and Mental Diseases*, 186(9): 566–73.

Vedhara, K., McDermott, M.P., Evans, T.G. *et al.* (2002) Chronic stress in nonelderly caregivers: psychological, endocrine and immune implications, *Journal of Psychosomatic Research*, 53: 1153–61.

Veldtman, G.R., Matley, S.L., Kendall, L., Quirk, J., Gibbs, J.L., Parsons, J.M. *et al.* (2000) Illness understanding in children and adolescents with heart disease, *Heart*, 84(4): 395–7.

Vits, S., Cesko, E., Enck, P., Hillen, U., Schadendorf, D. and Schedlowski, M. (2011) Behavioural conditioning as the mediator of placebo responses in the immune system, *Philosophical Transactions of the Royal Society of Biological Sciences*, 366: 1799–807.

Vlaeyen, J.W.S. and Linton, S.J. (2000) Fear-avoidance and its consequences in chronic musculoskeletal pain: a state of the art, *Pain*, 85: 317–32.

von Baeyer, C.L., Spagrud, L.J., McCormick, J.C., Choo, E., Neville, K. and Connelly, M.A. (2009) Three new datasets supporting use of the Numerical Rating Scale (NRS-11) for children's self-reports of pain intensity, *Pain*, 143: 223–27.

Vydelingum, V. (2006) Nurses' experiences of caring for South Asian minority ethnic patients in a general hospital in England, *Nursing Inquiry* 13(1): 23–32.

Vygotsky, L.S. (1978) *Mind in Society: The Development of Higher Mental Processes*. Cambridge, MA: Harvard University Press.

Waatkaar, T., Borge, A.I.H., Fundingsrudc, H.P., Christiea, H.J. and Torgersen, S. (2004) The role of stressful life events in the development of depressive symptoms in adolescence – a longitudinal community study, *Journal of Adolescence*, 27: 153–63.

Wales, K. (2000) North and south: an English linguistic divide?, *English Today*, 16(1): 4–15.

Walker, J. (1994) Caring for elderly people with persistent pain in the community: a qualitative perspective on the attitudes of patients and nurses, *Health and Social Care in the Community*, 2: 221–8.

Walker, J. (2000) Women's experiences of transfer from a midwife-led to a consultant-led maternity unit, *Journal of Midwifery and Women's Health*, 45(2): 161–8.

Walker, J. (2001) *Control and the Psychology of Health*. Buckingham: Open University Press.

Walker, J. and Sofaer, B. (1998) Predictors of psychological distress in chronic pain patients, *Journal of Advanced Nursing*, 27: 320–6.

Walker, J., Brooksby, A., McInerney, J. and Taylor, A. (1998) Patient perceptions of hospital care: building confidence, faith and trust, *Journal of Nursing Management*, 6: 193–200.

Walker, J., Holloway, I. and Sofaer, B. (1999) 'In the system': patients' experiences of chronic back pain, *Pain*, 80: 621–8.

Walker, J., Sofaer, B. and Holloway, I. (2006) The experience of chronic back pain: accounts of loss in those seeking help from pain clinics, *European Journal of Pain*, 10: 199–207.

Wall, P. (1999) *Pain: The Science of Suffering*. London: Weidenfeld & Nicolson.

Wallston, K.A., Wallston, B.S. and DeVellis, R. (1978) Development of the Multidimensional Health Locus of Control (MHLOC) scale, *Health Education Monographs*, 6: 161–70.

Walter, T. (1996) A new model of grief: bereavement and biography, *Mortality*, 1(1): 7–25.

Walter, T. (1999) *On Bereavement: The Culture of Grief*. Buckingham: Open University Press.

Wang, S-M., Kulkarni, L., Dolev, J. and Kain, Z.N. (2002) Music and preoperative anxiety: a randomized, controlled study, *Anesthesia & Analgesia*, 94(6): 1489–94.

Wasserman, D. (2006) *Depression, the Facts: Expert Advice for Patients, Carers and Professionals*. Oxford: Oxford University Press.

Watson, A. and Visram, A. (2000) The developing role of play preparation in paediatric anaesthesia, *Paediatric Anaesthesia*, 10: 681–6.

Watson, J.B. and Raynor, R. (1920) Conditioned emotional reactions, *Journal of Experimental Psychology*, 3(1): 1–14.

West, R. (2005) Time for a change: putting the Transtheoretical (Stages of Change) Model to rest, *Addiction*, 100: 1036–9.

WHO (World Health Organization) (1946) *Preamble to the Constitution of the World Health Organization as Adopted by the International Health Conference*, New York, 19–22 June 1946, and entered into force on 7 April 1948. Geneva: WHO.

WHO (World Health Organization) (1997) *Measuring Quality of Life: The World Health Organization Quality of Life Instruments*. Geneva: WHO. www.who.int/mental_health/media/68.pdf (accessed 16 August 2011).

WHO (2010) *International Statistical Classification of Diseases and Related Health Problems*, 10th revision, 2nd edition, Ch. 5. Geneva: WHO.

Wiese, B.S., Freund, A.M. and Baltes, P.B. (2002) Subjective career success and emotional well-being: longitudinal predictive power of selection, optimization, and compensation, *Journal of Vocational Behavior*, 60: 321–35.

Williams-Piehota, P., Schneider, T.R., Pizarro, J., Mowad, L. and Salovey, P. (2004) Matching health messages to health locus of control beliefs for promoting mammography utilization, *Psychology and Health*, 19(4): 407–23.

Witte, K. and Allen, M. (2000) A meta-analysis of fear appeals: implications for effective public health campaigns, *Health Eduction and Behaviour*, 27(5): 591–615.

Wittouck, C., Van Autreve, S., De Jaegere, E., Portzky, G. and van Heeringen, K. (2011) The prevention and treatment of complicated grief: a meta-analysis, *Clinical Psychology Review*, 31: 69–78.

Wolf, M.S., Davis, T.C., Shrank, W., Rapp, D.N., Bass, P.F., Connor, U.M. *et al.* (2007) To err is human: patient misinterpretations of prescription drug label instructions, *Patient Education and Counseling*, 67: 293–300.

Wolpe, J. (1958) *Psychotherapy by Reciprocal Inhibition*. Stanford, CA: Stanford University Press.

Wood, W. (2000) Attitude change: persuasion and social influence, *Annual Review of Psychology*, 51: 539–70.

Wortman, C.B. and Silver, R.C. (1989) The myths of coping with loss, *Journal of Consulting and Clinical Psychology*, 57(3): 349–57.

Zhao, Z.-Q. (2008) Neural mechanism underlying acupuncture analgesia, *Progress in Neurobiology*, 85(4): 355–75.

Zwakhalen, S.M.G. Hamers, J.P.H., Abu-Saad, H.H., Martijn, P.F. and Berger, M.P.F. (2006) Pain in elderly people with severe dementia: a systematic review of behavioural pain assessment tools, *BMC Geriatric*, 6(3): 1–15.

Index